I0813000

IMAGES
*of America*

# ARTHUR RICKERBY'S NEW YORK CITY

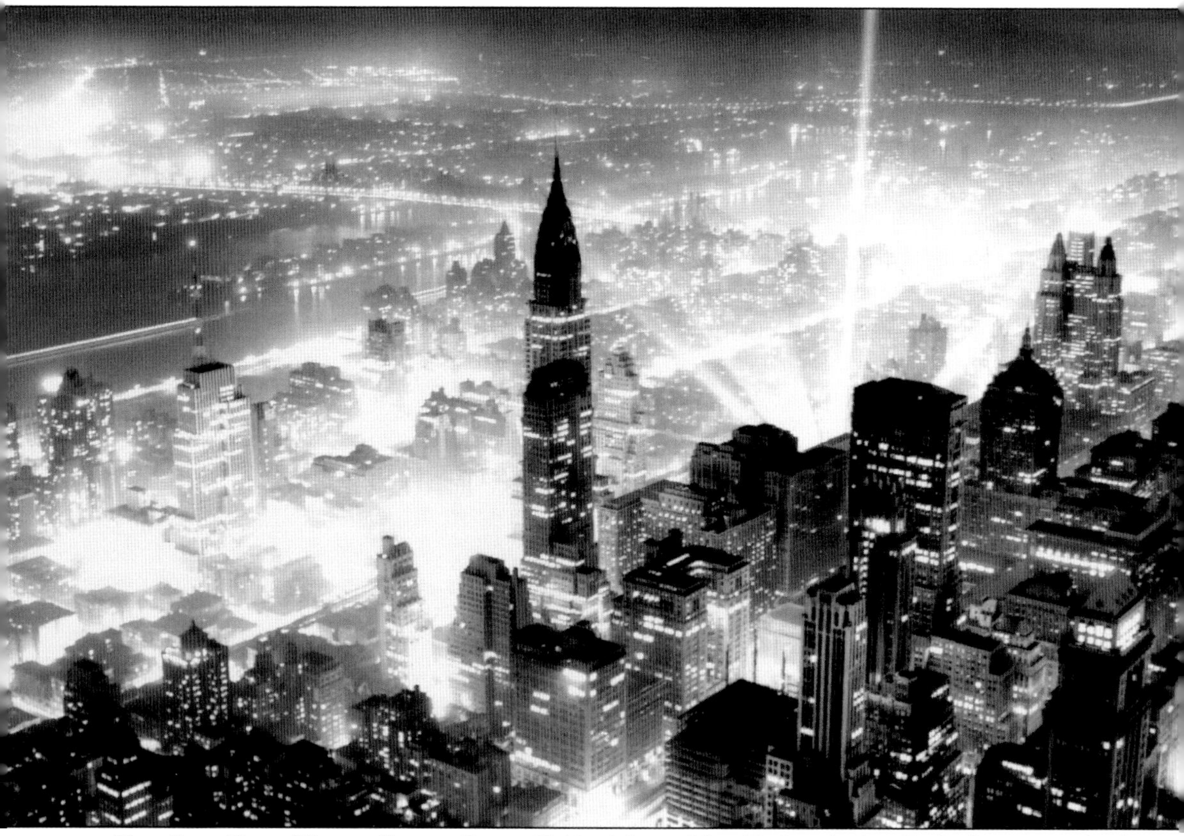

**THE CITY THAT NEVER SLEEPS, LATE 1940S.** Native New Yorker Arthur Rickerby went as high as he could get in his hometown—the top of the Empire State Building—to test out a new camera lens. The result was this stunning view of New York City at night that sizzles with excitement.

*On the cover*: **SAILORS IN TRAINING.** Cold sailors line the deck of the United States Navy destroyer the *Kyne* as the ship departs New York on a Naval Reserve training cruise. Between shivers, the sailors reminded one another that they were heading for sunny Florida. (Courtesy of John Rogers.)

IMAGES
*of America*

# ARTHUR RICKERBY'S NEW YORK CITY

Frank Ceresi and Carol McMains
with John Rogers,
Foreword by Wanda Rickerby

ARCADIA
PUBLISHING

ISBN 978-0-7385-4900-2

Published by Arcadia Publishing
Charleston, South Carolina

Printed in the United States of America

Library of Congress Catalog Card Number: 2006928596

For all general information contact Arcadia Publishing at:
Telephone 843-853-2070
Fax 843-853-0044
E-mail sales@arcadiapublishing.com
For customer service and orders:
Toll-Free 1-888-313-2665

Visit us on the Internet at www.arcadiapublishing.com

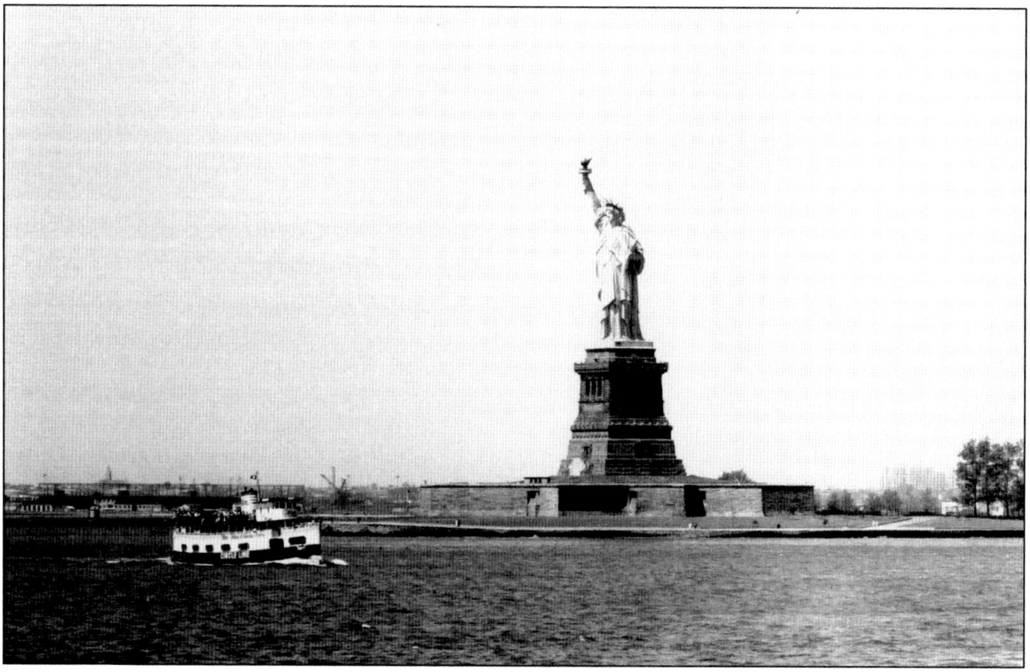

**SWEET LAND OF LIBERTY, 1950S.** There is no greater symbol of the nation and its promise of freedom and opportunity for all than the Statue of Liberty, which has held the flame of liberty above New York Harbor since 1886. Originally intended to stand in Egypt and at first regarded in the United States as a waste of money, Lady Liberty may be America's most famous landmark.

# Contents

# ACKNOWLEDGMENTS

This book is not meant to be a definitive work of all Arthur Rickerby photographs taken during his illustrious career. The images contained within these pages are just a small sampling of the photographs that Arthur took that capture his early years as well as those spent roaming around the streets of New York City and its environs after World War II. Most of the photographs have never been published before and provide a glimpse of life during a simpler age.

We owe a debt of gratitude to many, including Wanda Rickerby, Arthur's longtime spouse and confidant, the Rickerby family, Zoe Dalis, and Micah Gulledge, as well as Frank Goodyear, Ann Shumard, and Lizanne Garrett at the Smithsonian National Portrait Gallery. We would especially like to thank John Rogers, the owner of the Arthur Rickerby Photographic Archive, and business partner Art Jafee, who have provided support and assistance during this project. We, of course, could not have written this book as we have wanted to without the help and support of the good folks at Arcadia Publishing, particularly our editor, Erin Vosgien. It was Erin who immediately recognized the significance of the Arthur Rickerby Photographic Archive and provided encouragement every step of the way.

On a personal level, we wish to thank our families and friends whose support and belief in us makes everything possible and worthwhile. To Angelica, Lexie, John Matthew, and Gabriel Rogers, Dan and Nicole Ceresi, and Les and Brady McMains, we are eternally grateful for your loving support, understanding, and patience. To our cheerleaders, Richard, Barbara, Ricky, and Vicki Sellner, Patricia McMains, Holly Mahla, Gayle Rice, Barbara Grimm-Crawford, Marianne Horinko, Karen Adams, Beth Monroney, Valerie Dulany, Patrice Shaw, Gene Burroughs, and Rick Spees, your inspiration and encouragement are deeply appreciated. Thank you all for being our biggest fans!

Finally, of course, this book is dedicated to the memory of Arthur Rickerby, who we never had the pleasure of personally knowing but whose creative work is still treasured today and will be forever.

# FOREWORD

Arthur Burroughs Rickerby was born in New York City on March 15, 1921. His father, Frank, was connected to the garment industry, but Arthur was never clear about what the connection was because Frank died when his son was only three years old. "After that," Arthur said, "my mother was too busy working to spend much time giving lessons in family history."

They lived in the Bronx, and Arthur attended public schools there, working his way through the grades up to DeWitt Clinton High School. In those years, the Bronx was his world. Although he eventually traveled over the entire globe, he always treasured memories of that part of New York City: the echoing halls of an Episcopalian church, a grassy, rock strewn public park, and, with special fondness, a Horn and Hardardt cafeteria where his mother, exhausted from her workday, would send him alone to get his supper.

Arthur was a good scholar, but, as he told the story, one particular class at DeWitt Clinton, botany, had him stumped. He badly needed the goodwill of the man who taught the class, and this teacher was also the faculty advisor for the school Camera Club. Arthur knew nothing of photography, but he knew he had to pass botany if he was going to college, so he joined the Camera Club.

"It was love at first sight," he told people. "I knew immediately that this was what I was meant to do." Those who knew him in later years will attest: he was rarely seen anywhere without a camera in his hand.

Having passed botany, Arthur was admitted to Duke University in Durham, North Carolina. Duke was a relatively young university back then, a slow-paced southern place, with massive, dignified stone buildings, set on wide open acres of emerald green grass, a very different culture from the bustling city he was used to. The impetuous city boy did not adapt; he continued to hustle. He and his camera seemed to be everywhere recording campus life—but in particular campus sports. Fortuitously, Duke's various teams were doing well, and newspapers wanted Arthur's pictures. Eventually, because they really were remarkable images, the editors at Acme Newspictures (eventually United Press) proposed that he come to work in their New York bureau after graduation.

By then, however, there was a world war to be attended to. Arthur signed on with the United States Navy, and some wise personnel officer, noting his interest in photography, sent him to work under Capt. Edward Steichen in the Pacific.

There was magic in that unit. Steichen, of course, was on his way to being a giant in the world of photography. He had much to teach the young photographers assigned to him, and none of them were more eager to absorb that wisdom than Arthur Rickerby.

When World War II ended, Arthur returned to his native New York and to the job waiting for him there. It was, however, not the city in which he had grown up, nor was he the hotshot youth who had rushed off to college. Both the city and the man had lived through a war; they had matured the hard way.

The first order of the day was to outfit himself with the tools of his trade. Arthur spent every penny he could lay his hands on to buy camera bodies, lenses, lighting equipment, and a myriad of optical gadgets. Then he set out to test not only his new toys but his own ability to chronicle his city.

For the most part, the pictures in this book are the result. Night and day, he prowled the streets and tall buildings of Manhattan. A street violinist in front of an opera house, a little girl with her hula hoop waiting for mom to come out of the grocery store, a tired bagel peddler in the 14th Street retail district, a Salvation Army band serenading the workers of Wall Street: everywhere he saw images he deemed worthy of recording. And when he had done that, he went home and spent half the night in his darkroom so that he could judge the quality of his own work.

At the United Press office, he was learning to listen to a more strident city heartbeat. The subjects his editors chose for him were more formal than the ones he made on his own. He took pictures of union leaders and Yankee catchers, subway engineers and blind girls learning ballet, mayors and mobsters, and a million other details within the skeleton and tissue that comprised New York City.

Don Larsen pitched the only perfect game in World Series history. Arthur, by now exploring the advantages of the smaller 35 millimeter cameras, left the press box and snapped the last pitch against a scoreboard full of zeroes. His picture ran front page on every newspaper in the world that was a United Press subscriber. He was nominated for a Pulitzer Prize, not for the photograph, but for his leadership in the world of news photography.

He was starting to be noticed. Annual prizes from several national photograph contests helped. So did United Press's decision to send him to cover national political conventions, and international Olympics, baseball spring training, farming along the real tobacco road, not to mention China and Japan and Brazil and Spain.

Because his photographs were both sensitive and hard hitting, because of his ability to weave important details into his reportage, thus broadening the impact of his stories, United Press began to send him out to do larger, longer features. He loved it, but he could not get enough of it working for what was, essentially, a news organization.

He left United Press and became a freelancer, seeking human interest assignments from magazines. Since he had no idea how successful he might be, he moved his family to a rough cabin in the Connecticut woods. He need not have worried. Within a year, his income had tripled, and *Life* magazine searched him out, asked him to join its prestigious staff, and moved him to Washington to cover the Kennedy White House.

Arthur Rickerby shot exclusive stories in the Oval Office, vied with hundreds of colleagues when Mrs. Kennedy toured India, captured Bobby Kennedy smashing at a tennis ball as if it were Jimmy Hoffa, photographed Ted's plane when it crashed in Massachusetts, and was riding in the official procession that fateful day in Dallas.

Heartbroken at the loss of a leader he had grown to admire, Arthur willingly returned to *Life*'s Manhattan headquarters and the city he knew best in all the world.

He was not, however, to make many pictures there. *Life* was known for lengthy stories about faraway places, and Arthur spent weeks at a time in Asia creating a story about rice as the world's foremost food crop, in northern South America where he made the pictures for a *Life World Book* on Colombia, Venezuela, and the three Guianas, and in a host of other venues.

His major New York City essay was on the Rockettes at Radio City Music Hall, which ran with a Gatefold cover and pages of swirling color action shots. He also began a series of major color essays on various sports, so that sometimes, he said, it seemed that he was right back where he started, in Yankee Stadium and Madison Square Garden.

Indeed, the last photograph in a retrospective of his work, which toured the country in the 1990s, shows Willie Mays at bat in the spring of 1972. Arthur died a few months later, unexpectedly, in a hospital in Connecticut. It was less than a hundred miles from the hospital where he had been born. It was a lifetime and a universe away from where it all began.

He had made photographs in every style and every arena, but it may be that his gentle, whimsical images of New York City represented the heart of Arthur Rickerby.

—Wanda Rickerby

# INTRODUCTION

We knew of Arthur Rickerby and some of his photographs from a special exhibit that we curated featuring many of his better known sports images at the National Sports Gallery in Washington, D.C., in 1999. The popular exhibit, Sports Images from the Lens of Arthur Rickerby, was one of our favorite creations because it gave us an opportunity to watch patrons of all ages stare, sometimes in awe and wonderment, at the striking shots that recall the glory of sports in America.

Our pleasure in discovering Arthur's work intensified once we got to know his widow, Wanda Rickerby. Wanda initially telephoned to entice us with the proposed exhibit in its early stages. Truth be told, once we saw the remarkable image of Don Larsen throwing the final pitch in the first and only perfect game in World Series history, we needed little convincing. Wanda proceeded to do what every museum curator dreams about. She professionally framed the images, hopped in her car, and drove what would become the finished exhibit to us in Washington, D.C.! She even composed concise story lines for each shot. All we had to do was paint a wall and put the pictures up. The photographs did the rest. The exhibit was one of the longest running and most popular showcased during our tenure at the museum.

In 2004, another telephone conversation with Wanda eventually led to the writing of this book. Wanda casually mentioned that she had more of her late husband's work in the basement of her home. Arthur had passed away at the young age of 51 back in 1972. But Wanda had the wherewithal to keep his creative flame glowing bright. "I have more negatives and prints," Wanda said, "I mean thousands more!" Within days, we paid Wanda a visit, and what we saw was thrilling.

Wanda's basement was what can only be described as a laboratory dedicated to one man's passion for photography. On one table was a stack of Arthur's vintage prints featuring everything from President Kennedy's early "Camelot" years at the White House to searing photographs of raids over Tokyo during World War II. Across the room were boxes containing thousands of negatives neatly labeled and preserved in their individual glassine envelopes. Against another wall were rows and rows of filing cabinets containing even *more* negatives, some in black and white and others in color, but each drawer with enticing labels reading titles of magazines, news service agencies, and periodicals to which Arthur contributed. Our imagination went wild as we read names such as *Life*, *Look*, *Collier's*, *Sport*, *Sports Illustrated*, *Saturday Evening Post*, Acme, United Press, and more. All in all, there were 20,000 negatives and 7,000 vintage prints in the basement laboratory. We were suitably impressed.

It did not take a rocket scientist to appreciate the significance of the gold mine we entered into. Want to know about basketball at Madison Square Garden in the early 1940s? There were rows of classic images, most never published, taking us into the Garden. How about the early days of the United Nations? There were hundreds of shots to choose from. Or World War II? Or Babe Ruth Day at Yankee Stadium in 1947? It was staggering.

The Arthur Rickerby Photographic Archive spans four decades. It is now organized and in the possession of John Rogers, a true sports and photograph connoisseur of the highest order. John acquired the collection and is dedicated to preserving and promoting Arthur's work. Having a keen eye for history, photography, and sports, John has taken on Wanda's mission: to expose Arthur's treasures on film to the largest possible audience. This time, however, the keeper of the flame does not have to pack up a car and tote the photographs to a willing institution, for we are now in the digital age. That is something Arthur likely never envisioned, but we think he would certainly approve. Now, even if you are a sports fan in Europe or a young history student in California, all you have to do is go online, click on www.arthurrickerby.com, and a world of wonderful images is yours to enjoy.

The photographs featuring New York City, Arthur's hometown, is a natural first book dedicated to Arthur and his creativity. There will be more. We think you will enjoy the trip down memory lane that these timeless images provide.

And what about Arthur, the man who passed on way too young but left us with an extraordinary visual legacy? What about this man who made our book possible? Perhaps Colin Westerbeck, associate curator of photography at the Art Institute of Chicago, summed it up as well as we can when he said, "Art died at the height of his powers, at a time when both his talent and opportunities to use it were still growing. None of us can ask more than that."

# *One*

# A Career Begins at Duke University

Born in New York City in 1921, Arthur Rickerby's dream as a youngster was to become a dancer on the bright lights of Broadway. It was, however, a dream that he would give up after joining the Camera Club at DeWitt Clinton High School in the Bronx. It was there that he discovered his passion for photography. Arthur carried that enthusiasm on to college when he entered Duke University, where he supported himself by selling sports and other photographs. His college years were quite a learning experience, particularly as he honed his skills as an expert lensman.

Clutching an old four-by-five speed graphic, Arthur, in four years at Duke, built up an impressive freelance business. Although he was studying political science and government, he was living and breathing the art of photography. One of his first influences was the renowned Harold Blumenfeld of Acme Newspictures (later United Press). At one point, in fact, when Arthur considered leaving Duke to work for United Press full time, the fatherly Blumenfeld urged him to stay in school and earn his degree. "That was only the first of a lot of good advice I got from Mr. Blumenfeld," Arthur recalled while being interviewed in the 1969 issue of *U.S. Camera World Annual*.

The enormous Arthur Rickerby Photographic Archive contains hundreds of superior quality early Duke photographs. This chapter features an impressive array of images as Arthur began his love affair with the camera over 50 years ago.

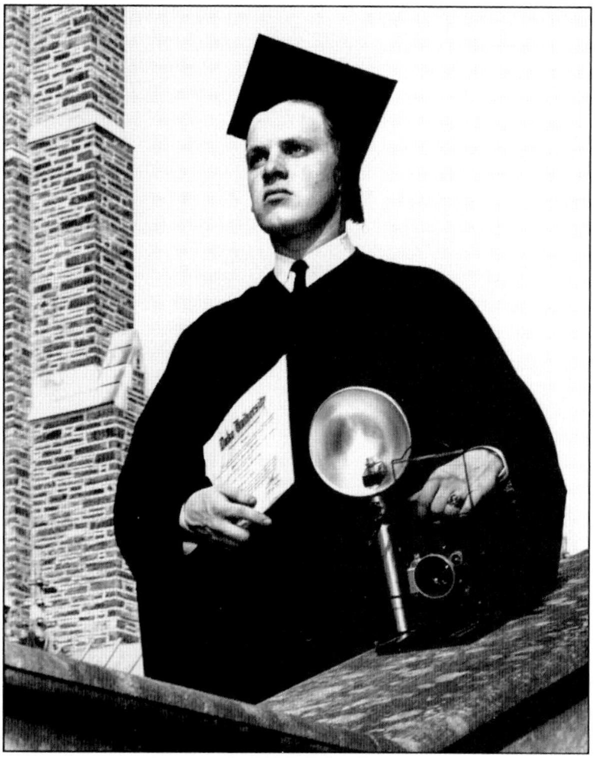

**DUKE GRADUATE ARTHUR RICKERBY, 1942.** Arthur Rickerby discovered his passion for photography after joining the Camera Club at DeWitt Clinton High School in the Bronx. He carried that fervor to Duke University where he supported himself by selling photographs of the school's sports teams, events, and athletes.

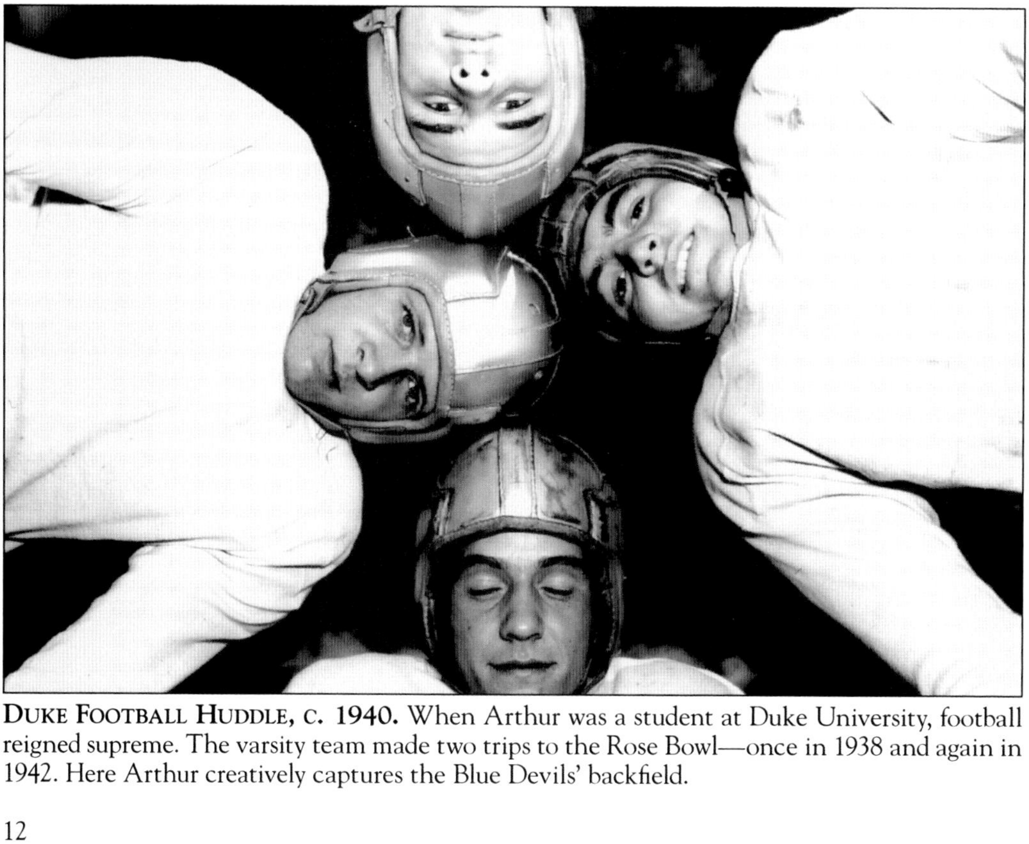

**DUKE FOOTBALL HUDDLE, C. 1940.** When Arthur was a student at Duke University, football reigned supreme. The varsity team made two trips to the Rose Bowl—once in 1938 and again in 1942. Here Arthur creatively captures the Blue Devils' backfield.

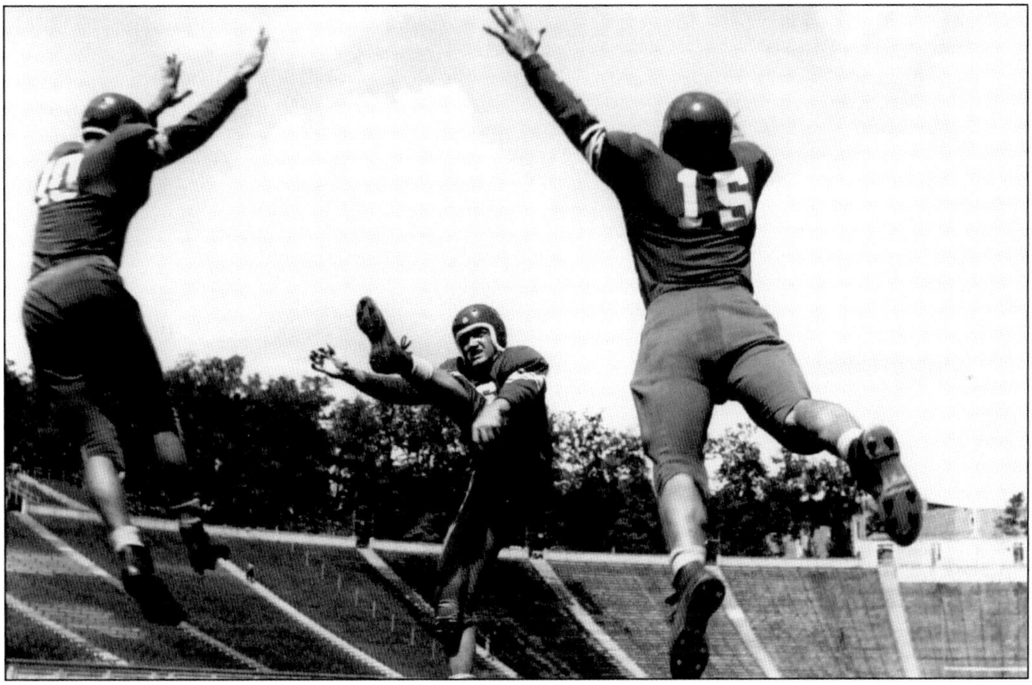



**The Varsity Team Takes Flight, c. 1940.** "Sunday used to be a day of rest and quiet," lamented the Duke *Chronicle* in the 1940s. But the Duke football team created gridiron excitement for several years as the campus rallied behind its team during the fall football season. From the 1938 through 1942 seasons, the team won two Southern Conference championships, went to the Rose Bowl twice, and only lost five regular-season games.

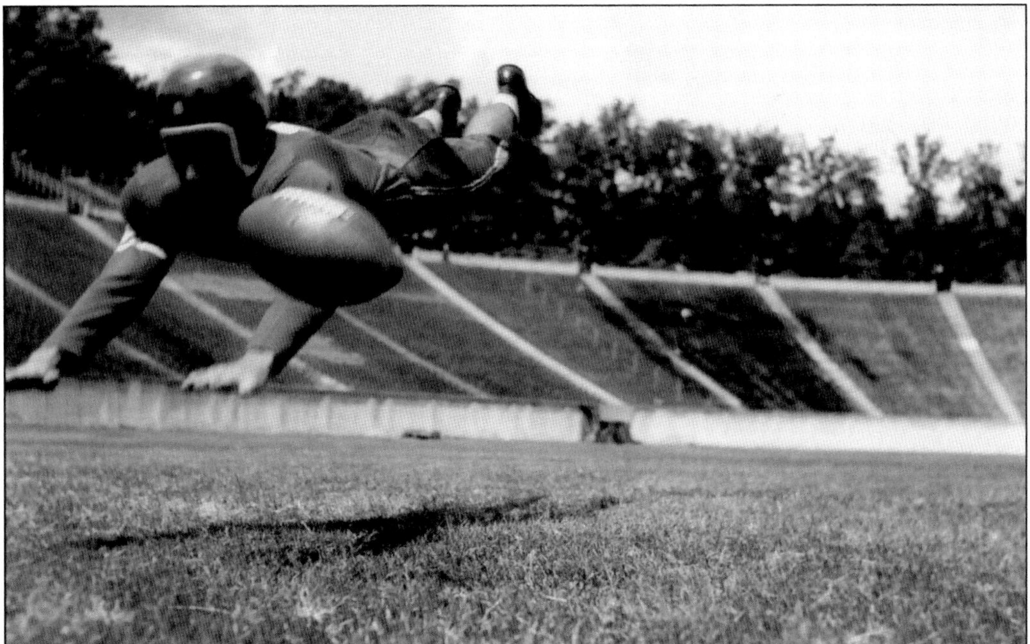

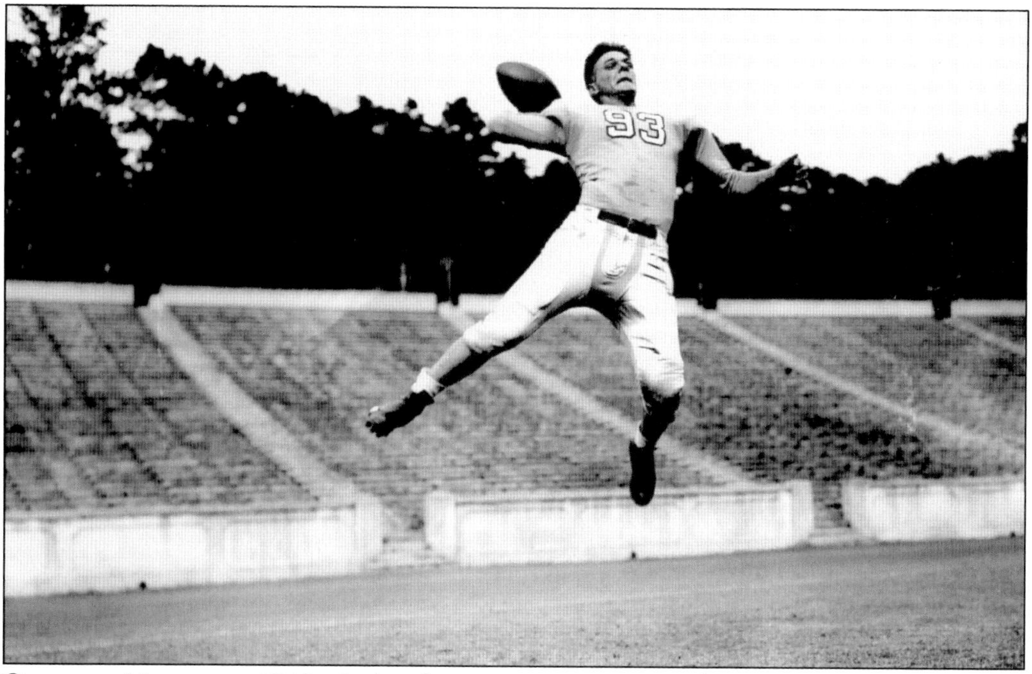

GRIDIRON MAGIC, C. 1940. Arthur began to earn money taking interesting and unusual photographs of the Duke sports teams. Here he used the Duke stadium practice field as a backdrop to have the campus football heroes pose creatively. These photographs sold well and captured the eye of Harold Blumenfeld at Acme. Within a short period of time, Arthur's freelance business blossomed, and he was able to buy the latest photography equipment and partially pay for his college tuition.

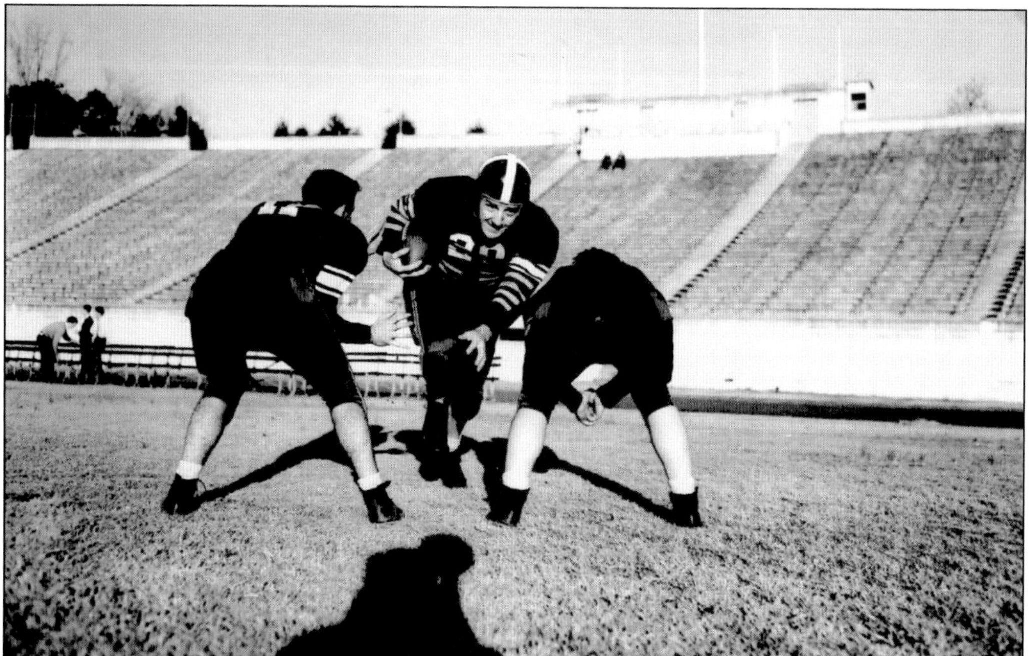

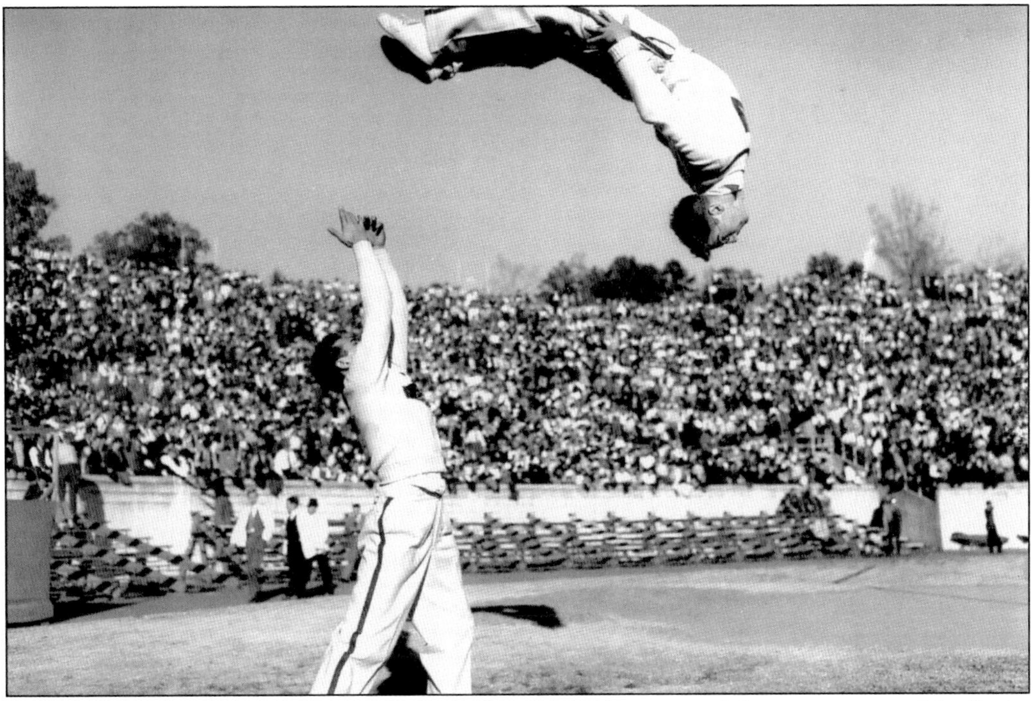

**Flipped Out for Football, c. 1940.** Arthur perfectly captured the excitement of the Duke fans and cheerleaders during games throughout his college career. Because the football team was nationally ranked every year that he was a student, home games and the crowds gave Arthur many "Kodak moments."

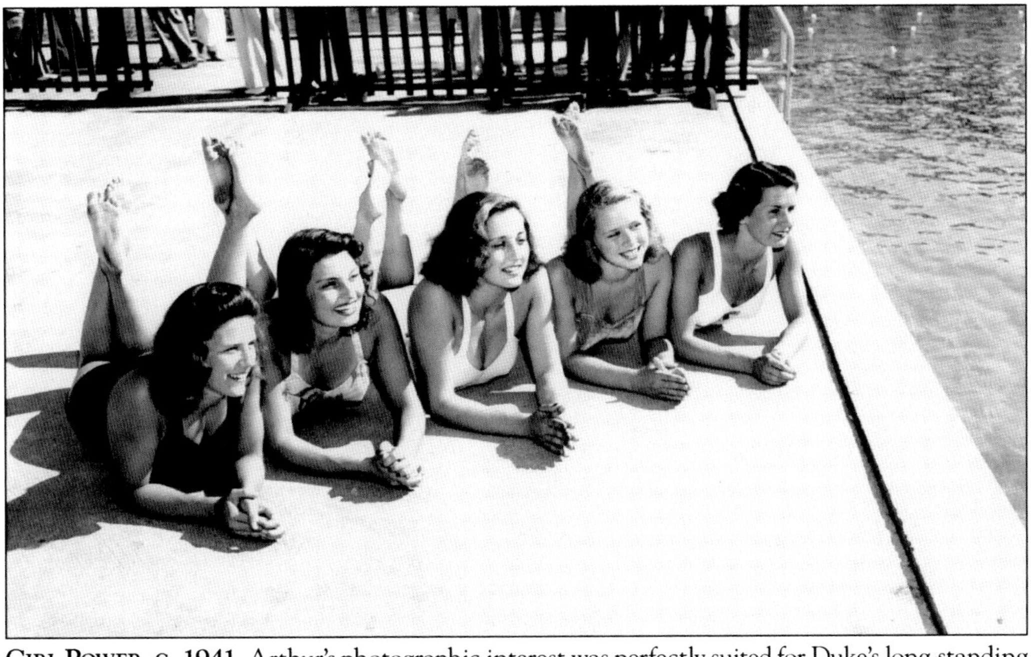

**Girl Power, c. 1941.** Arthur's photographic interest was perfectly suited for Duke's long-standing and early concern with women's athletics. He shot women athletes who played baseball, rode horses, participated in track and field, and those who enjoyed swimming as well.

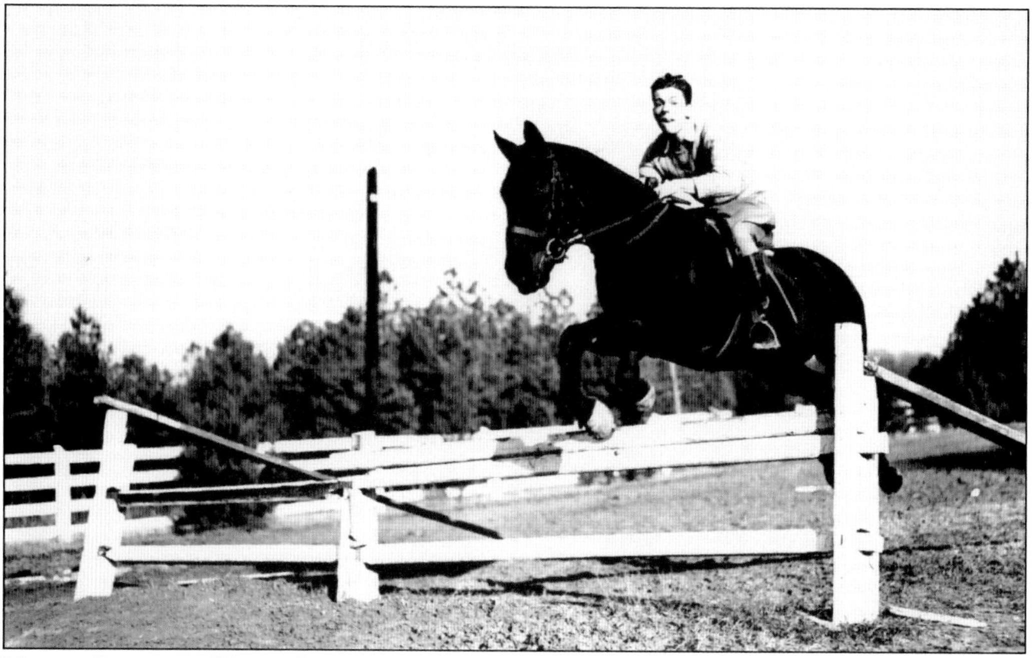

**NORTH CAROLINA HORSE COUNTRY, C. 1941.** The area surrounding Durham, North Carolina, home of Duke University, is to this day popular horse country. Arthur enjoyed covering equestrian events and developed a knack for capturing action shots such as this jumping horse.

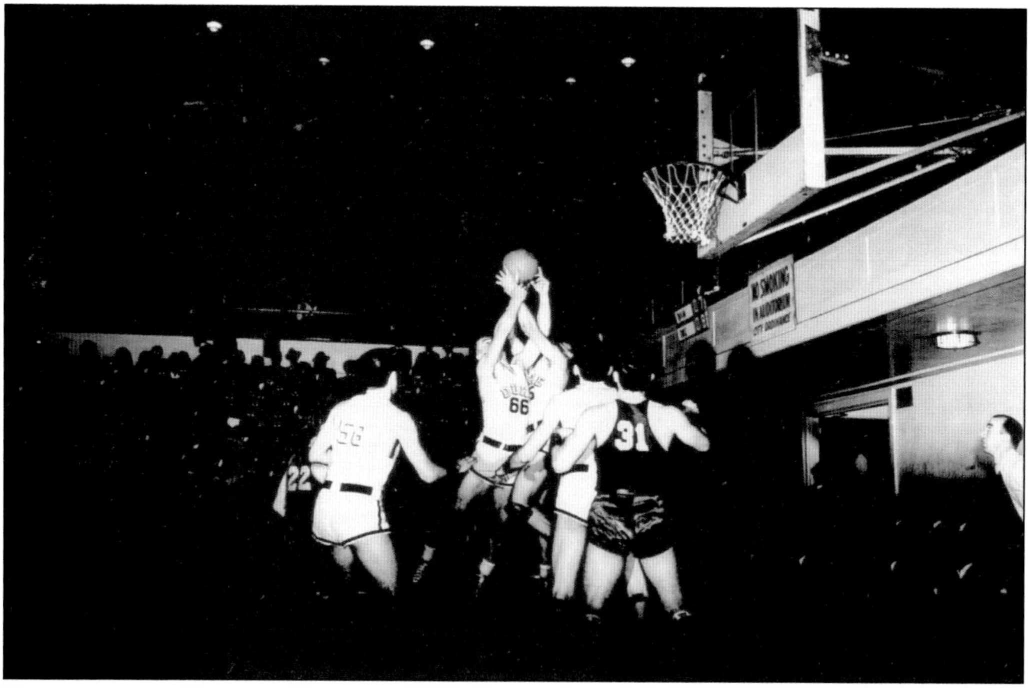

**BASKETBALL IN TOBACCO ROAD, C. 1941.** Even today, when one thinks of college basketball, thoughts automatically turn to Duke University. During Arthur's years on campus, he covered many exciting Southern Conference games, including this contest against the William and Mary Tribe.

# *Two*

# THE CLOUDS OF WAR

Like many of his Duke classmates in early December 1941, Arthur Rickerby was looking forward to graduating the following May. Life was good for the young photographer as he prepared for a career with Acme Newspictures. Also, the campus was filled with unbridled excitement and why not? The Blue Devil varsity football team had just buttoned up their second Southern Conference championship in four years, and on December 1, 1941, they were invited to play at the Rose Bowl in the prestigious Tournament of Roses.

But Arthur's plans, along with countless other college-age Americans, were derailed a week later when the campus was jolted into reality upon hearing the news that the Japanese had bombed Pearl Harbor in Honolulu, Hawaii. Pres. Franklin D. Roosevelt spoke for the nation when he said that "December 7, 1941, is a day that will live in infamy," and it certainly did for Arthur's generation. The Duke Blue Devils did play football on January 1, 1942, but not in Pasadena, California, as part of the Tournament of Roses as originally planned. That location was precipitously close to Hawaii, and the tournament organizers, fearing another Japanese attack, moved the game for the only time in Rose Bowl history out of Southern California to Durham, North Carolina.

Arthur did graduate on time, but instead of plying his trade as a photographer with Acme, he joined the United States Navy and quickly ended up in Capt. Edward Steichen's famed Naval Photographic Unit in the Far East. Arthur's wartime experience would help define him not only as a person but also as a photographer. The young soldier landed with the Marines at Iwo Jima and Okinawa, creating unforgettable images, and also photographed Tokyo just after its horrific bombing. Additionally he was given free reign to record life in a POW camp run by the United States military on Guam and was aboard the USS *Missouri*, capturing history as it happened, when the Japanese surrendered in 1945, ending the bloody conflict.

Under Steichen's direction, Arthur's photography became interpretive, and the images gained a new clarity. He seemed to have the knack and tenaciousness to be at the exact right place at just the right time. This would become his hallmark, a trait that continued during his career as a photojournalist. Soon his work gained prominence and recognition. For an essay in which his pictures told the story of the plight of civilians in Okinawa, he won the prestigious United States Navy Photographic Citation "for exceptionally meritorious photography . . . for one of the great picture records of the war, which reflects the highest credit on Lieutenant Rickerby."

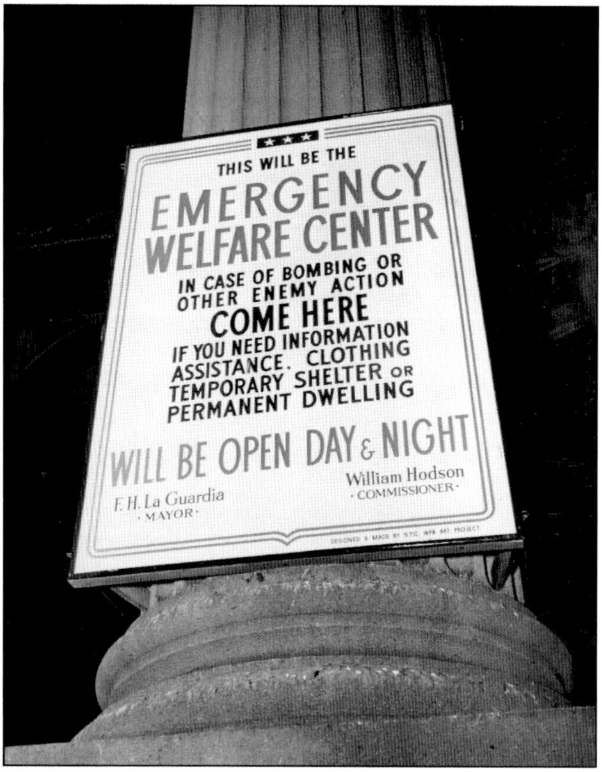


**SIGN OF THE TIMES, 1942.** After the start of World War II, numerous air raid emergency centers were set up around the country. Shortly before departing for military service, Arthur Rickerby photographed this sign, which hung outside of the Tweed Courthouse in New York City, one of 70 such shelters in the city.

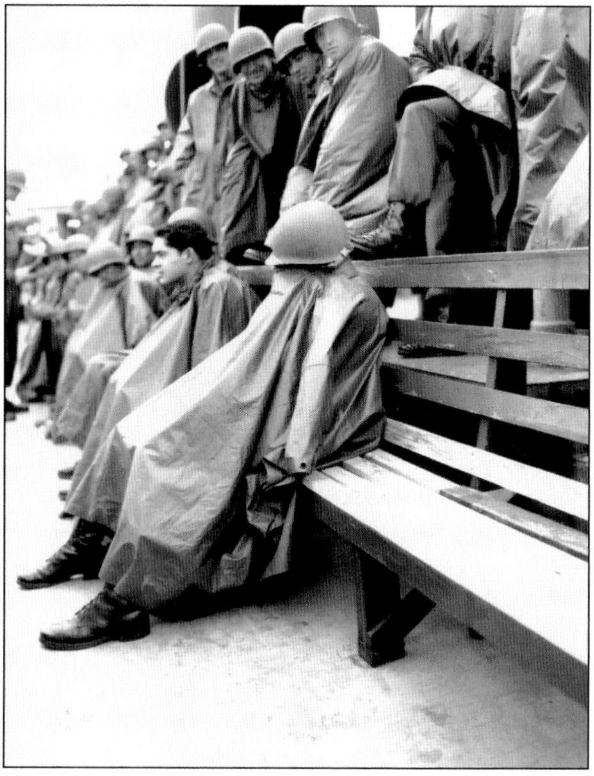

**GOING OFF TO WAR, 1942.** Immediately following graduation from Duke University, Arthur and many others put their lives on hold to serve their country during the war. Here Arthur perfectly captures United States soldiers as they leave New York Harbor for parts unknown.

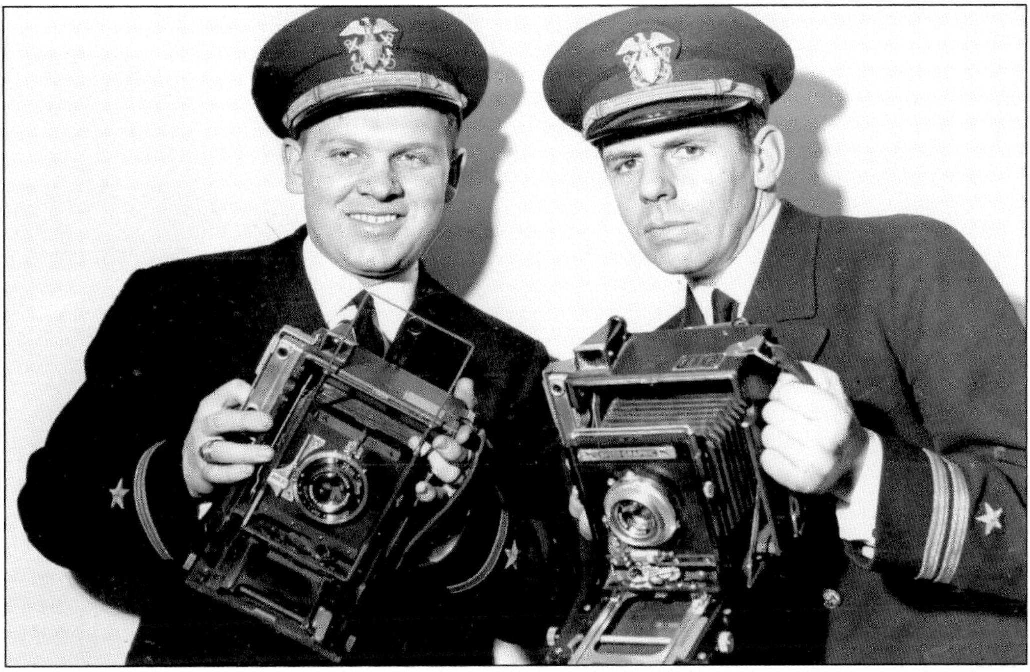

**A Soldier's Life, 1942.** It is all smiles for Arthur Rickerby (left) and a colleague as they begin their military careers under the command of the legendary Edward Steichen, the director of the U.S. Naval Photographic Unit. It was their mission to document on film key parts of the country's war effort in the Pacific campaign.

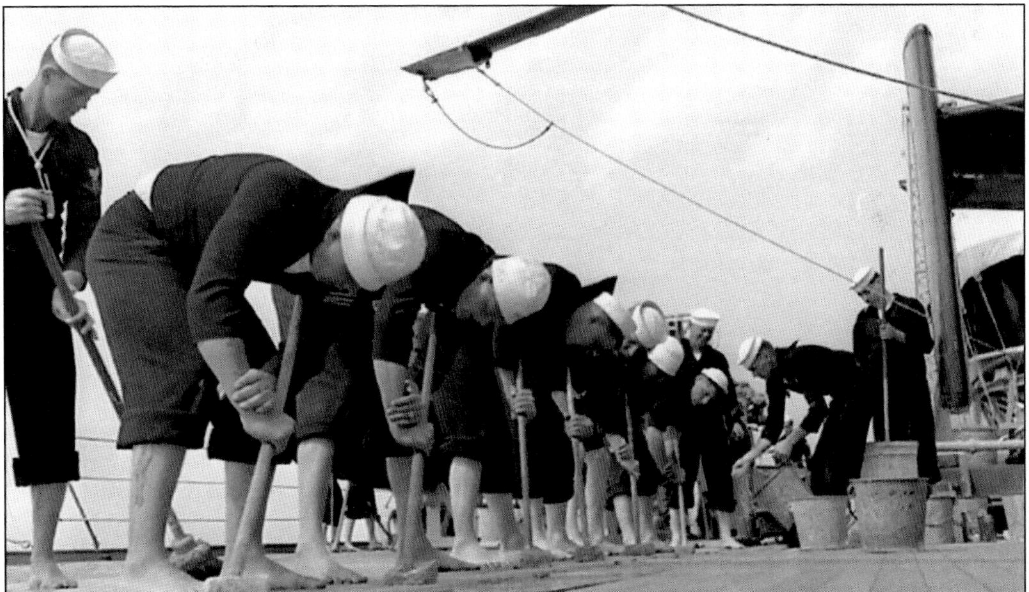

**All Hands on Deck, 1942.** As soon as Arthur boarded his ship and began the long journey by water from the United States to the South Pacific, he began to record the daily routine of his fellow sailors. It is clear that life for the men at sea can be demanding and difficult. Cleanliness was always the rule of the day. This image shows how swarms of sailors scrupulously scrubbed the ship's decks.

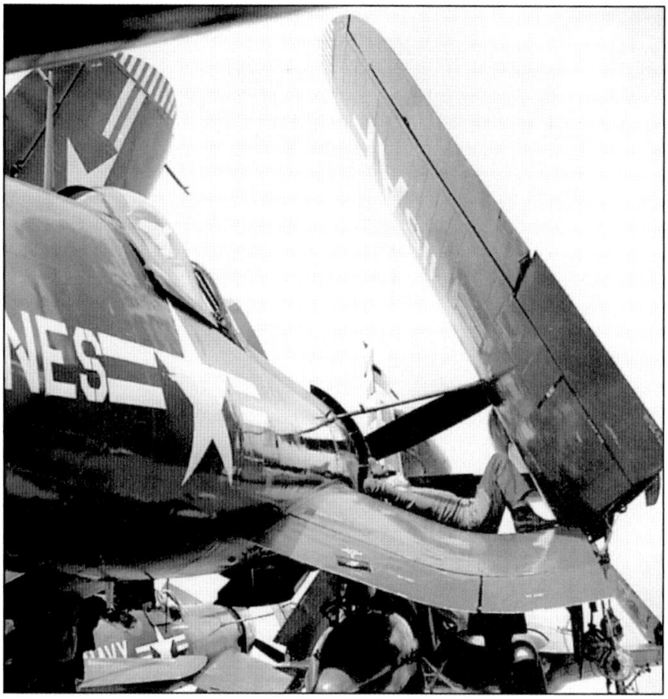

**Resting on an Aircraft Carrier, 1942.** After their duties on board the ship, the sailors enjoyed precious time alone, perhaps dreaming of their families back at home. Here Arthur perfectly captures one of his comrades catching some sun while resting comfortably on the wing of a jet.

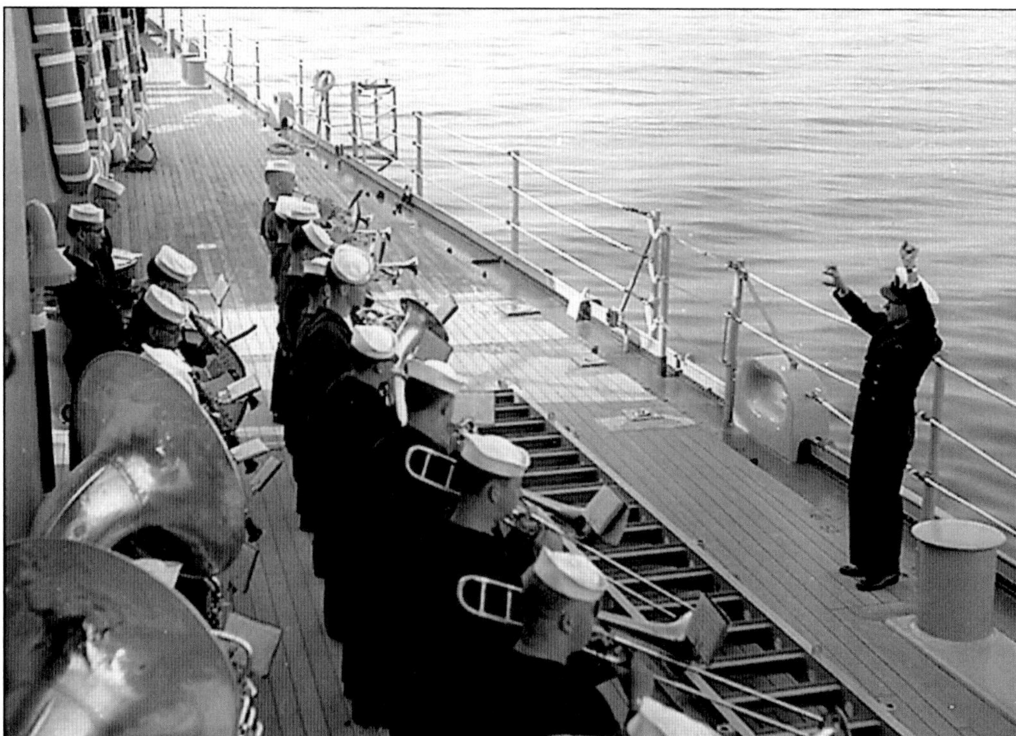

**And the Band Plays On, 1942.** To help relieve those long periods of loneliness that became part of everyday life while at sea, the ship's captain welcomed leisure activity. Here, as the band is facing the vast ocean, they play their music for all to hear.

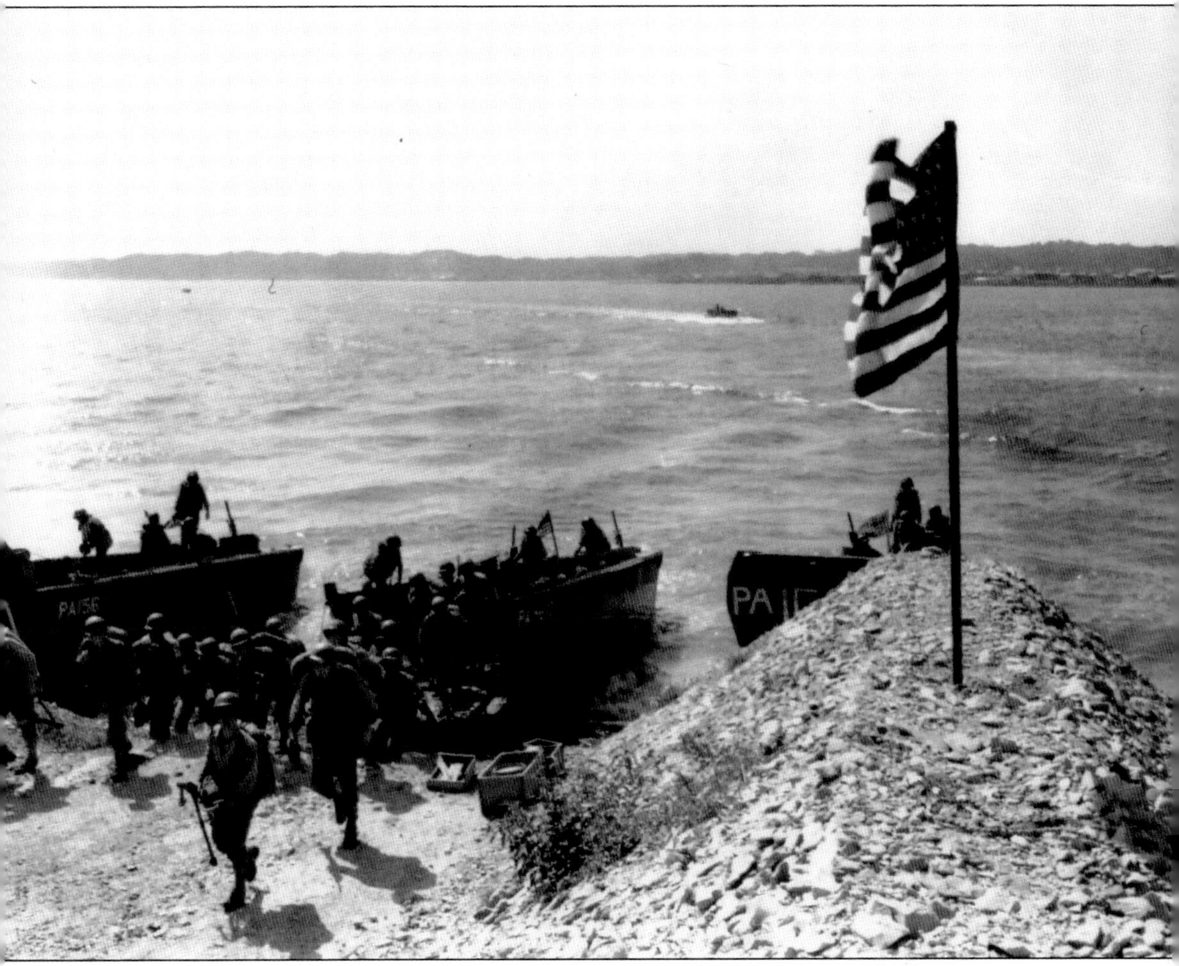

**RAISING THE FLAG AT IWO JIMA, 1945.** As the war raged on, Arthur with his ever-present camera seemed to be at the right place at the right time. This classic image was taken by Arthur when the Marines first landed at Iwo Jima in February 1945. It is believed that this shot predates the famous image taken by Joe Rosenthal showing American troops raising the United States flag atop Mount Suribachi signifying victory.

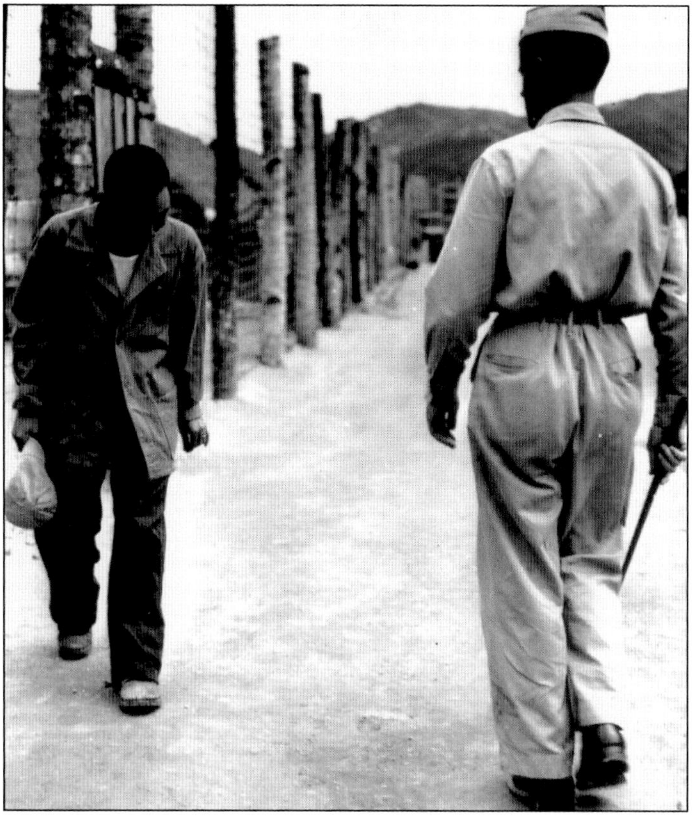

**JAPANESE PRISONER CAMP AT GUAM, C. 1945.** Japan invaded Guam shortly after attacking Pearl Harbor in 1941, but the Americans returned and liberated the island in July 1944. As a result, scores of Japanese POWs were held at the Guam Naval Station. They were assigned various construction, carpentry, and masonry duties under their captors' watchful eye.

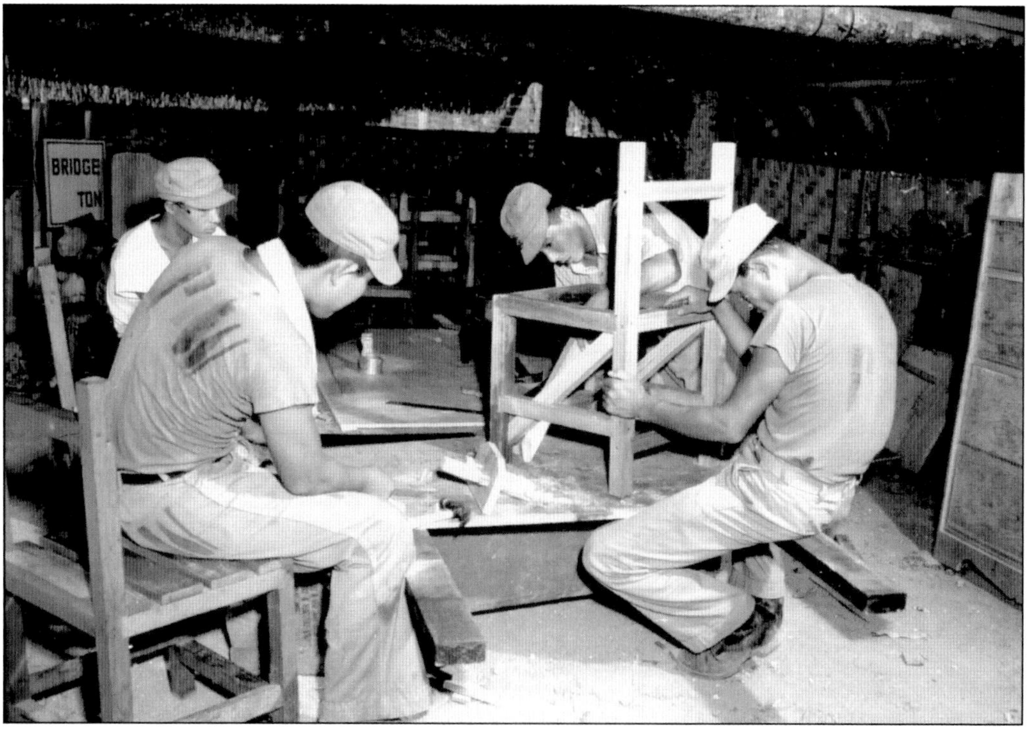

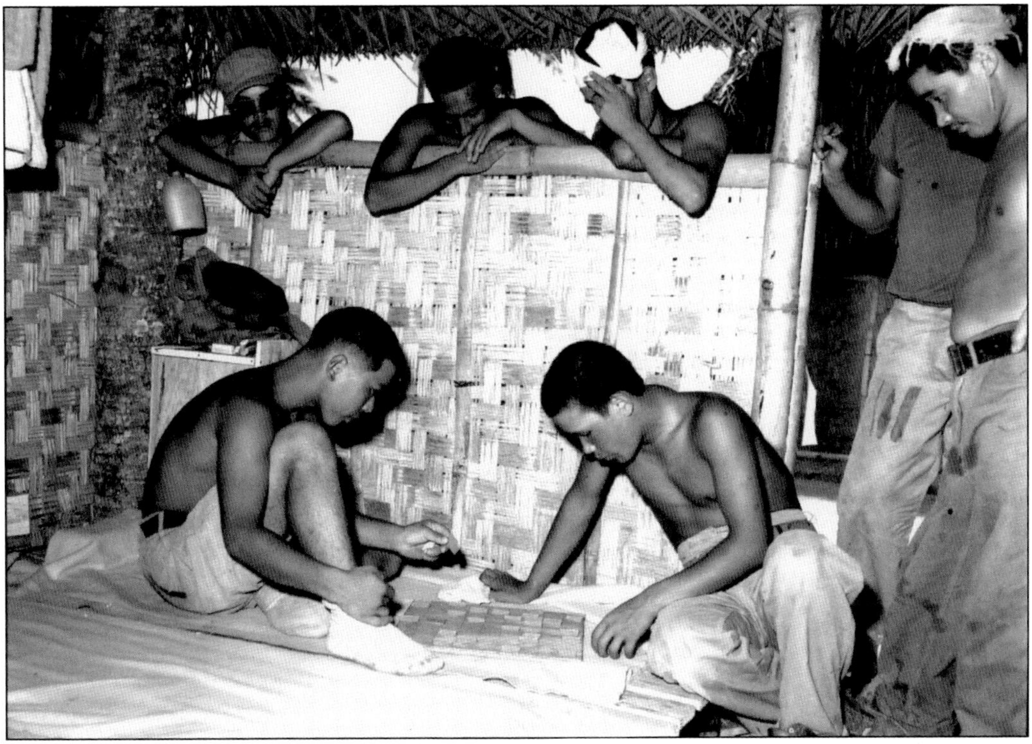

**LIFE AS A POW, C. 1945.** After the war, Arthur recalled that he made friends with and gained the confidence of many Japanese prisoners who were barracked at Guam before the war ended in 1945. These images show the humane treatment that was afforded the POWs. In the photograph above, the group looks on intently while two former soldiers play a board game, and pictured below, the prisoners have a hand at baseball, America's national pastime.

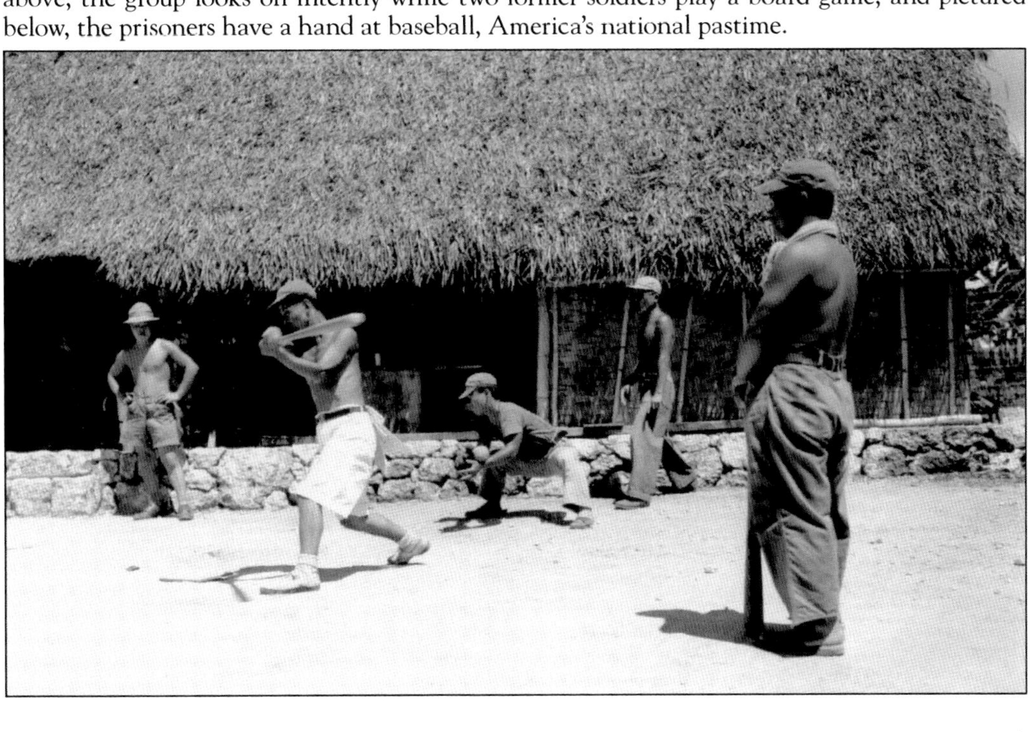

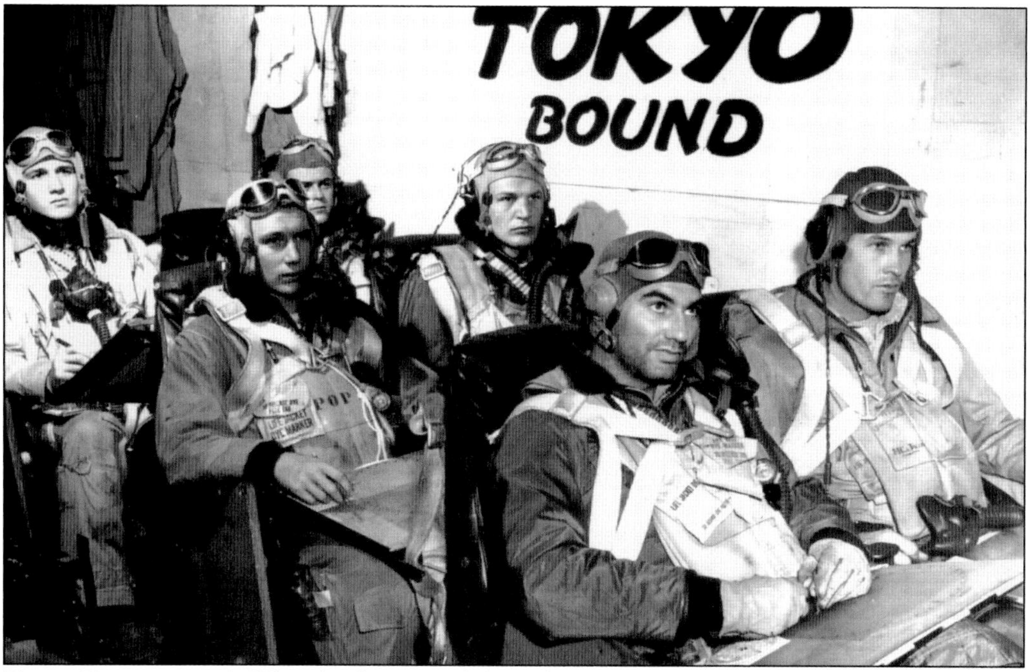


**TOKYO BOUND, 1945.** When he first joined the military, Arthur had no way of knowing that he would, in fact, be in the middle of some of the most famous and historic military activities of all time. Here Arthur takes the viewer inside a bomber plane that flew directly over and into Tokyo in 1945 as bombs were dropped. The war turned dramatically in favor of the United States and its allies shortly thereafter.

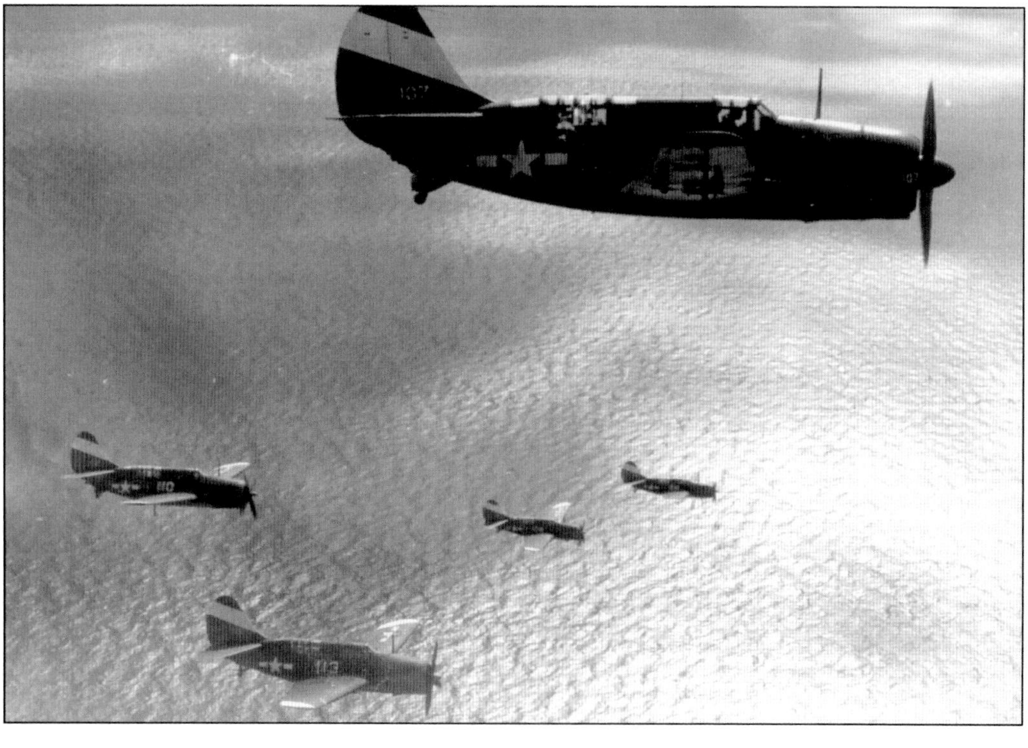

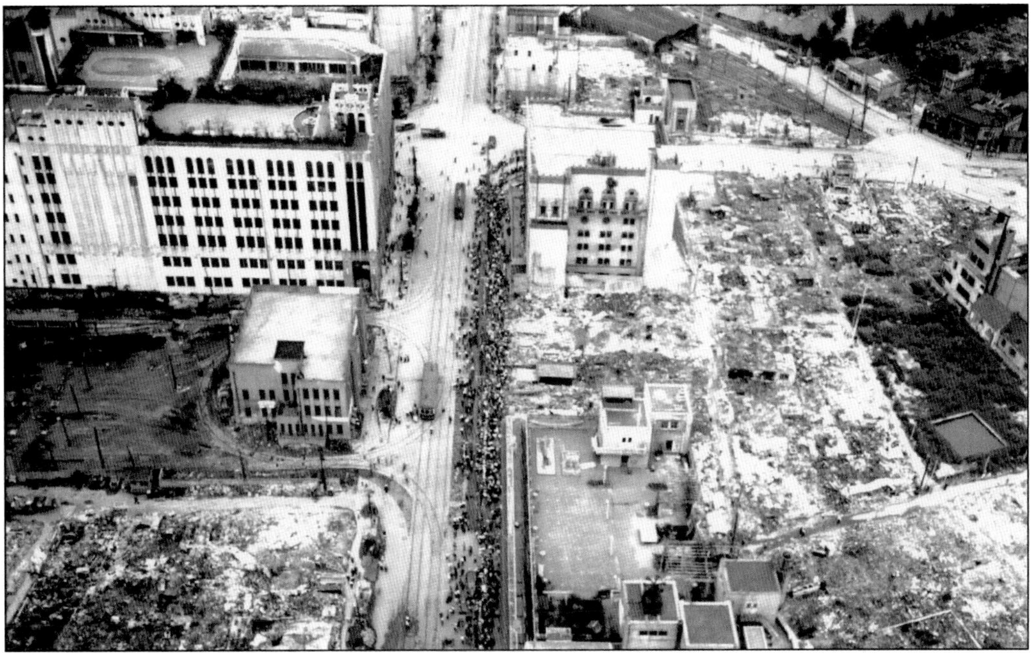

**THE DESTRUCTION OF WAR, 1945.** From a bomber plane, Arthur began to shoot furiously and documented the horrific scene directly after Tokyo was decimated by a relentless bombing attack. Here one can see what Arthur and his fellow soldiers saw as the pilot sought an area where they could land safely. Entire blocks of buildings in Japan's capital vanished into rubble as a result of the mission.

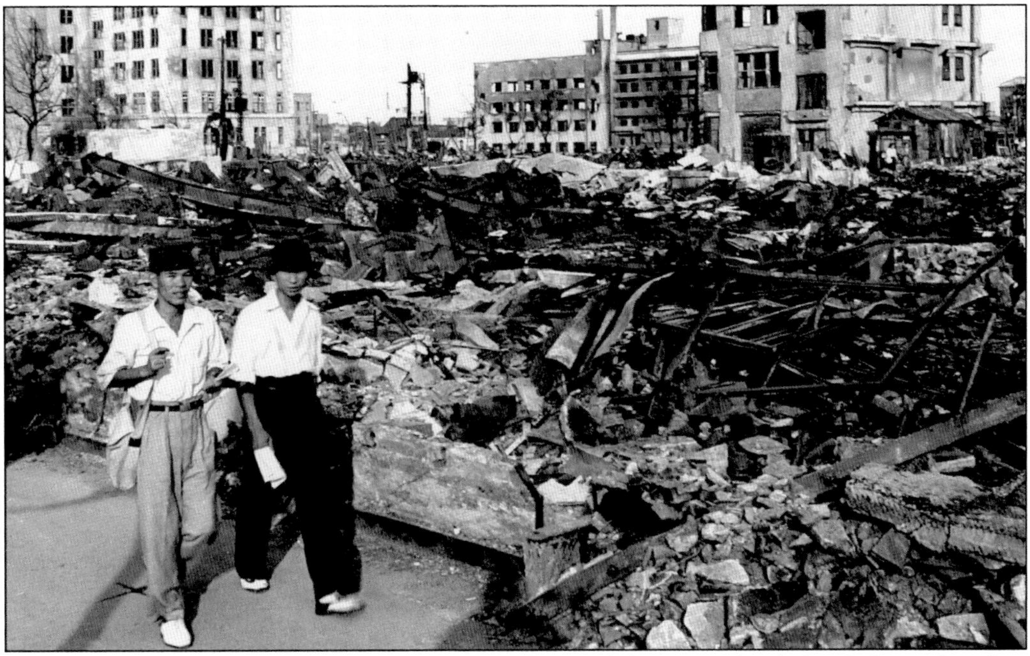

**WALKING AMONG THE RUINS, 1945.** When Arthur and the troops landed in Tokyo, what they witnessed was stunning. Japanese residents walked among the ruins of what had at one time been a vital and vibrant city. These gentlemen seem to be at ease as they glance at Arthur's camera.

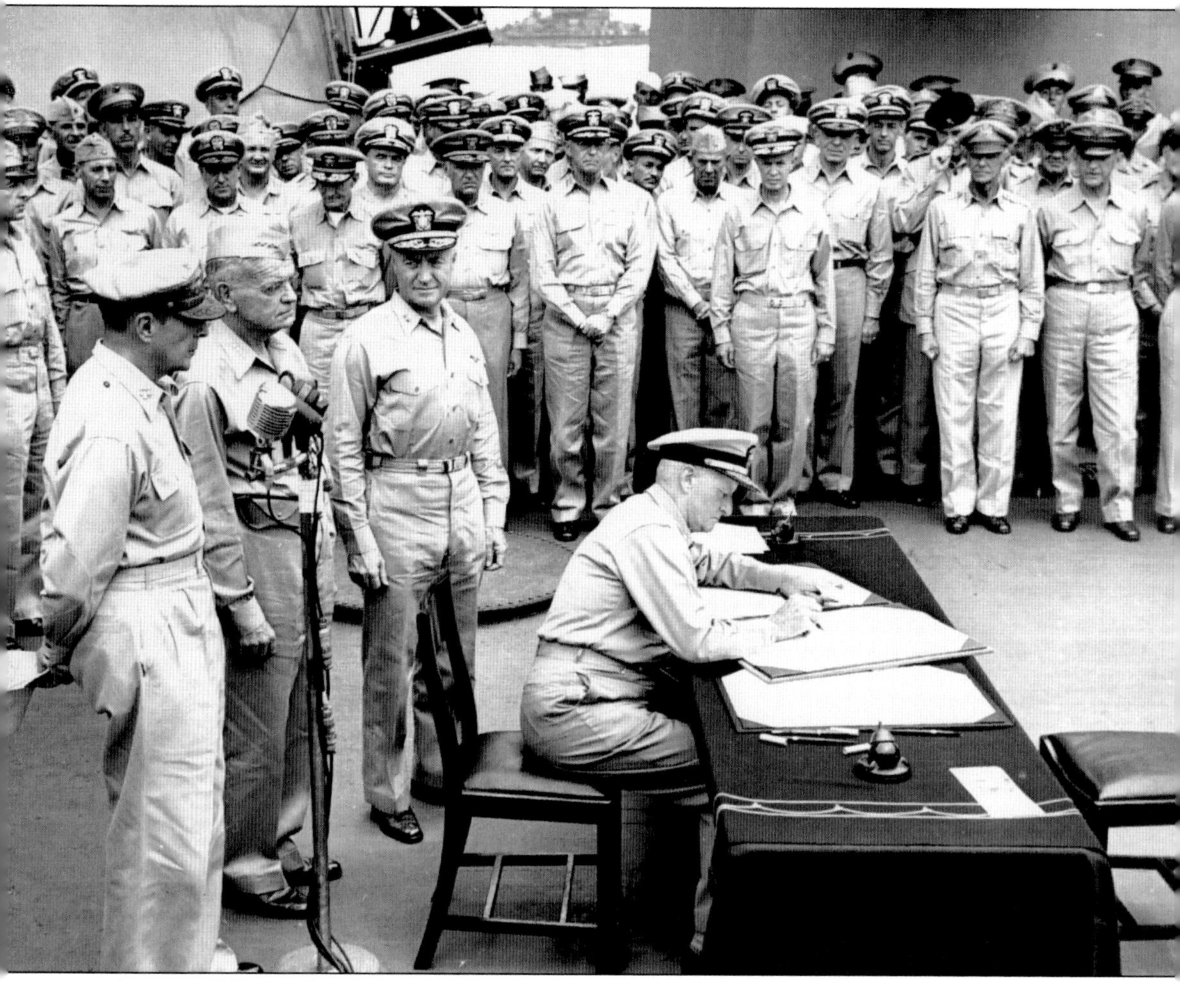

**ADMIRAL NIMITZ SIGNING THE INSTRUMENT OF SURRENDER, 1945.** Fleet Adm. Chester Nimitz, with Gen. Douglas MacArthur, Adm. William Halsey, and Rear Adm. Forrest Sherman standing behind him, signs the formal surrender document for the United States and makes it official. The Second World War is over. (Courtesy of the National Portrait Gallery, Smithsonian Institution.)

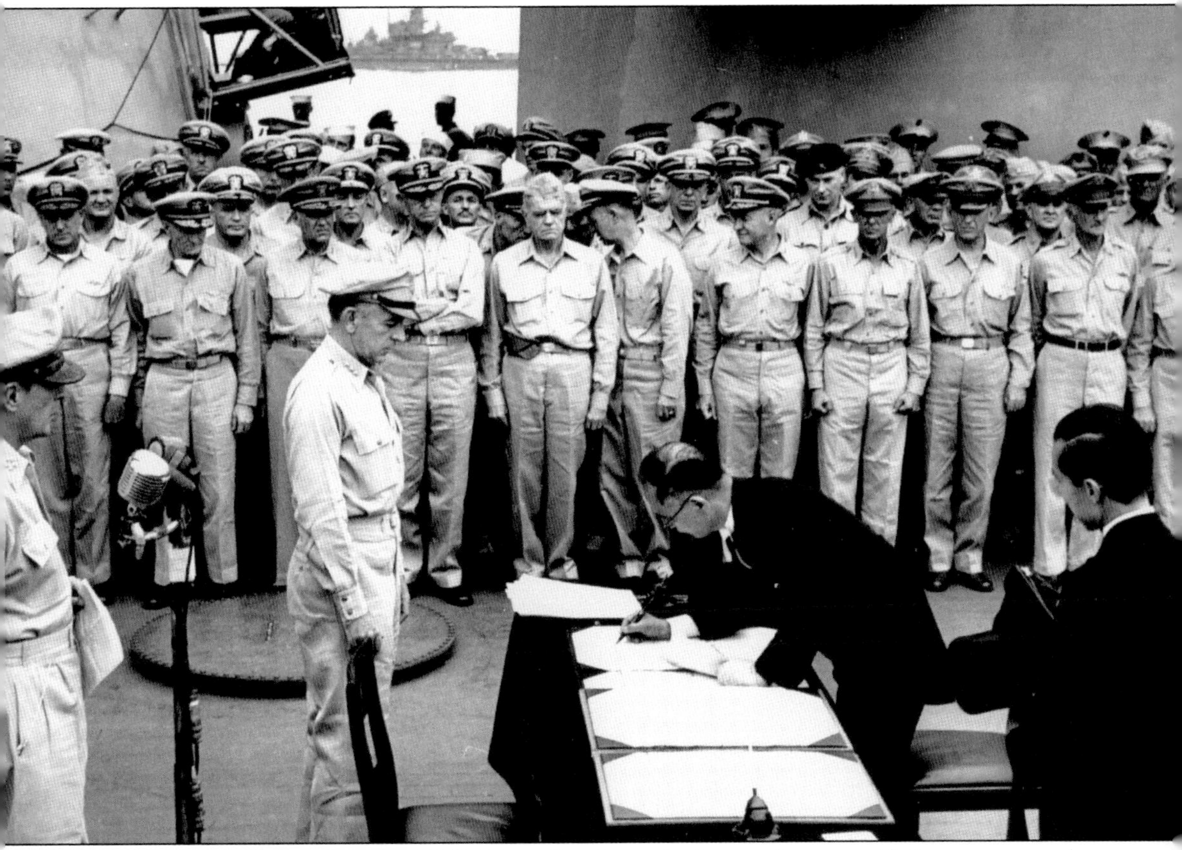

**FORMAL SURRENDER OF JAPAN, 1945.** The official conclusion to the war with Japan occurred on September 2, 1945, aboard the USS *Missouri*, the flagship of the U.S. Third Fleet, anchored in Tokyo Bay. Japanese foreign minister Mamoru Shigemitsu is shown here signing the formal Instrument of Surrender on behalf of the Japanese government. Arthur captured on film the historic signing ceremony, which lasted 23 minutes and was broadcast throughout the world.

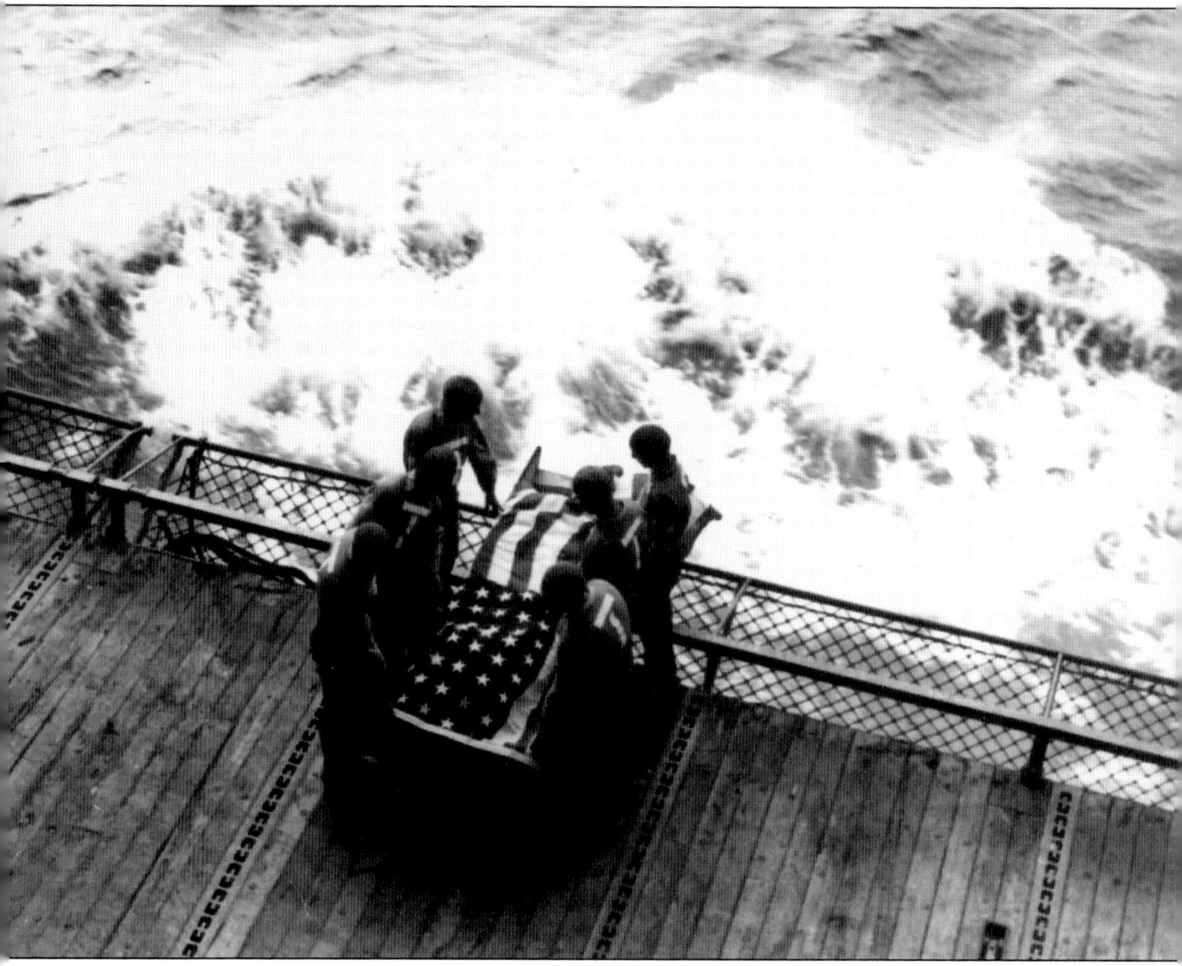

**BURIAL AT SEA, C. 1945.** During the fierce war, there were many causalities. Because of limited facilities aboard military ships, numerous burials occurred at sea. Arthur's photograph captures the stark reminder of the reality of war, as military personnel prepare to "bury" a flag-draped coffin in the ocean.

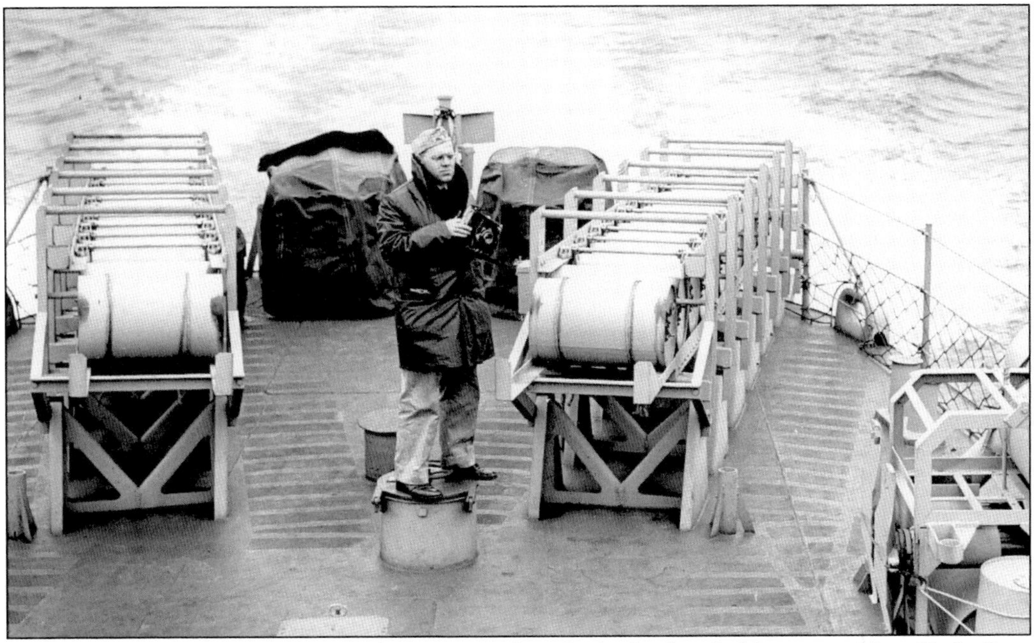

**A Pensive Soldier, 1945.** By the time Arthur Rickerby headed home to New York City, he had seen destruction and horror that was unimaginable only a few years before when he photographed sports and other activities at Duke University. Like millions of returning veterans, Arthur wondered what would come next.

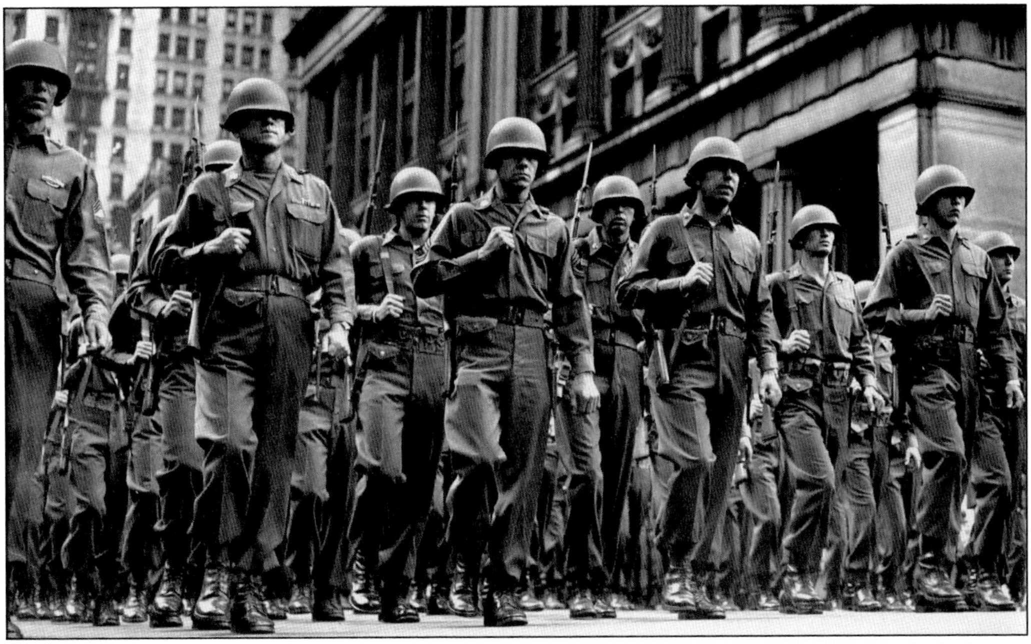

**In Perfect Military Form, 1946.** From August to December 1945, the 82nd Airborne Division conducted occupation in Berlin. There, while being reviewed by Gen. George Patton, the 82nd received its title "America's Guard of Honor." In January 1946, it returned to the United States aboard the *Queen Mary* and led the victory parade in New York City. Arthur was there to capture the moment.

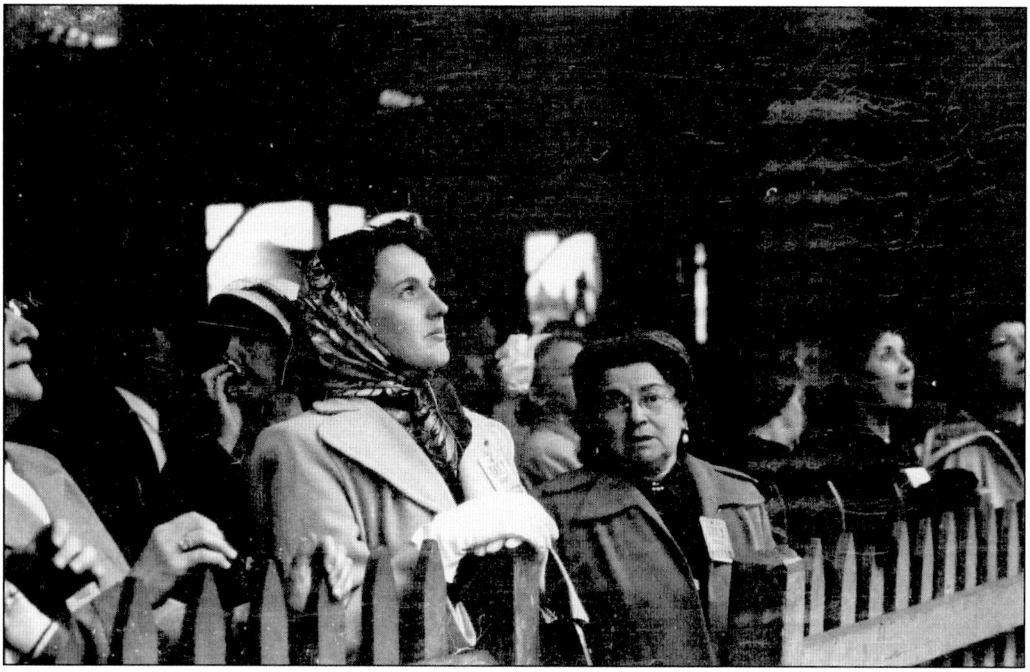

**New York City Victory Parade, 1946.** Thousands of people jammed Fifth Avenue as crack troops and snappy cadets marched through the streets of New York City in celebration of the end of World War II. Arthur was able to document a city that was now alive with joy as onlookers tearfully cheered on the returning troops in a ticker-tape parade that is recalled to this day.

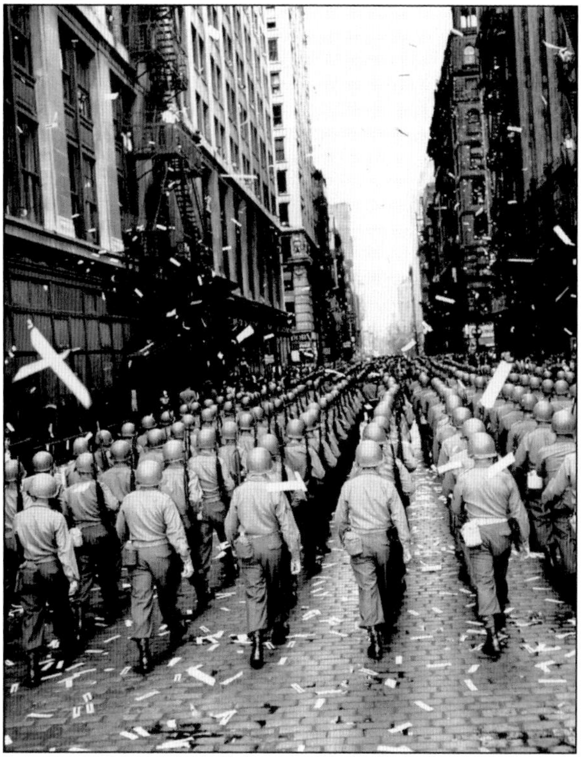

**War Weary Veterans Return Home, 1946.** It was a long struggle, but countless troops, weary and tired but ultimately victorious, made their way back to the United States at the war's end. Here they soak up the gratitude of a nation. Many would exchange their fatigues and steel helmets for civilian clothes when they returned to America.

# *Three*

# POSTWAR NEW YORK

Directly after serving his country while at war in the Pacific Theater, Arthur returned to New York City, the hometown he loved so dearly. He found himself in the midst of a city that, for its sheer size, vibrancy, and energy, had barely missed a beat during the World War II years. This was, in a sense, a culture shock to the veteran, since his photography work in the military had exposed him to the horrors of combat in a personal and intense way.

By 1946, as many of the world's great cities lay in ruin as a result of the horrific war, Arthur's hometown and its surrounding area assumed a new and vibrant global dominance. Its population was booming. By the mid-1940s, there were well over seven million people in the city, from all over the world. It was a cosmopolitan hub of activity that had impressive numbers of Asian, African, South American, and Caribbean immigrants joining the European families whose ancestors had settled in the area during the previous century and a half. But it was not only the sheer number and diversity of people that was extraordinary, it was the reality that New York City seemed to inherit the role as the cultural center of the world from heavily bombed global cities such as Paris, London, Berlin, and Tokyo.

Arthur Rickerby was a man who from a very early age developed a keen eye for the subtleties of the way people lived, worked, and played. Upon returning home, he continued his love affair with the camera and within short order began to record life in the Big Apple and the surrounding area as a war-weary metropolis began to settle in and move forward. It was an exciting and invigorating time for Arthur and his generation. He recorded events of serious international import such as tense proceedings at the United Nations and the birth of Israel, as well as strikes and demonstrations within a city poised to progress into a new age. He also covered people enjoying themselves by escaping the bustle of the city and going to the racetrack or simply enjoying the state fair in Syracuse. His first photographic foray into New York City life was an interesting series that he recorded at the City Center Opera, some of which is shown here for the very first time. Arthur was good at his trade and quickly found that his photographs were sought after by many.

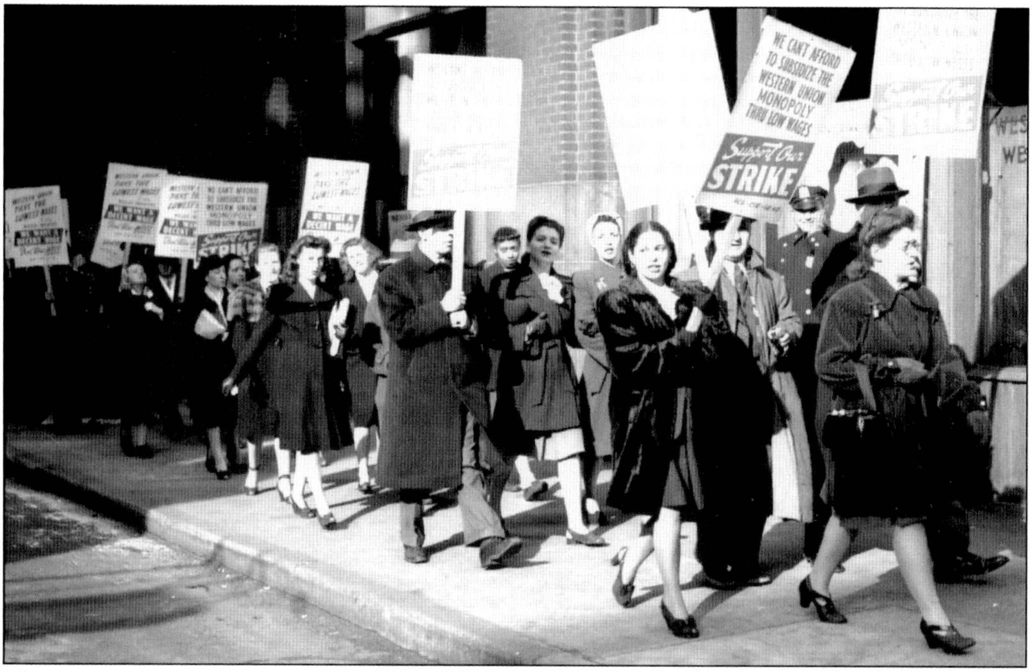


**WESTERN UNION STRIKE, 1946.** New York City can be a contentious place, and protests sometime seem just part of urban life. Arthur photographed the first day of a Western Union strike for higher wages that was eventually settled. These images show employees who were rather well dressed and, even though the police were called, well behaved.

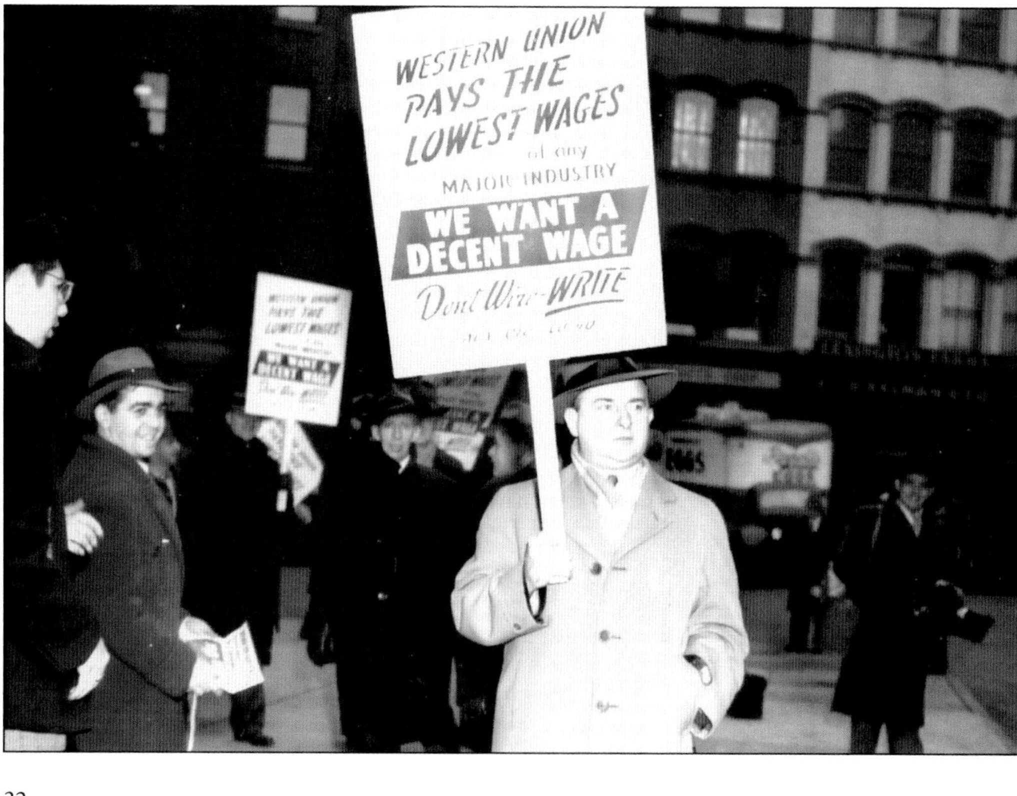

**CHILDREN PLEA FOR PEACE, 1947.** In an effort to prevent future conflicts between nations, the United Nations was founded in New York City in late 1945. The hope for peace was so widespread that schoolchildren decided to make their views known. The image to the right features a letter written by kindergartners from a city public school to United States delegate Warren Austin. The letter contains a plea by the children, denouncing war and simply asking why people could not get along together. In the photograph below, Arthur captured the attentive children as their teacher reads the reply letter sent to them by Delegate Austin acknowledging their hope for peace and exclaiming, "Little people make the whole world."

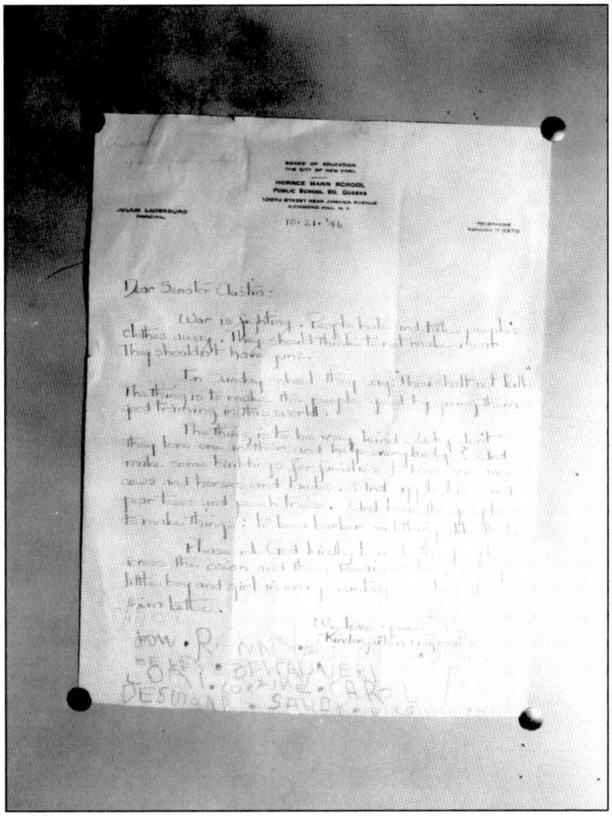

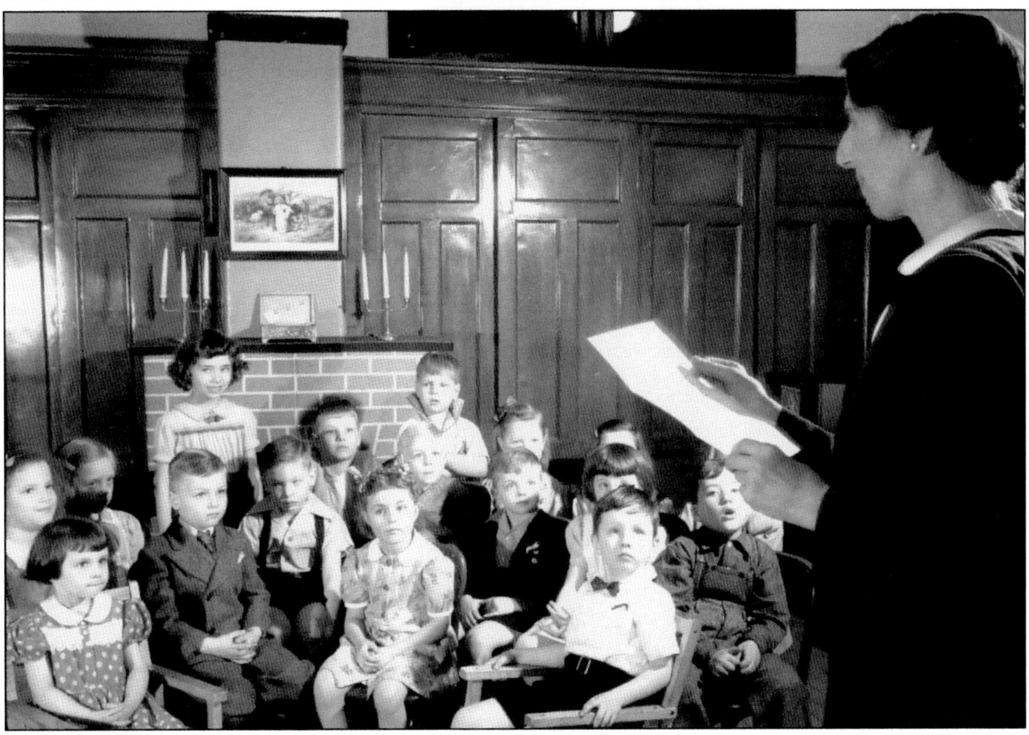

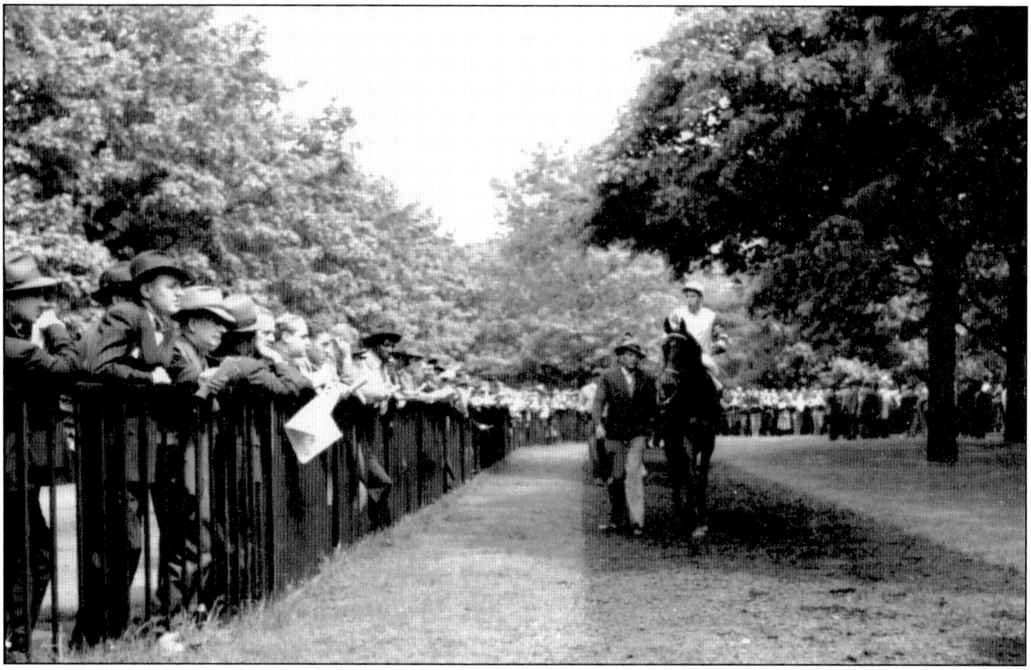

**BELMONT PARK, 1947.** Life in New York City was not always steeped in world events. New Yorkers enjoyed their leisure time as well. Drawing crowds of hopeful winners since it opened in 1905, Long Island's Belmont Park is the largest dirt course in Thoroughbred racing. In addition to being world-famous as the home of the Belmont Stakes, the third leg of the Triple Crown, Belmont is considered one of the most beautifully landscaped venues in American sports. Arthur photographed life at the track, including spectators carefully studying their racing sheets and gathering at the fence of the stately paddock area to inspect the competition, trying to determine which horse to wager on.

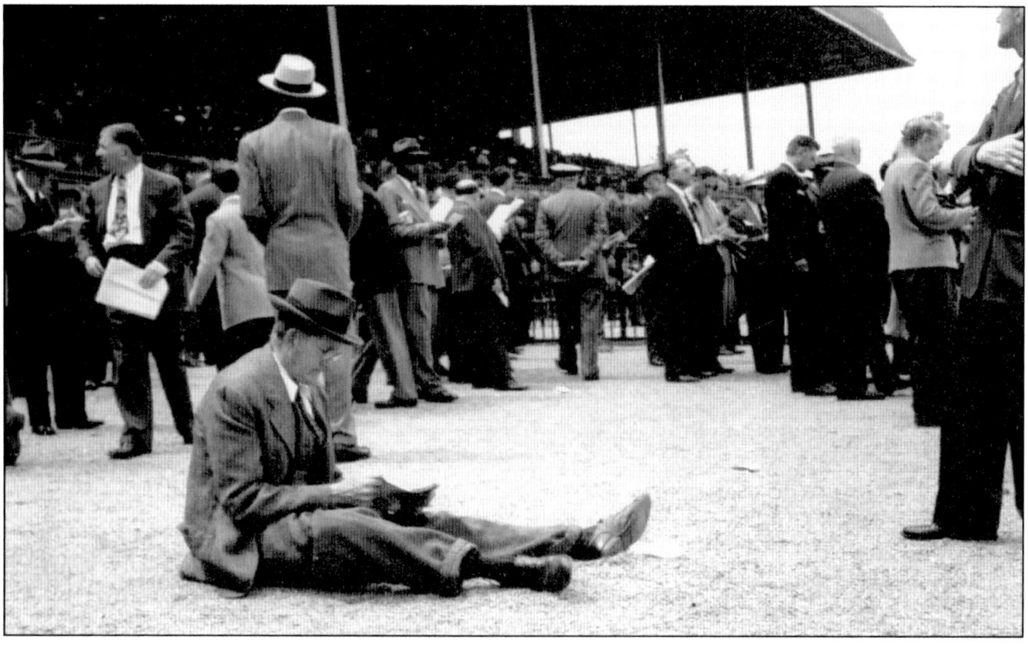

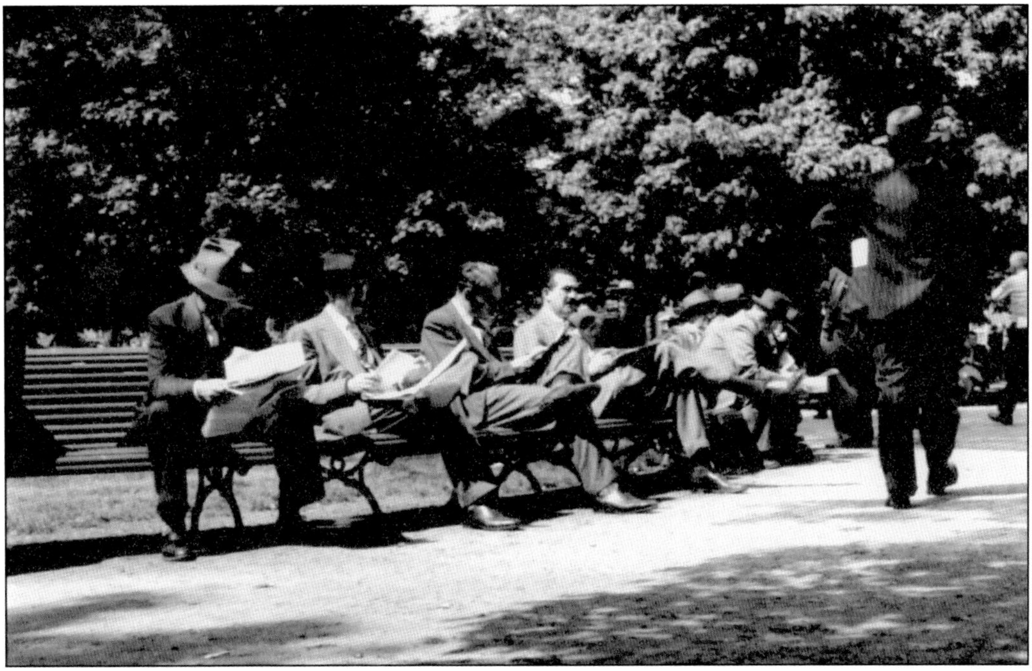

**SERIOUS BUSINESS, 1947.** Showing concentration that would make a college student proud, these bettors study tip sheets, programs, and racing forms in an attempt to give them every edge prior to placing wagers on their favorite horses. The ever-allusive hope of picking a surefire 50 to 1 shot is what keeps many racing fans coming back to the track again and again.

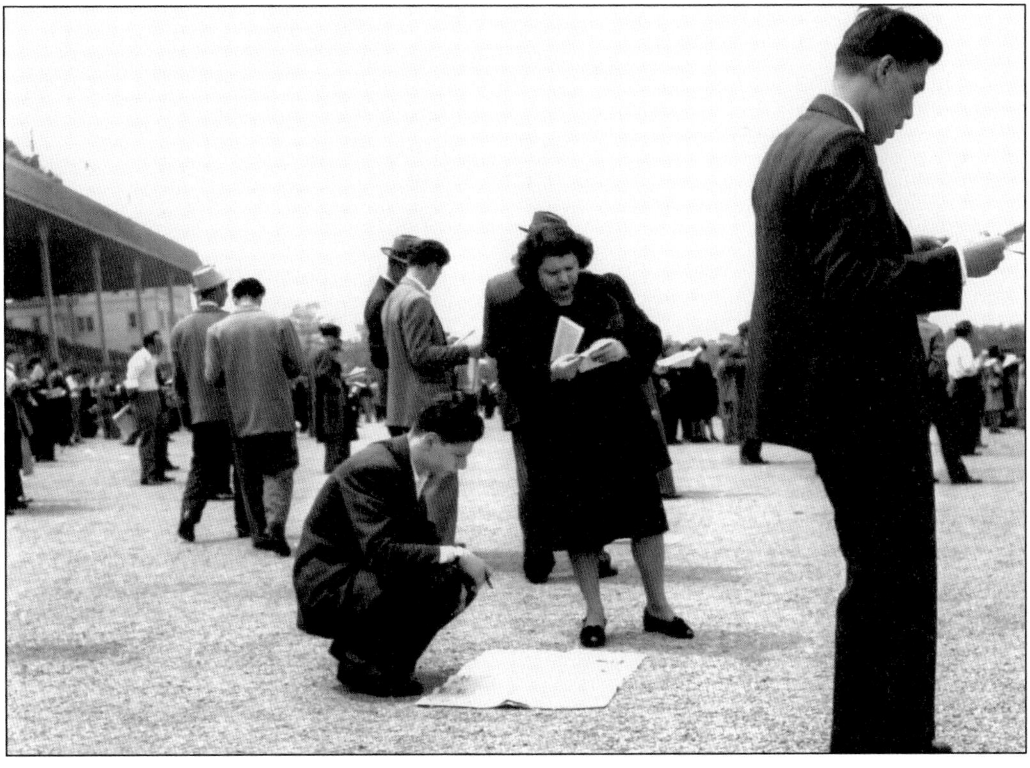

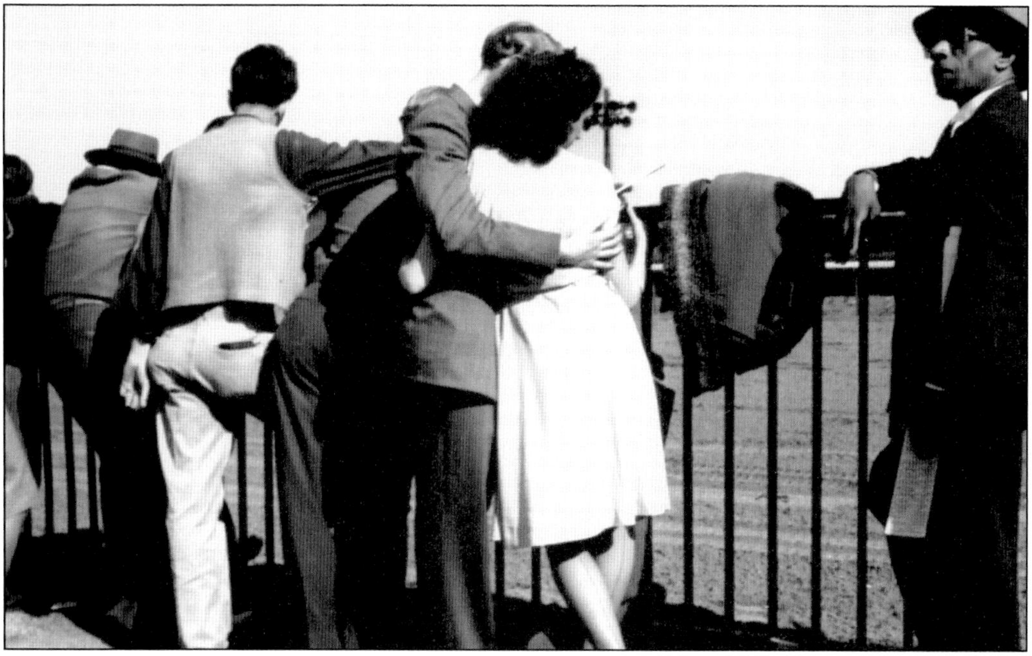

**AND THEY'RE OFF, 1947.** These photographs show the tension and excitement generated among men and women as post time approaches. The shot above shows a couple at the rail leisurely awaiting the start of the race, while two women below lean forward in earnest, hoping for a big payday.

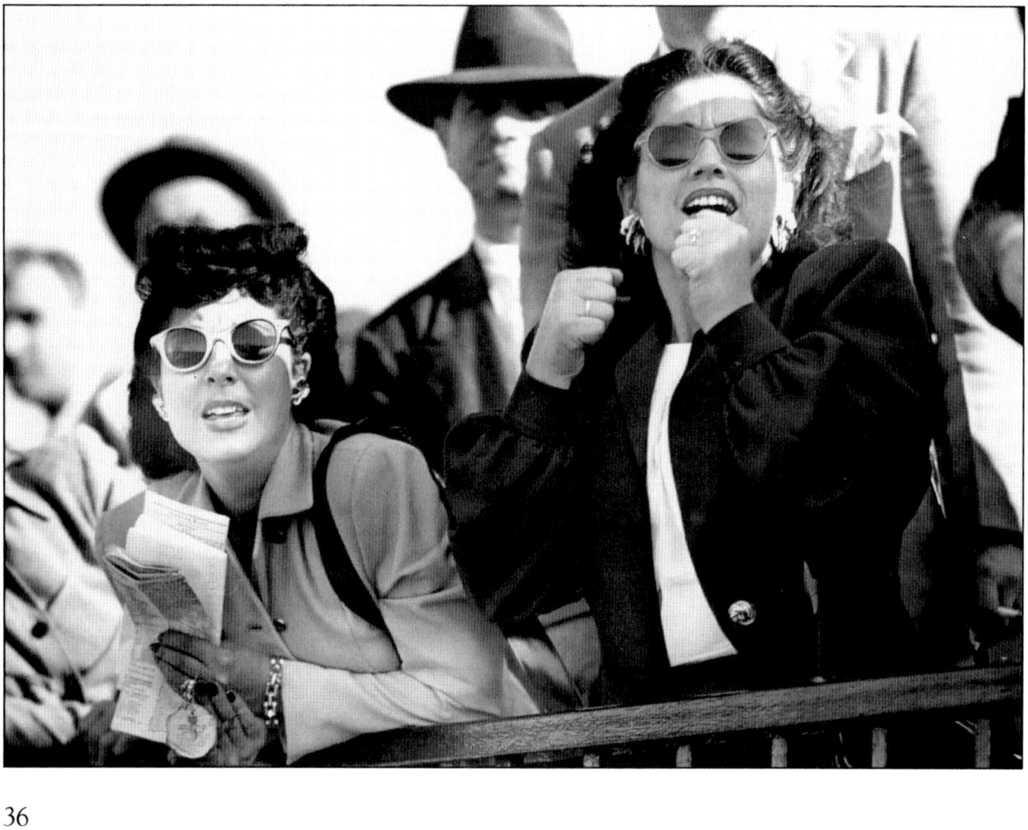

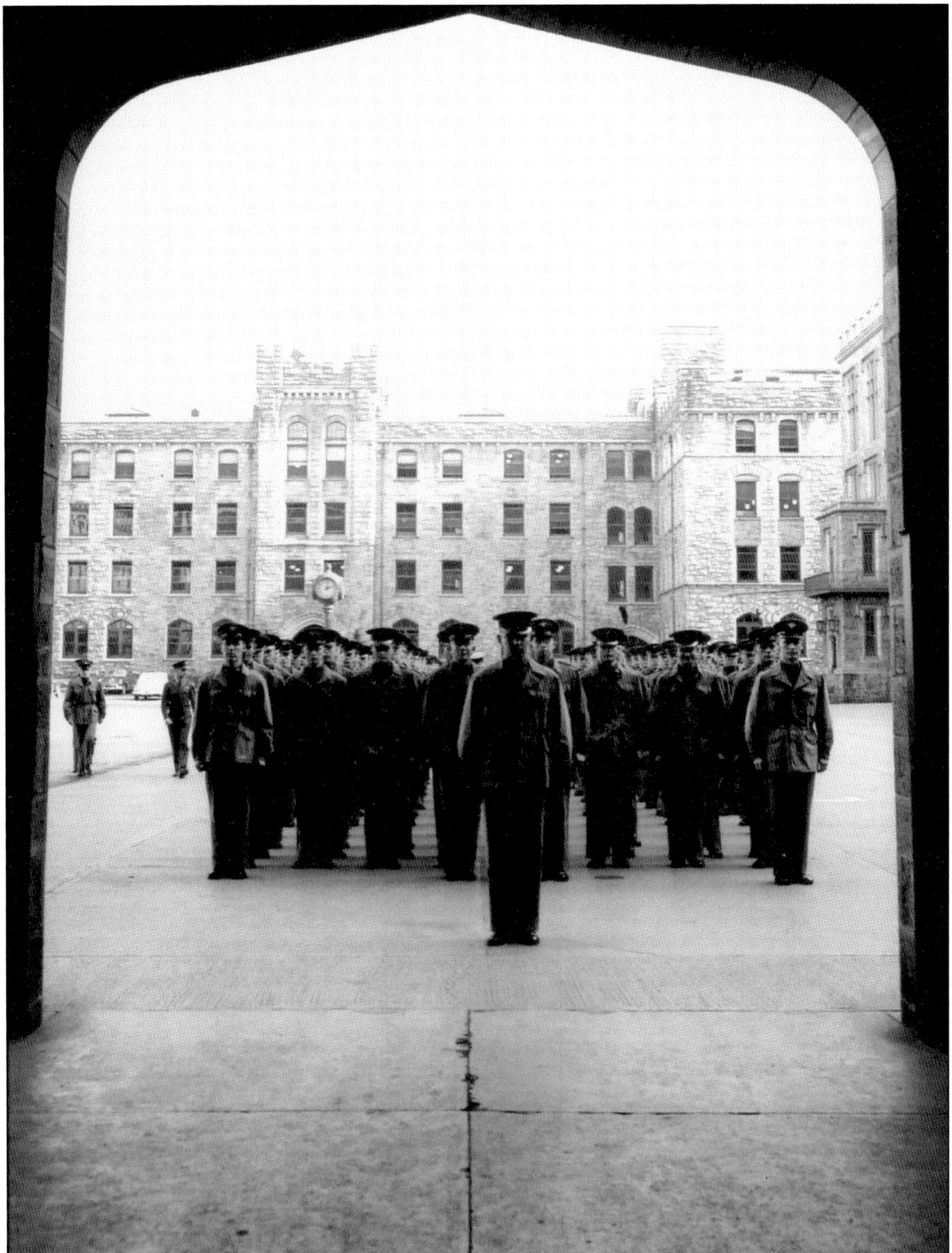

**THE WEST POINT EXPERIENCE, C. 1948.** "It is a regrettable fact that the United States Military Academy at West Point is a comparatively unknown institution insofar as an appreciation of its seriousness is concerned," so said Gen. Maxwell D. Taylor, outgoing superintendent in 1948. With those words, Arthur Rickerby decided that he would travel from the city into the Empire State in an attempt to capture "the West Point experience" through photography. Here, seen through the archway of one of the courtyards at the academy, cadets line up precisely at noon.

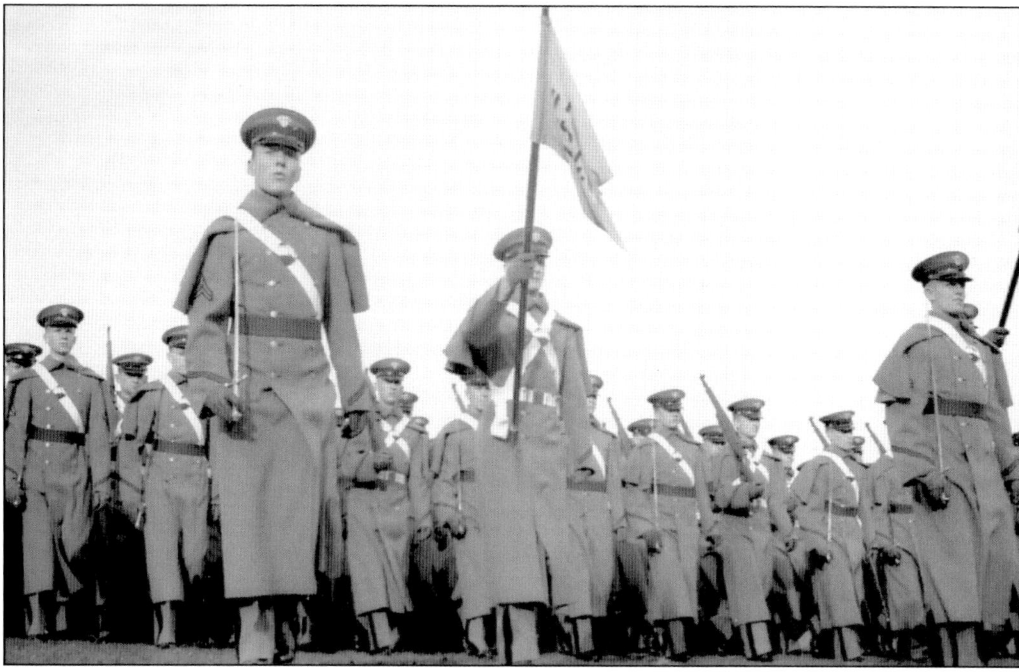

**THE TRADITION OF DISCIPLINE AND ORDER, C. 1948.** Drilling and marching in formation were familiar to former navy lieutenant Arthur Rickerby. Having seen combat action, Arthur knew all too well that military drills were an important part of creating an atmosphere of discipline and order that would serve a soldier well. Here the veteran photographer featured young cadets during drills at the United States Military Academy.

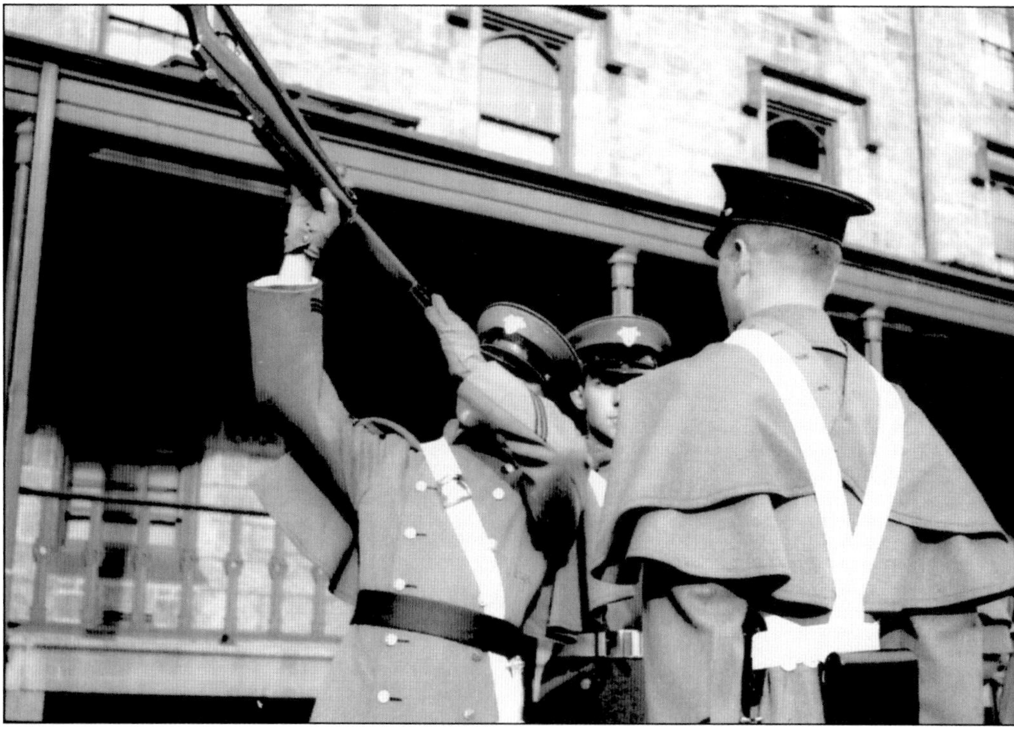

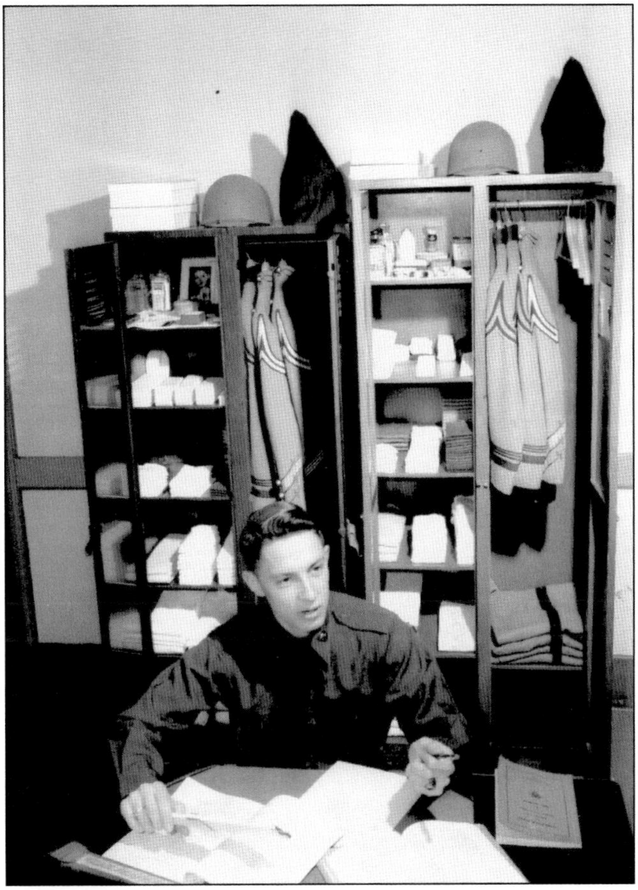

**MILITARY LEADERS IN THE MAKING, C. 1948.** Since the day it was established in 1802 by Pres. Thomas Jefferson, the United States Military Academy has produced numerous leaders of character for America's army, including Ulysses S. Grant, Stonewall Jackson, Douglas MacArthur, George Patton, and Dwight D. Eisenhower. These candid shots show one soldier studying in his room and another absorbing a military problem in the classroom.

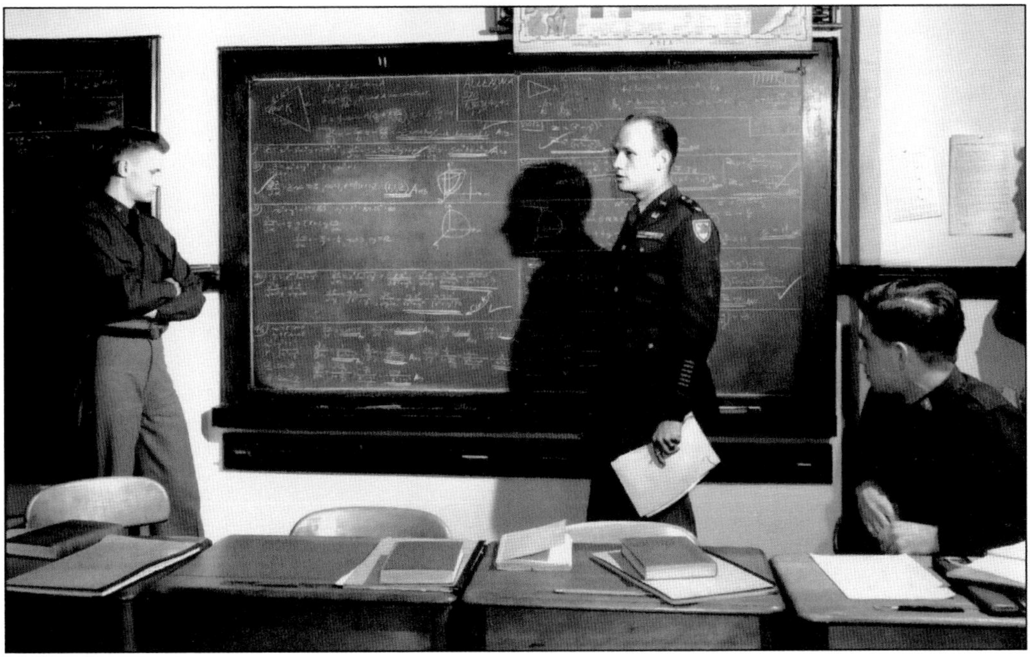

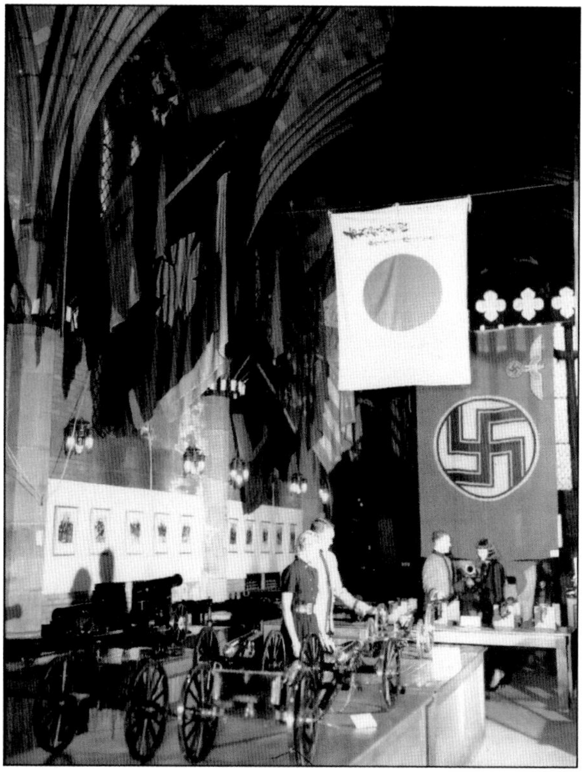

**All Work and Some Play, c. 1948.** Cadets at West Point prided themselves in their work at all times, but there was still time for leisure and visits from their girls back home. Here a small group of cadets shows off the many military artifacts at the point, while others enjoy an evening ball.

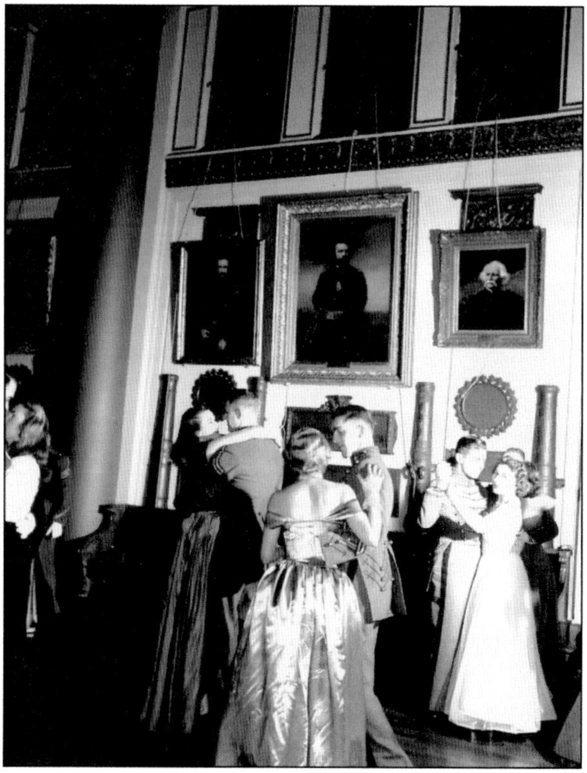

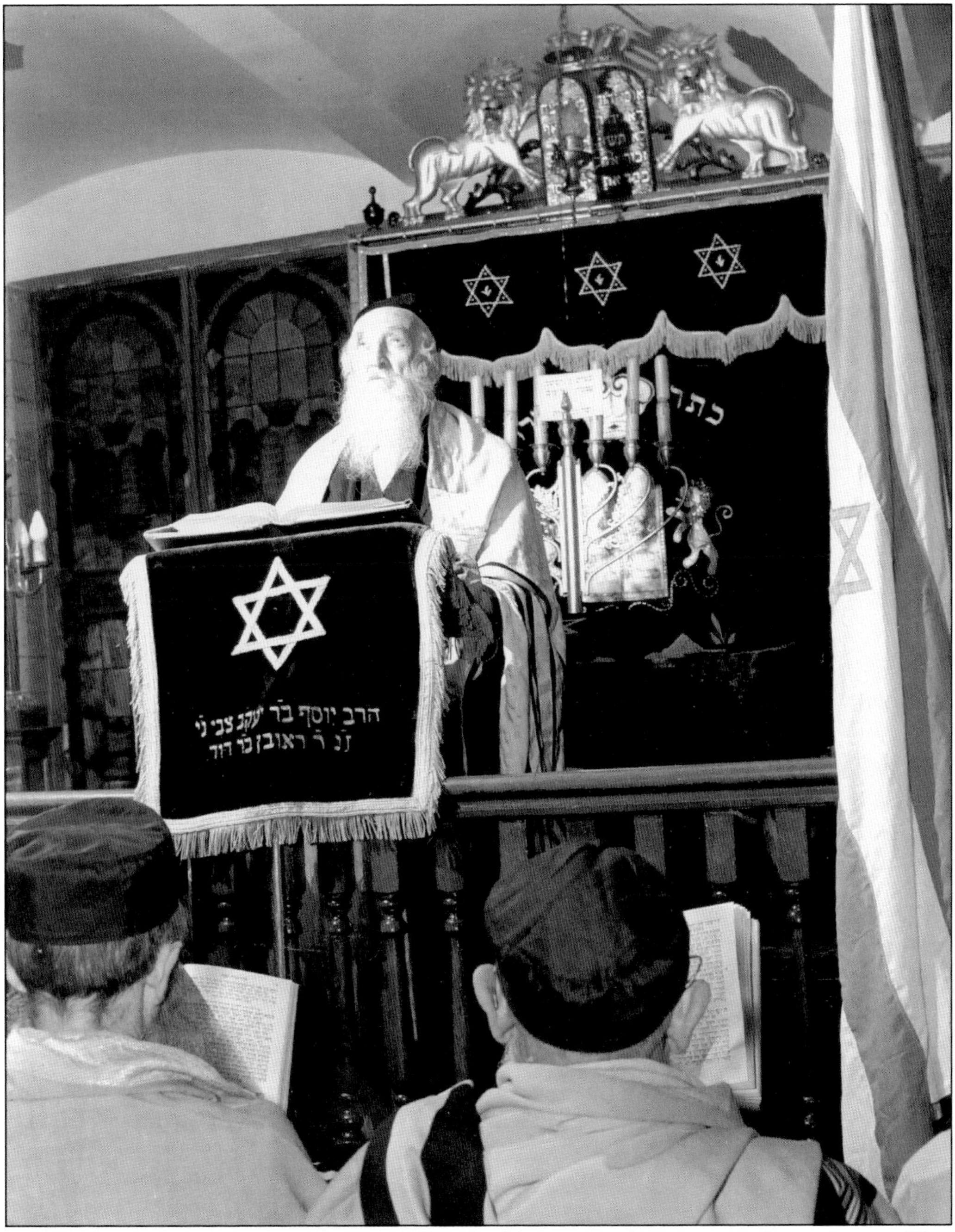

**THE BIRTH OF ISRAEL, 1948.** City news often had historic and international significance. This photograph shows Rabbi Hersh Belinsky leading the prayer of elders at the Home of Old Israel in Manhattan after hearing of the proclamation creating the new Jewish State of Israel. Pres. Harry Truman announced U.S. recognition of the new state 20 minutes after it was proclaimed in May 1948. All over New York, residents celebrated with prayer, song, dance, and cries of mazel tov!

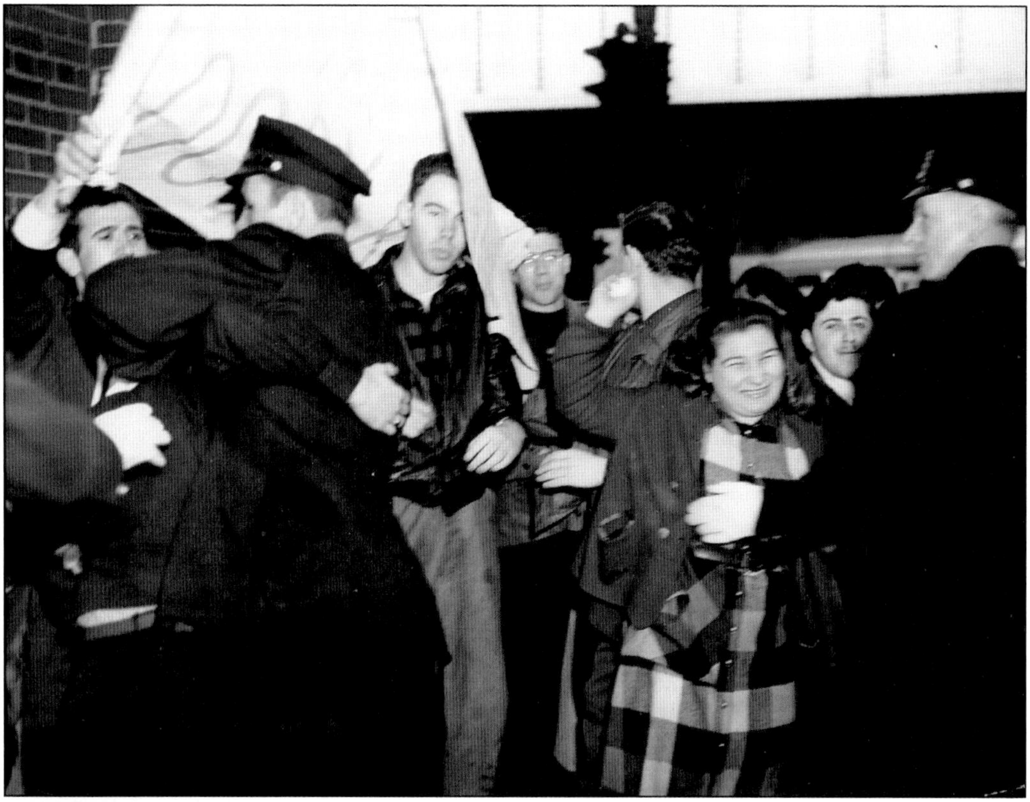

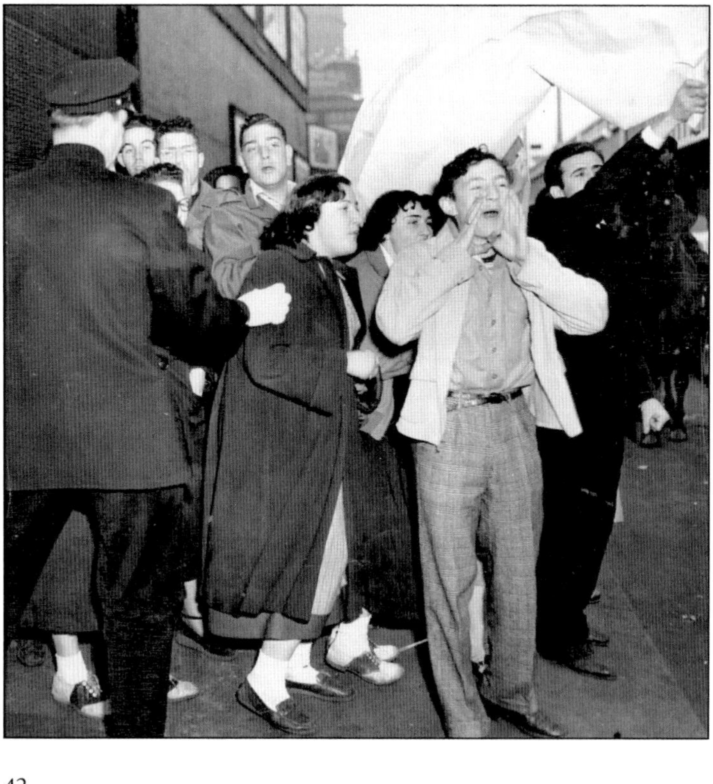

**EGGS FOR ERNIE, 1949.** A separate Israeli state did not end anti-Semitism even among friends and allies of the United States. These images show young Jewish picketers throwing eggs and booing Britain's foreign secretary Ernest Bevin after he made anti-Semitic statements just prior to his visit to New York City in March 1949. Bevin, a former English trade unionist, upon seeing the angry crowd, reportedly stated, "It reminds me of when I used to picket other people."

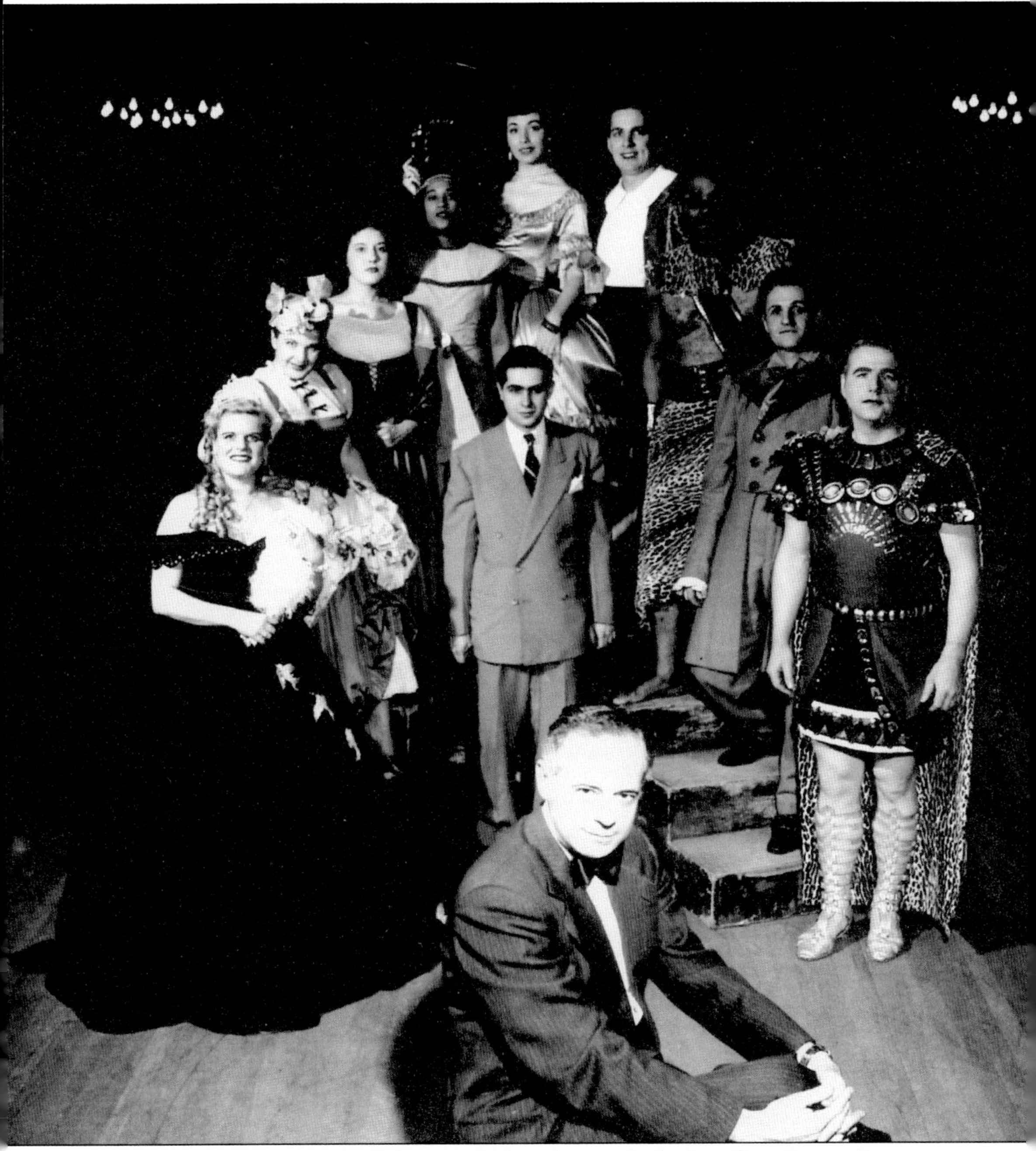

**CITY CENTER OPERA, 1949.** In February 1944, audiences flocked to City Center Opera to witness the start of what Mayor Fiorello H. LaGuardia dubbed "the people's opera company." Although skeptics doubted the decision to open a second city opera, particularly during a world war, the music-loving mayor believed that opera was essential to city life and wanted lower- and middle-class New Yorkers to enjoy it at affordable prices and without pretension. When it opened, ticket prices started at only 85¢ and topped out at $2.20.

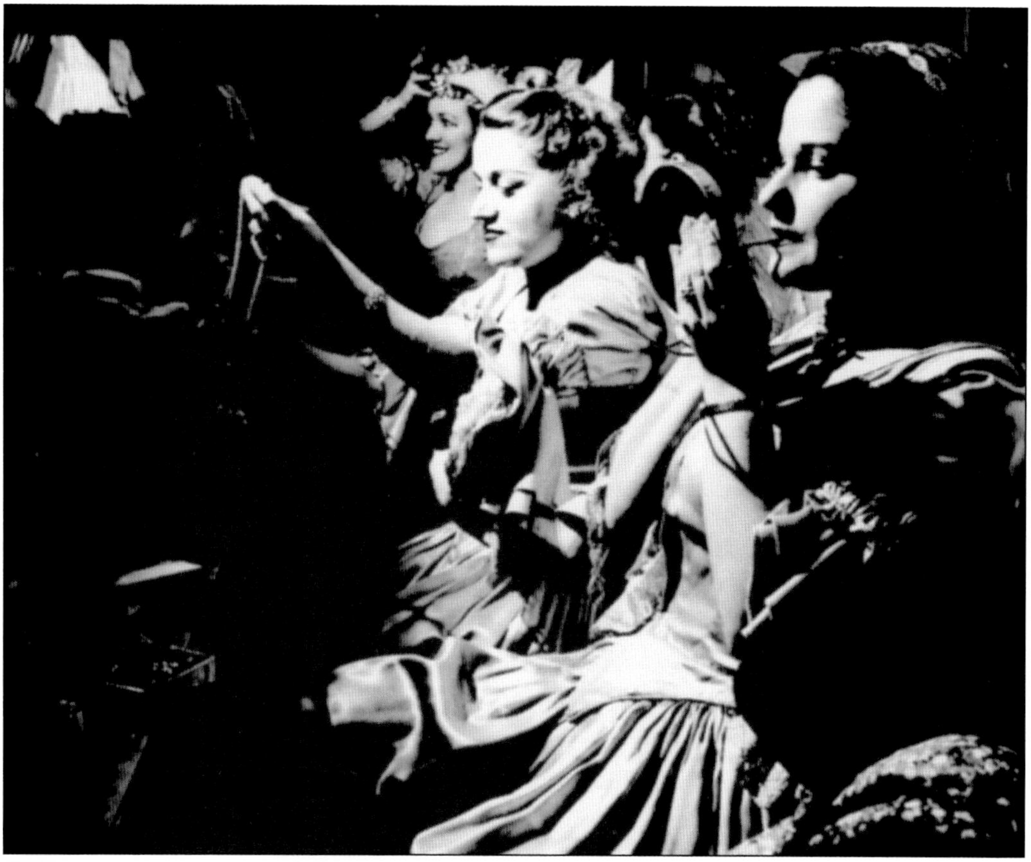

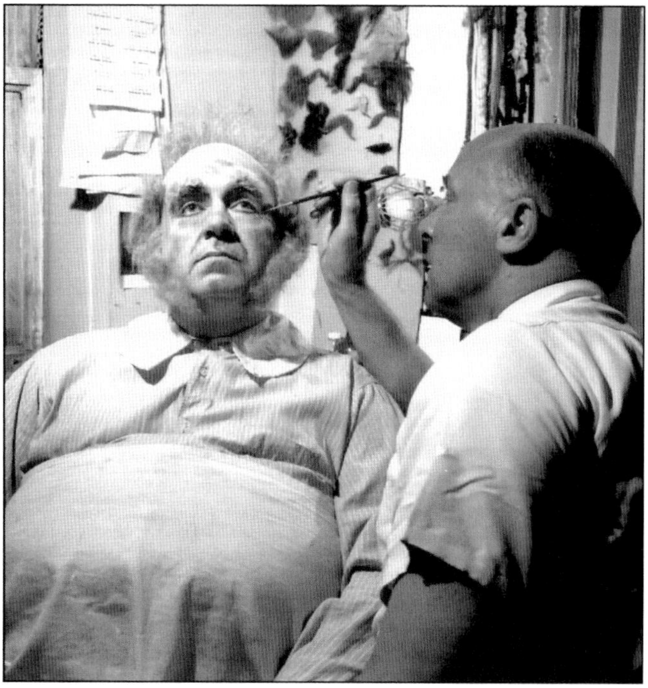

**The World of Make-Believe, 1949.** The composer-critic Deems Taylor called the City Center Opera "democracy in action, a democracy realizing the work of the individual." But even individuals, plying their trade as actors, need the all-important makeup to turn reality into make-believe. Here, several hours before the curtain went up at City Center Opera in 1949, Arthur photographed actors preparing for their night's work in the makeup room.

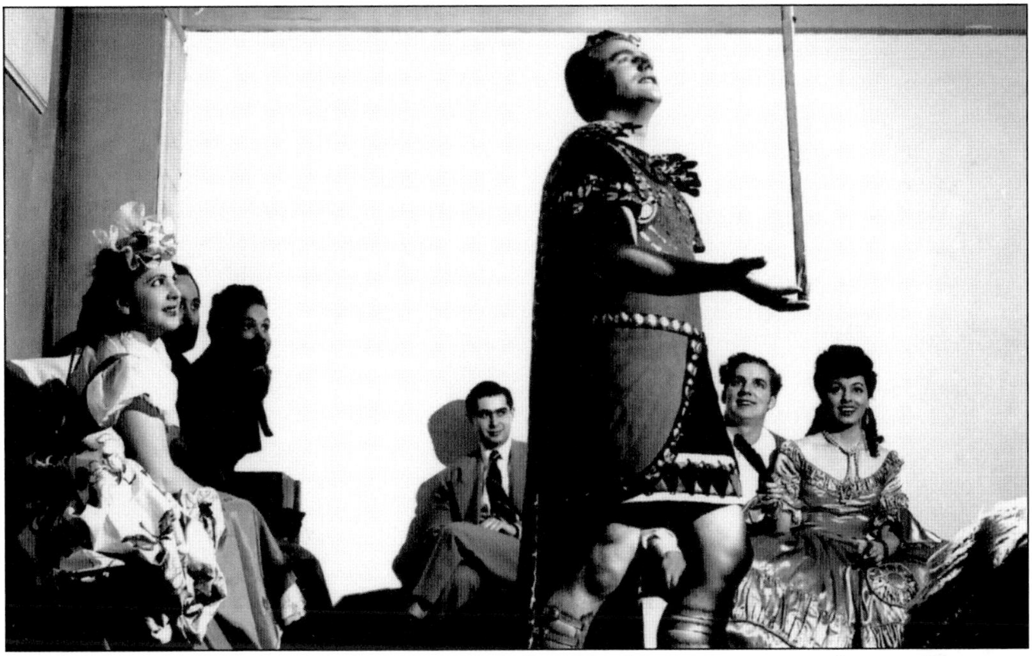

**ACTING NEW YORK CITY STYLE, 1949.** Legendary stars have given outstanding performances for many years at the City Center Opera. From Paul Robeson and Tallulah Bankhead to Jose Ferrer and Beverly Sills, actors have thrilled audiences for decades. By the end of the 1940s, the opera had become a cultural haven for New Yorkers as an affordable and fun complement to Broadway, Carnegie Hall, and the Metropolitan Opera House.

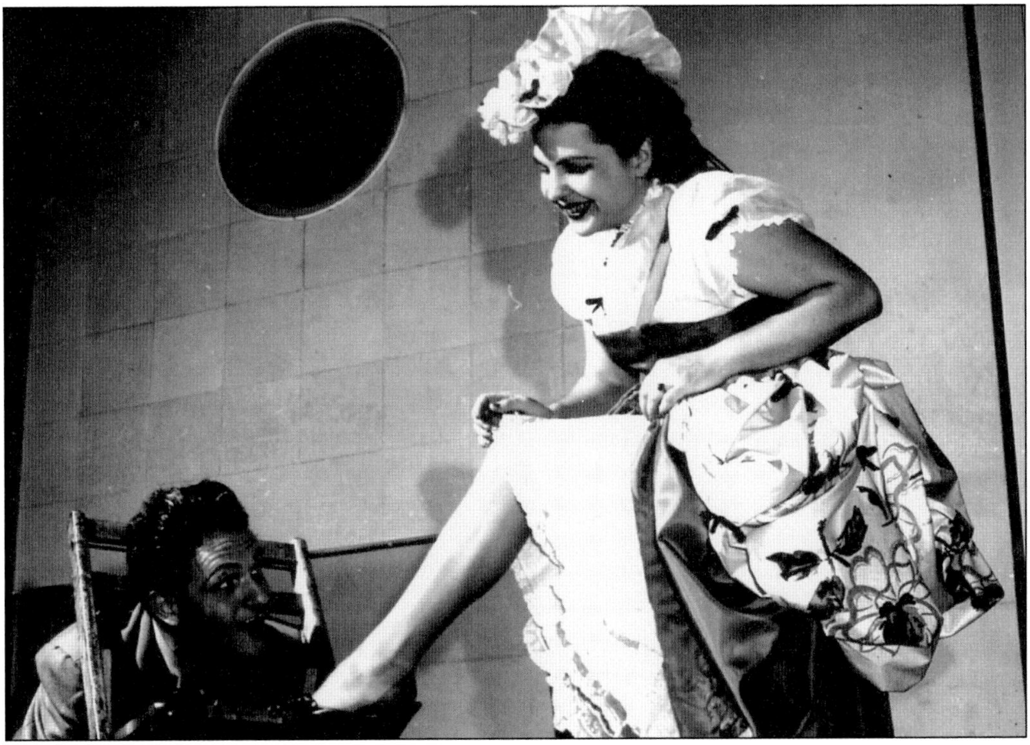

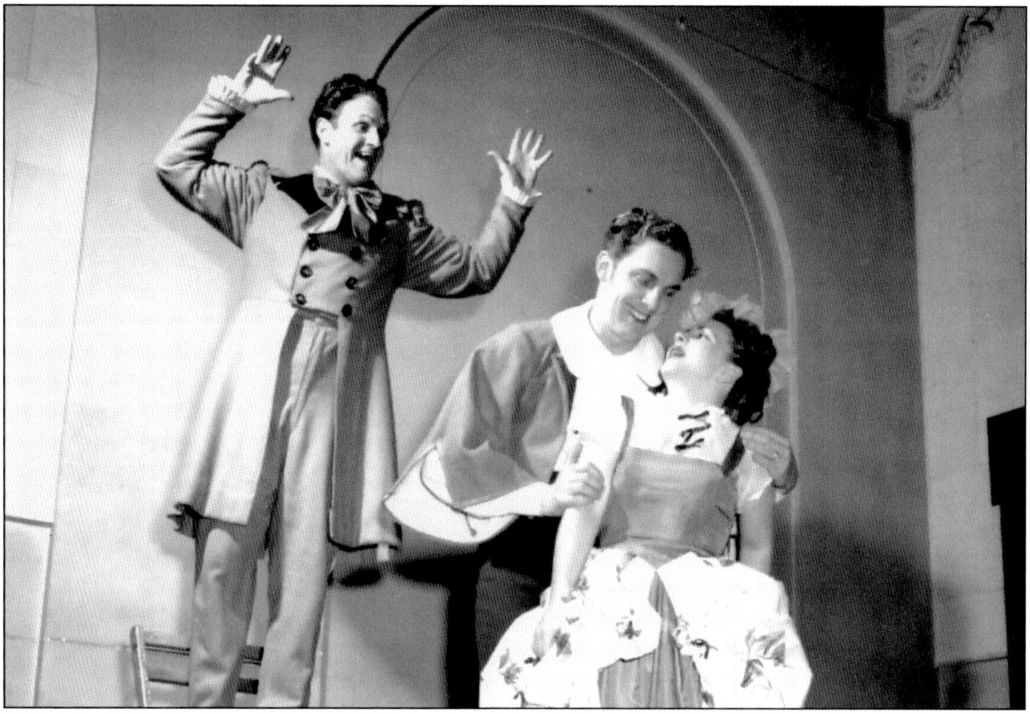

**PERFORMING ARTISTS, 1949.** Even with sparse sets and stage props, the City Center Opera became famous for getting "more from less." Here a prop as simple as a chair is used creatively by the actors as they weave an illusion to the spellbound audience. Also, by using elaborate period costumes, the actors are able to convey an authentic tale, be it romance or danger.

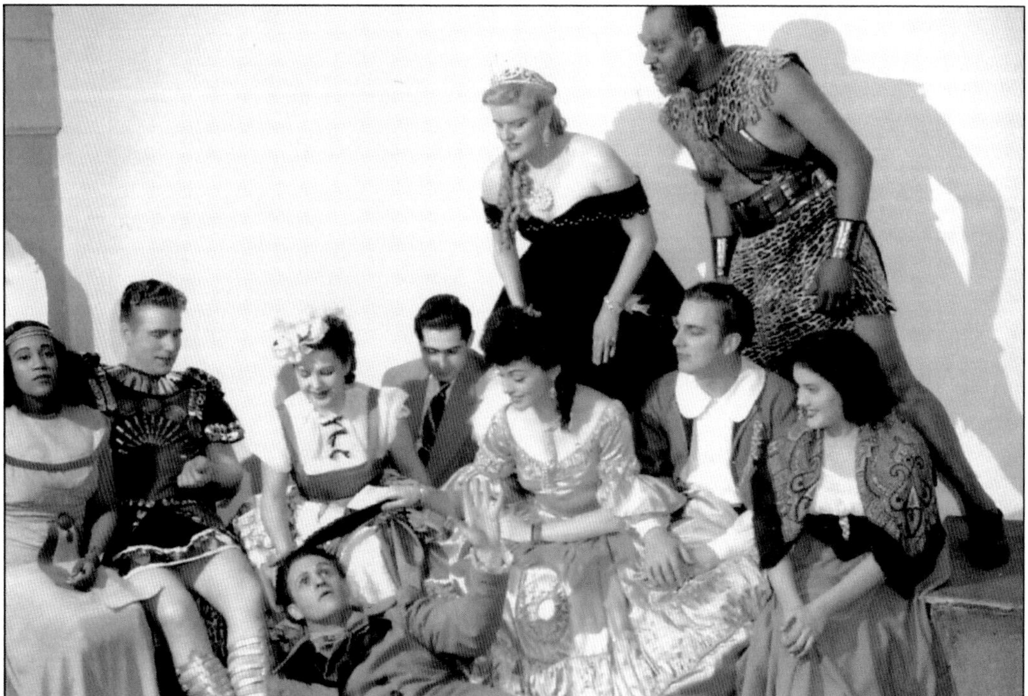

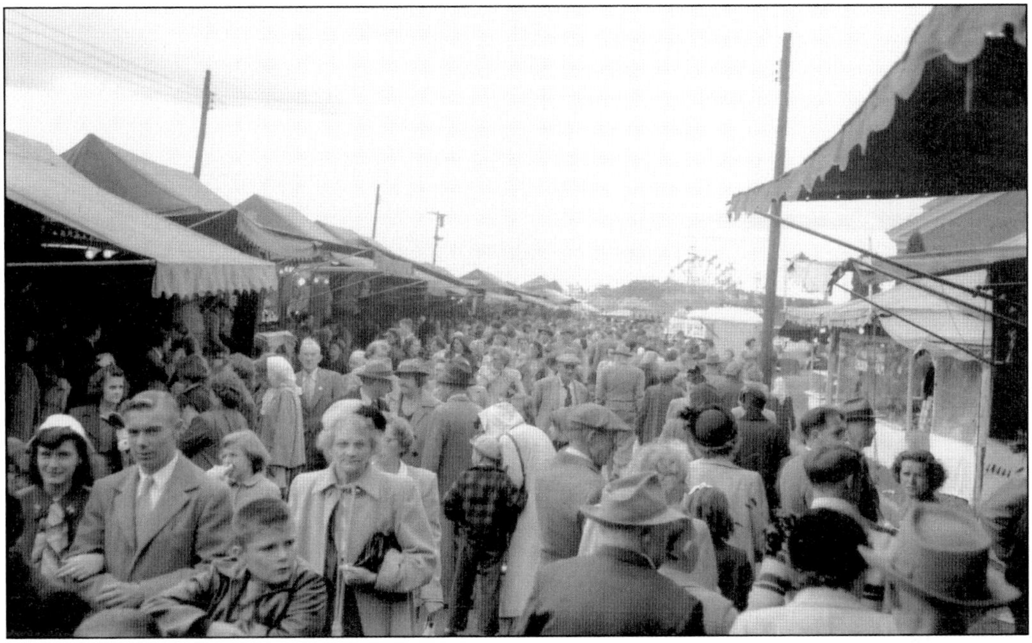

**The Mother of All State Fairs, 1950.** Started over a century ago, the New York State Fair is the largest and most historic exposition of its kind in the northeastern United States. Every year, throngs of fairgoers flock to Syracuse to enjoy the concessionaires and rides on the midway. Having grown up in the Bronx, Arthur thoroughly enjoyed his foray into rural New York, giving him an opportunity to record the pure joy of an old-fashioned country fair.

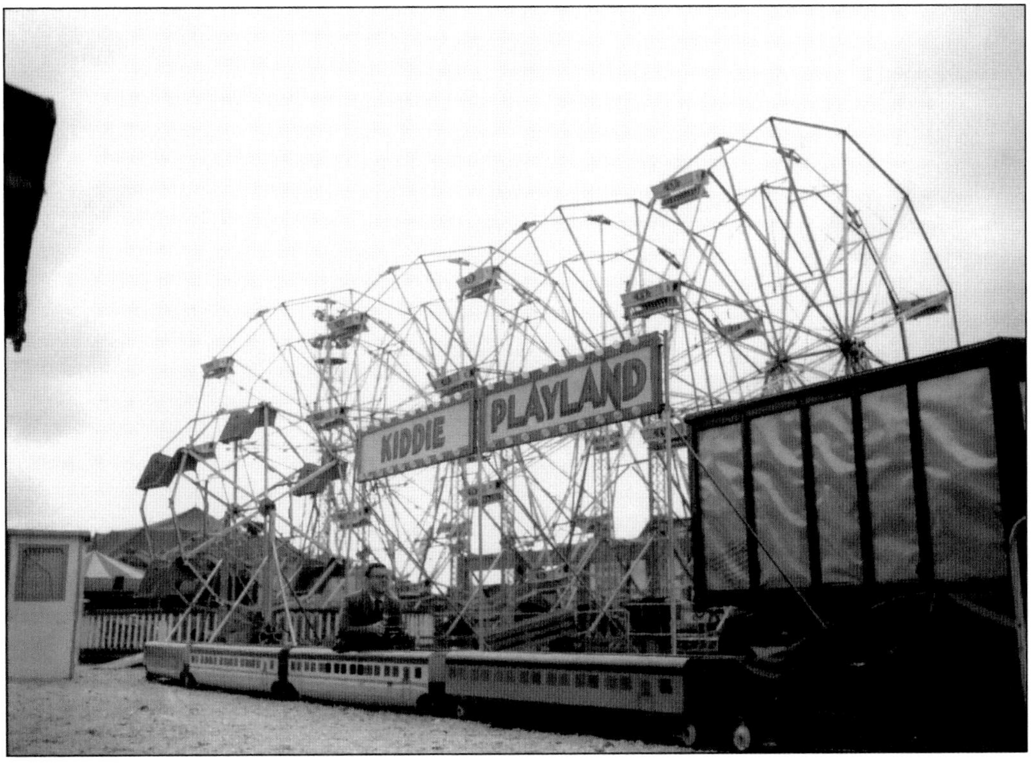

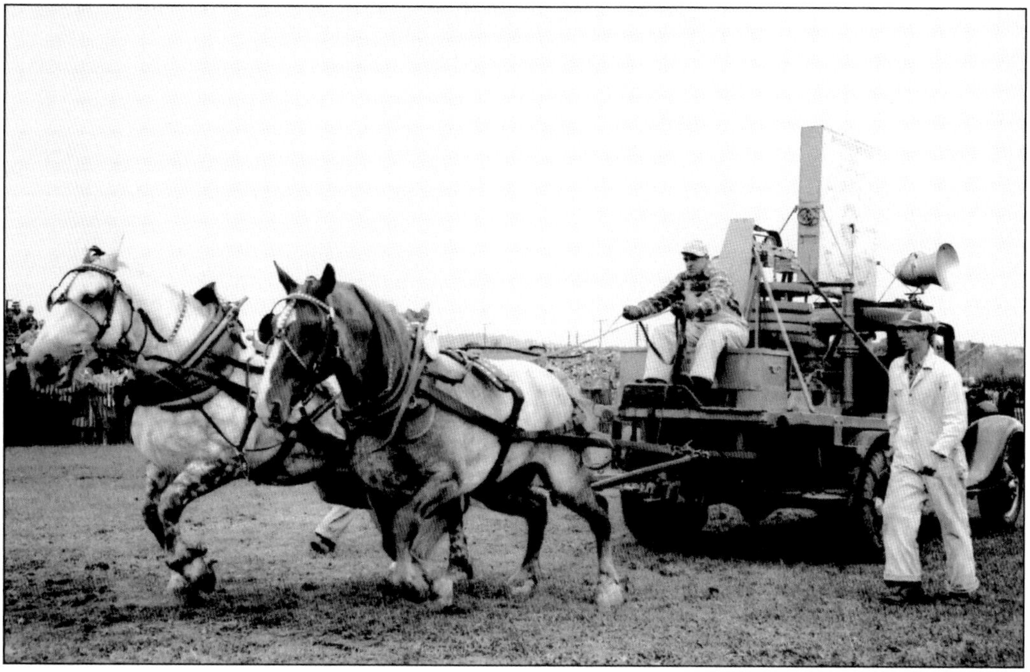

**A GRAND AGRICULTURAL EXHIBITION, 1950.** Traditionally the New York State Fair centered around agriculture and exhibits featuring farm animals. Tens of thousands of New Yorkers would annually make the trek to Syracuse and enjoy everything from tractor pulls to competitions showcasing prizewinning livestock. For several years in the 1940s, the fairgrounds were used as a military base, but by the time Arthur photographed the fair in 1950, it was back in full swing.

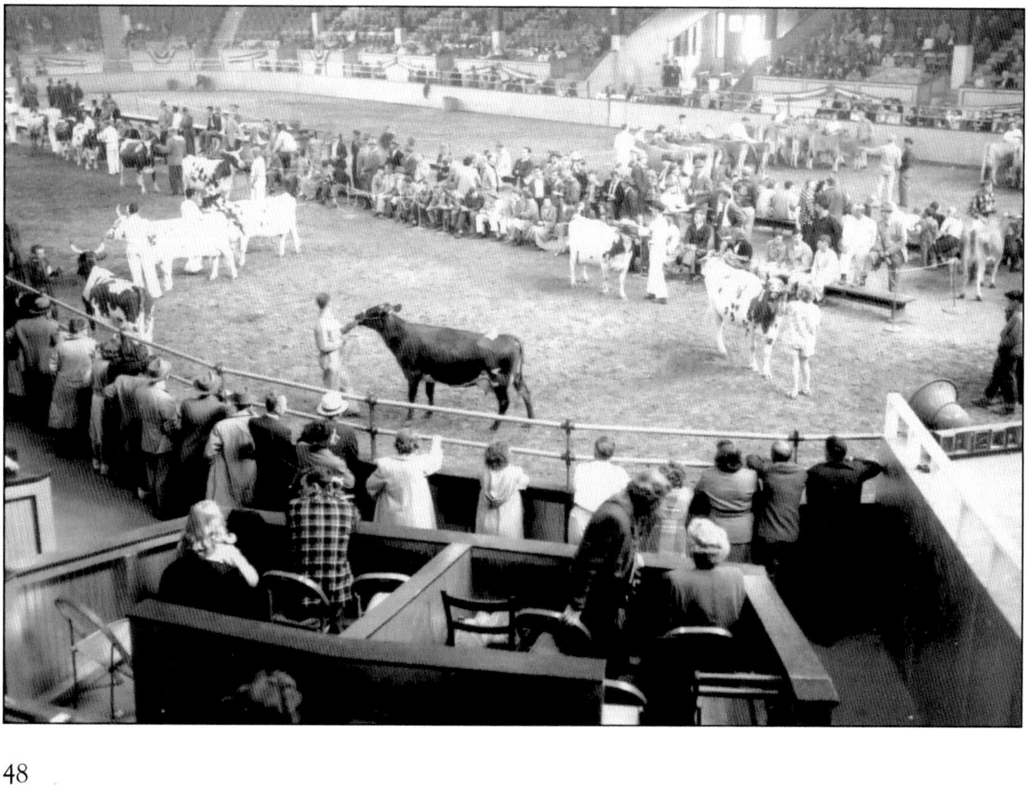

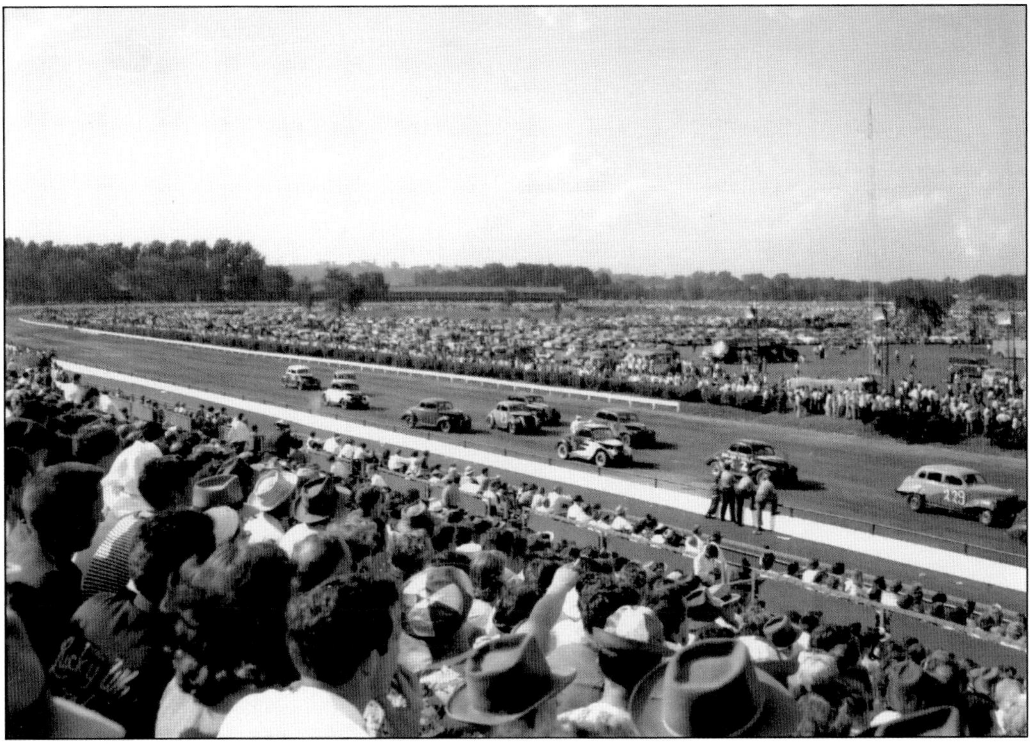

**GENTLEMEN, START YOUR ENGINES, 1950.** Long before there was NASCAR, a highlight of every country fair was automobile racing and spectacular car stunts. These attractions were fun to watch but sometimes dangerous, resulting in performer and spectator casualties. Jack Kochman's Hell Drivers, shown below during a dramatic stunt, was one of the most popular and daring acts of the day.

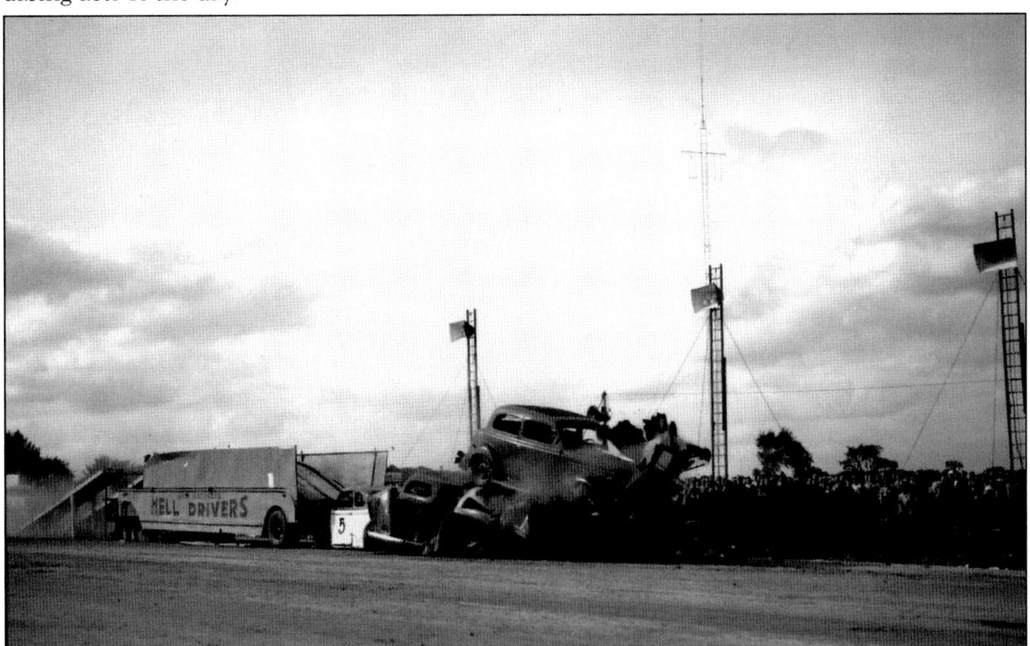

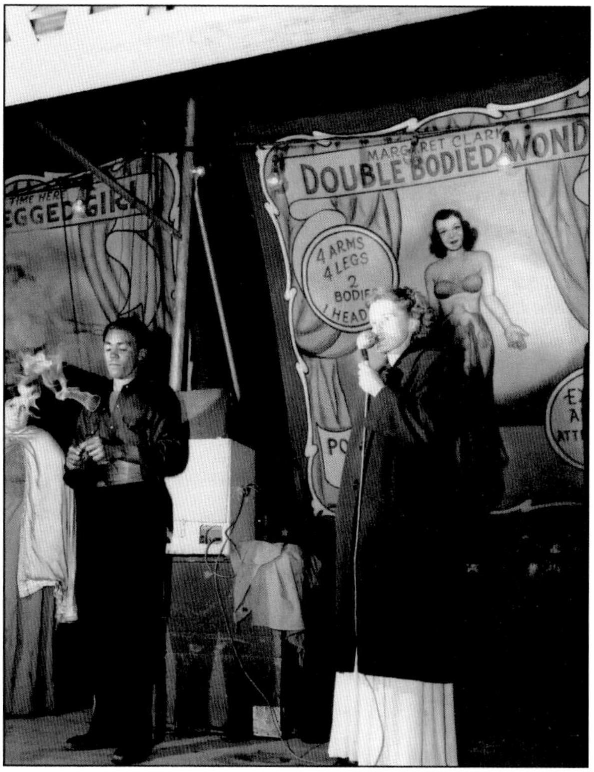


**FREAK SHOWS AND WONDERS OF THE WORLD, 1950.** As daylight turned to dusk, teenagers and adults alike flocked to the fair's famous freak shows. Arthur, no stranger to the bizarre side of life having visited exotic countries during the war, was able to record Margaret Clark, the "Double Bodied Wonder" with four arms, four legs, two bodies, and one head" as well as a rapt audience about to enjoy the thrills of *Arabian Night*.

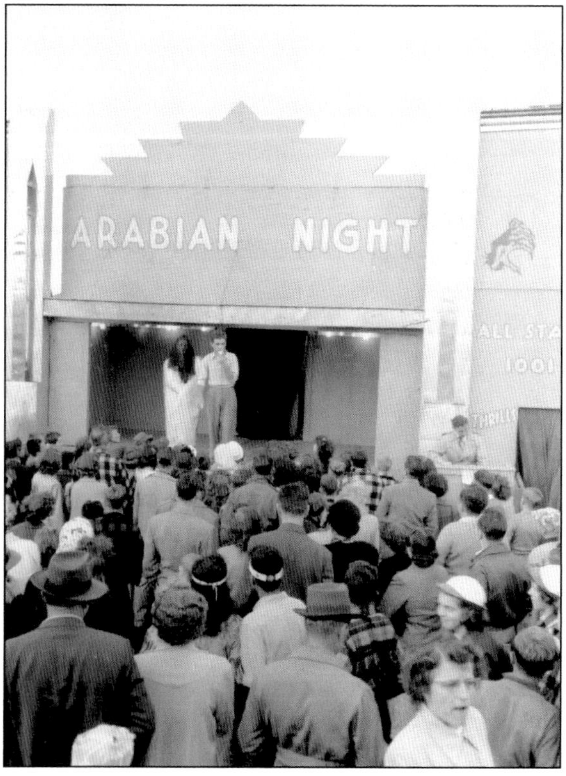

# *Four*

# The People and Places of the Big Apple

Arthur Rickerby and his trusty camera recorded everything New York, from theater scenes to children playing and Bryant Park chess players to teenagers ushering in the 1950s by enjoying treats at an ice-cream parlor. It becomes instantly apparent when one gazes at his work during this period that Arthur was not satisfied by merely taking pictures of people and things, rather he sought and succeeded in taking interpretive photographs of his subjects—images that evoke a story, a way of life. He was at home wherever he went whether it was to feature the world-famous Rockettes, leisurely recording people soaking up the fun of Coney Island or Times Square, or everyday life in areas as diverse as Harlem and Manhattan.

Arthur especially enjoyed those assignments that allowed him to chronicle simple but important everyday happenings. Through the lens of his camera, Arthur managed to capture the pulse beat of the time when he strolled through the city's streets constantly refining and perfecting the art of photography. Now, over 50 years after the images appeared on film, there is a historical record of a seemingly less complicated yet extraordinary time.

By the early 1960s, much of Arthur's work was seen by the very people he covered—the men and women of a vibrant city who started each day reading the morning newspaper. But also, luckily, a vast amount of his work has, until now, never been published before or seen anywhere in print. This chapter tells the story, through many of those images, of life in New York City and its environs during the 1940s and 1950s.

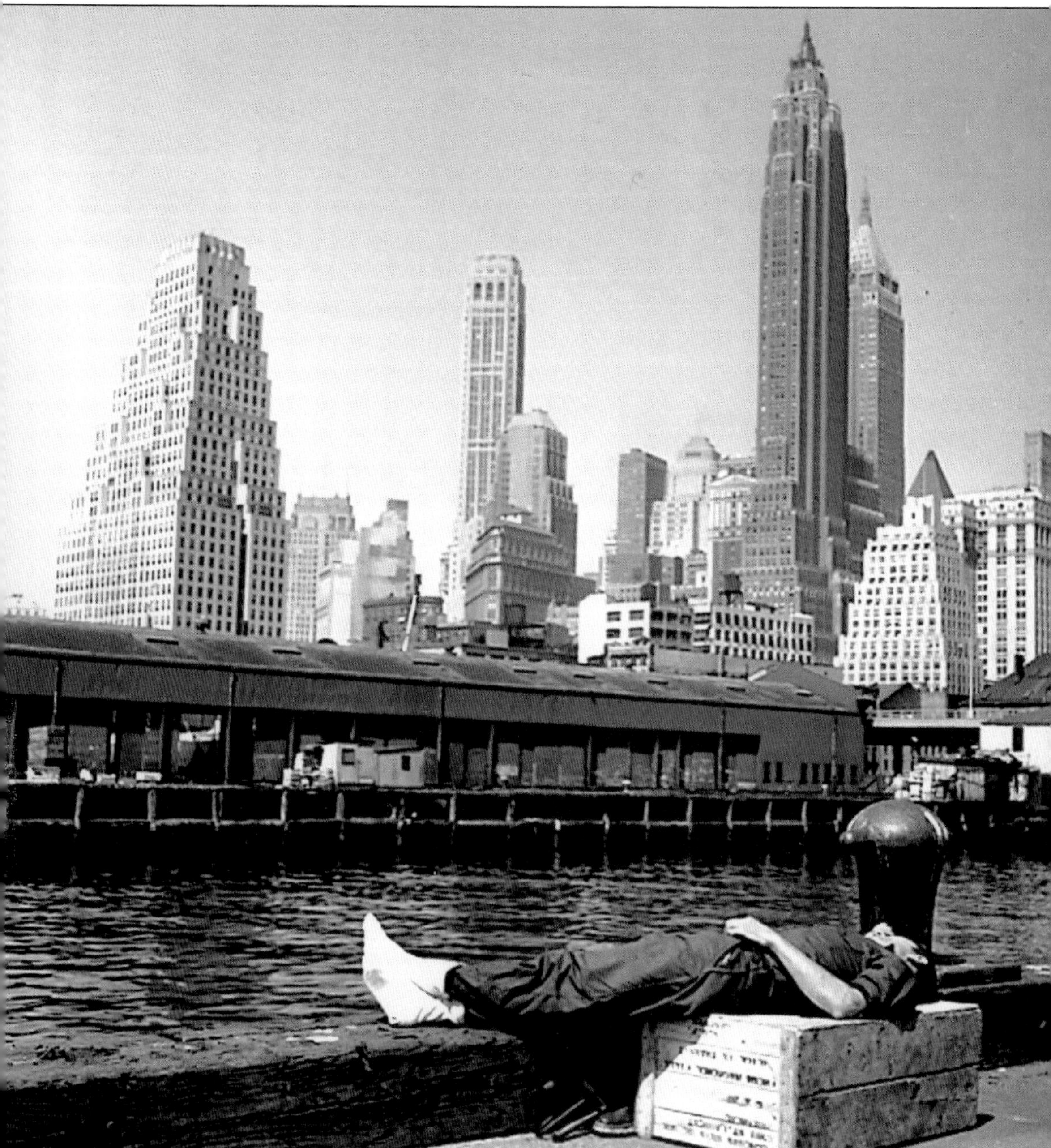

**JUST ADD WATER, 1950S.** The piers around New York City have long been inviting for sunbathers and loungers. Arthur photographed this particular spot, which features an added bonus—a magnificent view of the Manhattan skyline.

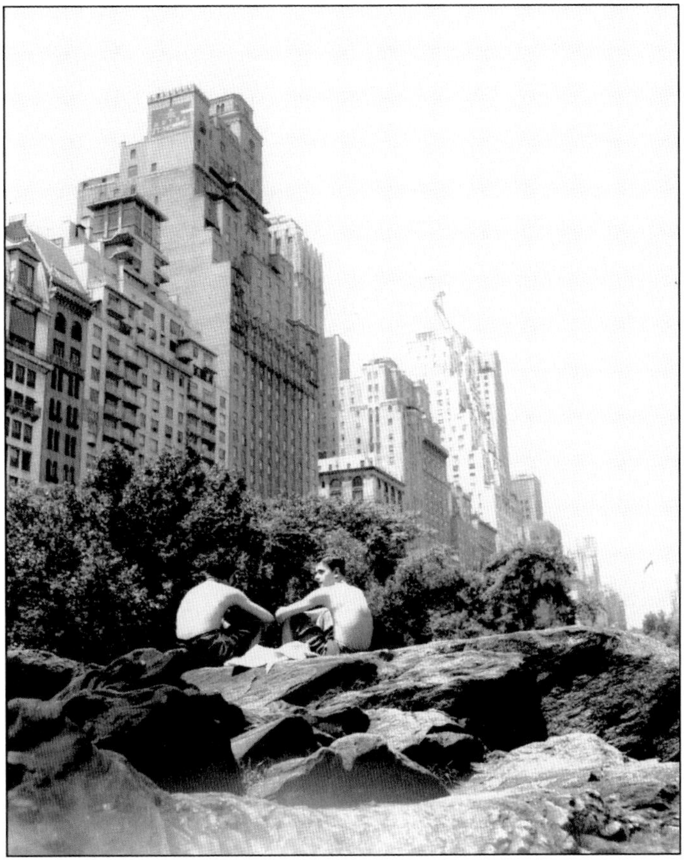

**SUMMER IN THE CITY, 1950S.** New Yorkers are able to enjoy the cityscape, even during the dog days of summer. One of the pleasures of being surrounded by tall buildings and cool water is that there always seems to be a place to beat the heat. Arthur delighted in finding those city dwellers who were comfortable relaxing or sunbathing in even the most public places like Central Park or along the Brooklyn Bridge enjoying a scenic view of the Manhattan Bridge over the East River.

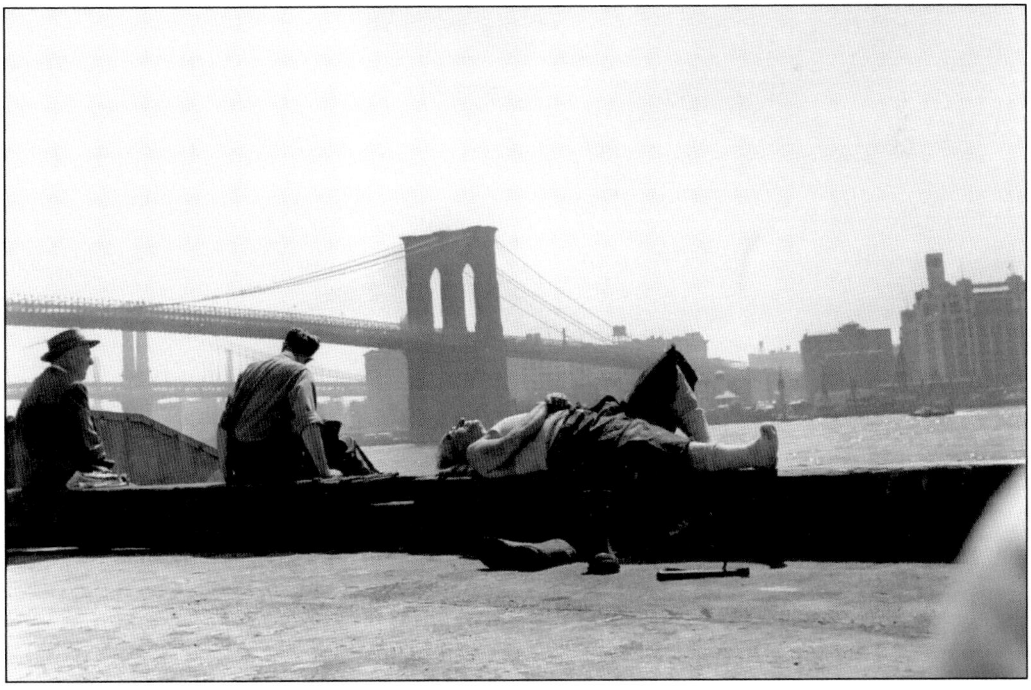

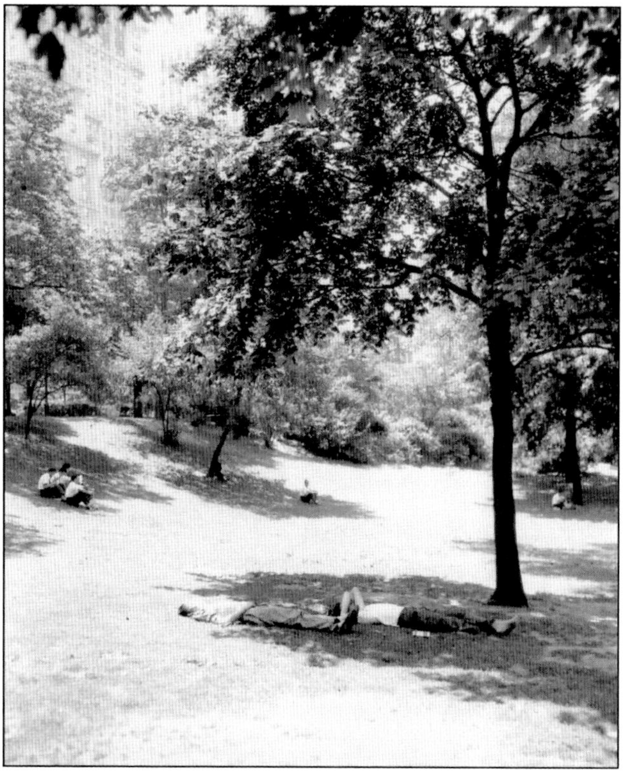

**TAKING A BREAK, 1950S.** What better way to soak up the city than to catch a quick snooze at Central Park or simply on a street side bench? Arthur, fascinated by every conceivable type of city dweller, enjoyed featuring those who unabashedly took a break from the sights and sounds of city life.

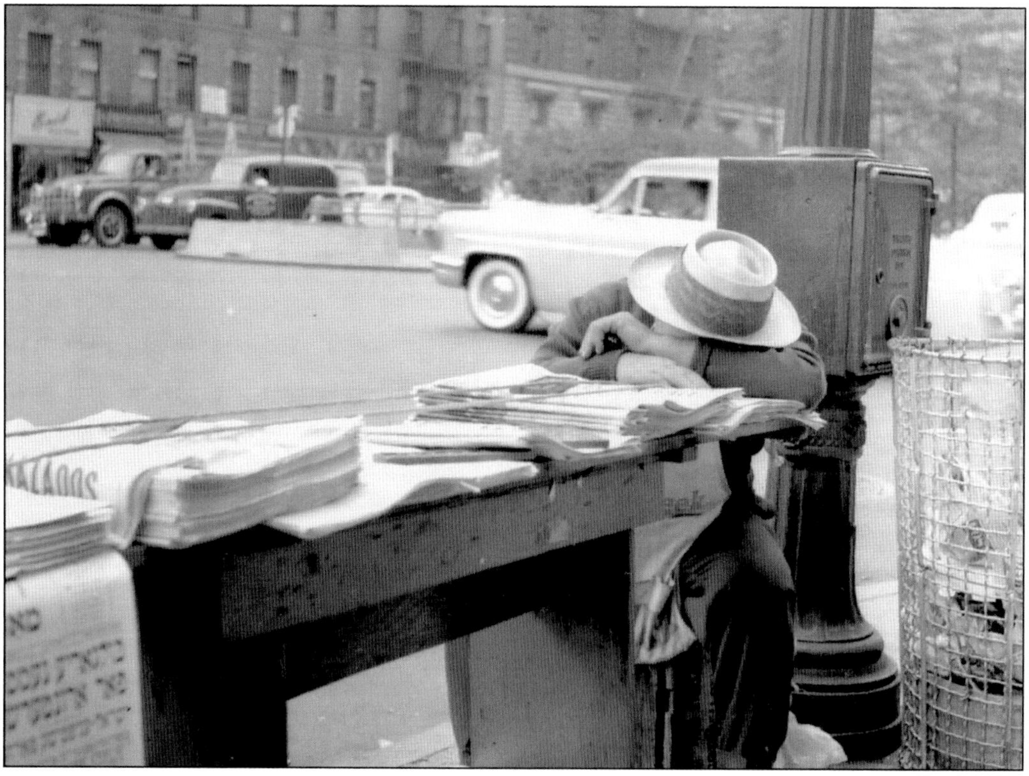

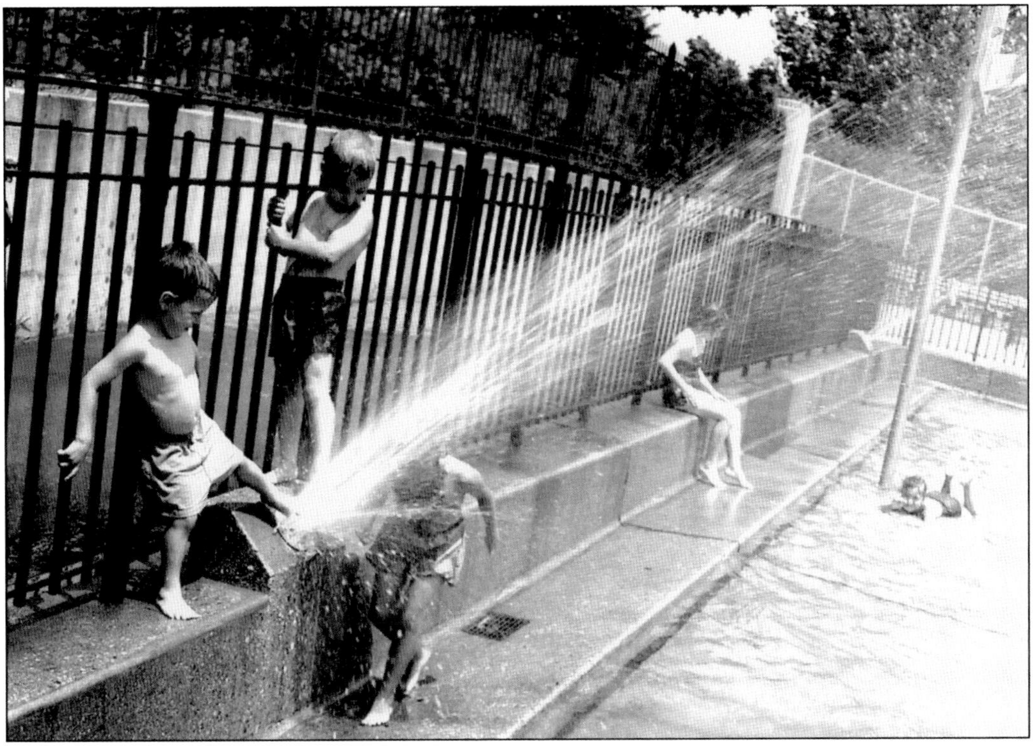

**HOT FUN IN THE SUMMERTIME, 1950S.** A requirement for summer play has always been water, and city kids find it where they can. Over the years, New York boroughs have provided more swimming pools and water access for their residents, but these photographs prove that sometimes the old ways are the best. These youngsters are having a blast with spray from a fire hydrant. Arthur's camera perfectly caught the smiles on the faces of the children, as the water offered a refreshing break from the summer heat.

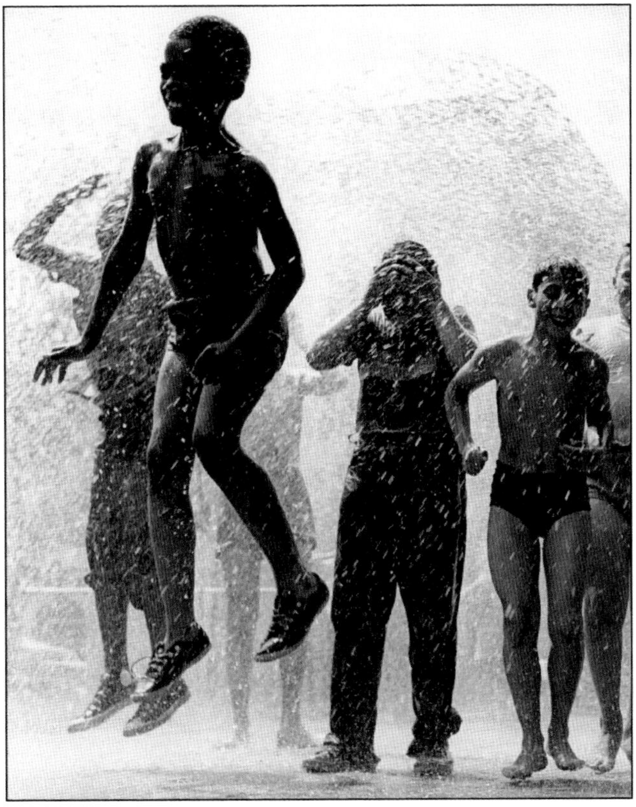

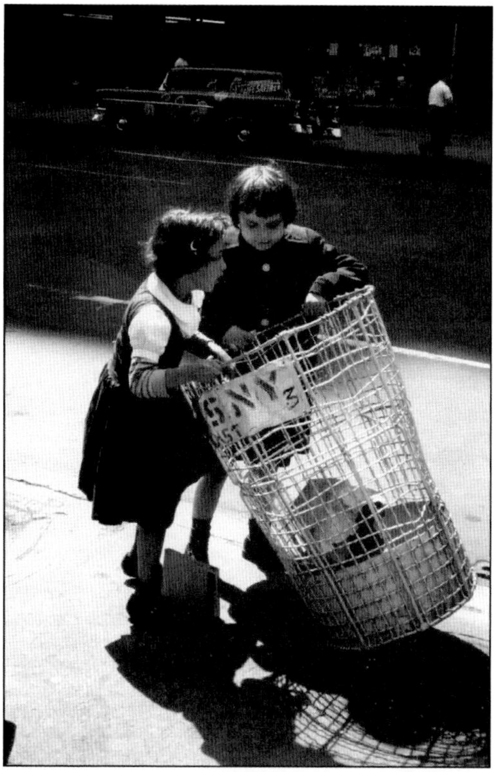

**TRASH OR TREASURE, 1955.** As he roamed the streets of the city, Arthur found enjoyment in the simplest of things. On their way home from school, these two young girls stop to search a city trash can for something to play with.

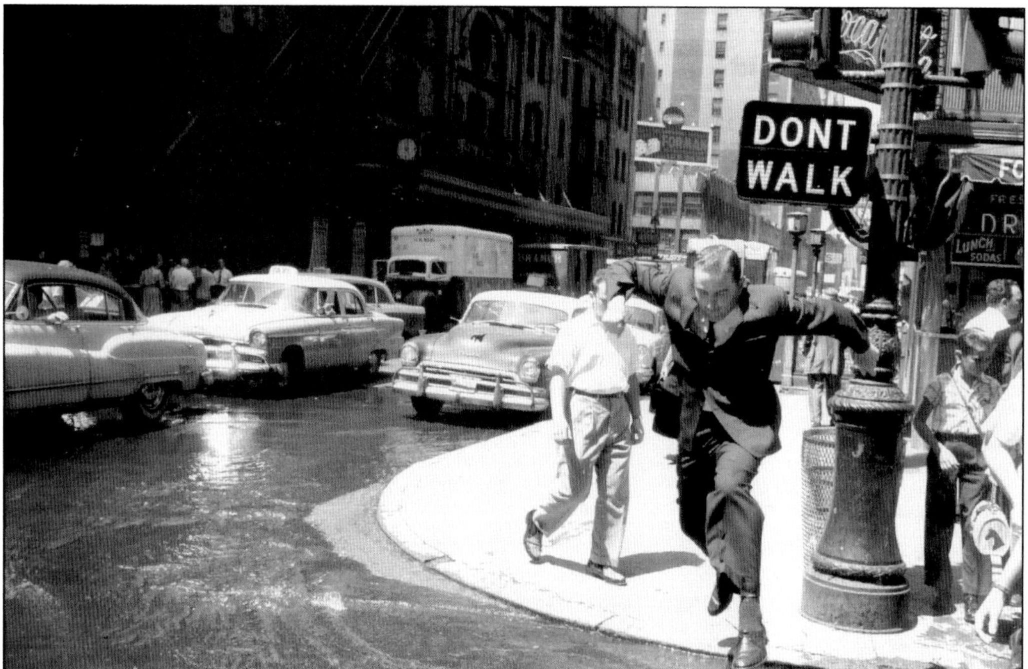


**JUMP, DON'T WALK, 1958.** When the streets of Times Square were flooded following the rupture of a water main, Arthur caught this young man jumping over a puddle of water, actually obeying the Don't Walk sign at Broadway and 40th Street.

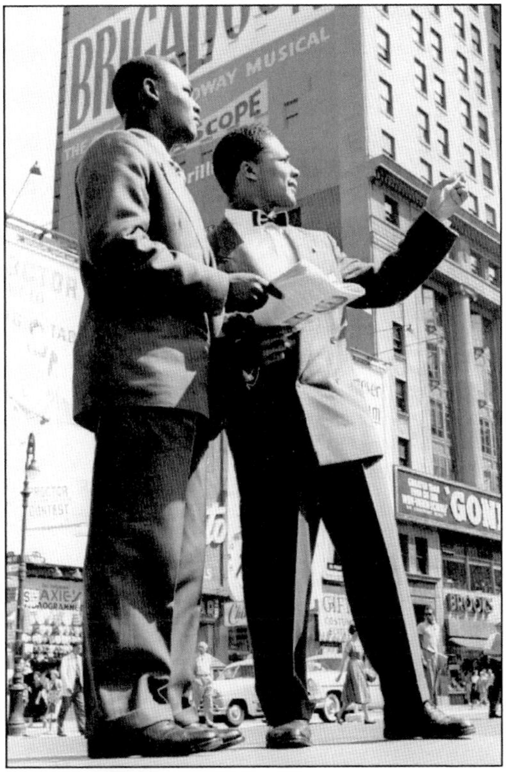


**TIMES SQUARE, 1950S.** With its gaudy giant billboards advertising the latest movies and Broadway shows, Times Square has always attracted visitors from all over the world. Arthur caught up with these two well-dressed men feeding the pigeons and taking in the sights.

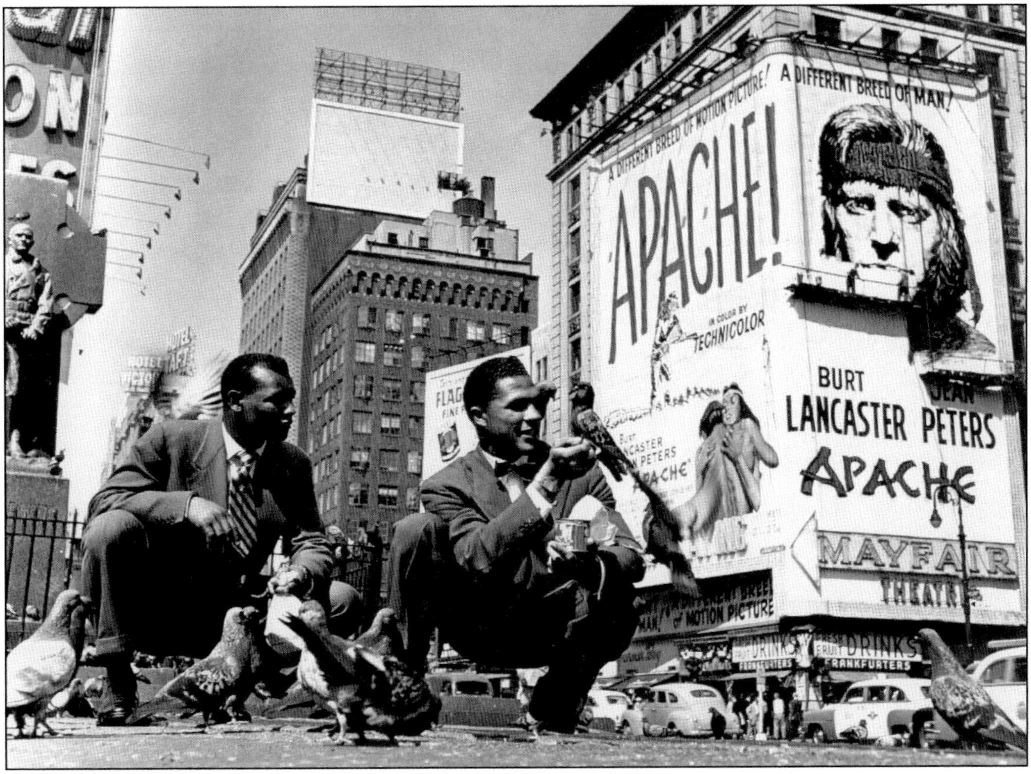

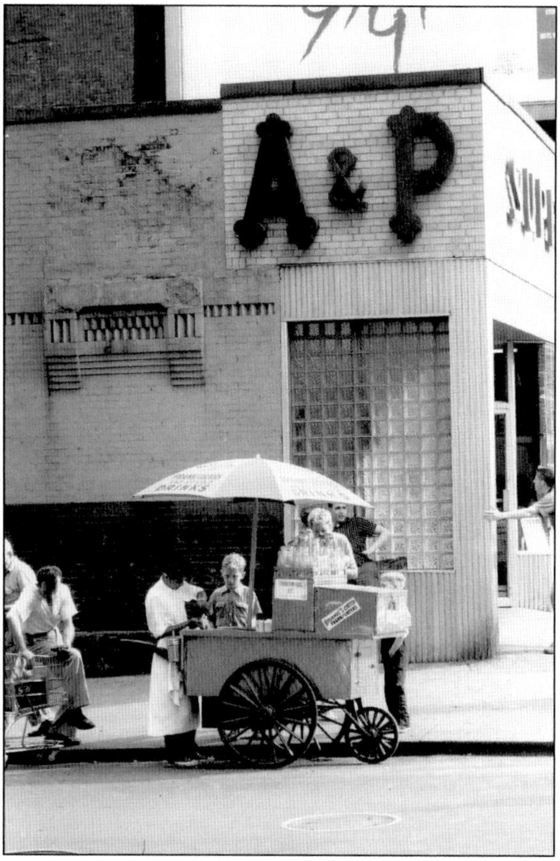


**Street Vendors, 1950s.** Street vendors and their carts laden with food, toys, and souvenirs have been part of the New York cityscape for decades. These photographs feature a popular hot dog stand in front of a supermarket and another cart filled with stuffed animals.

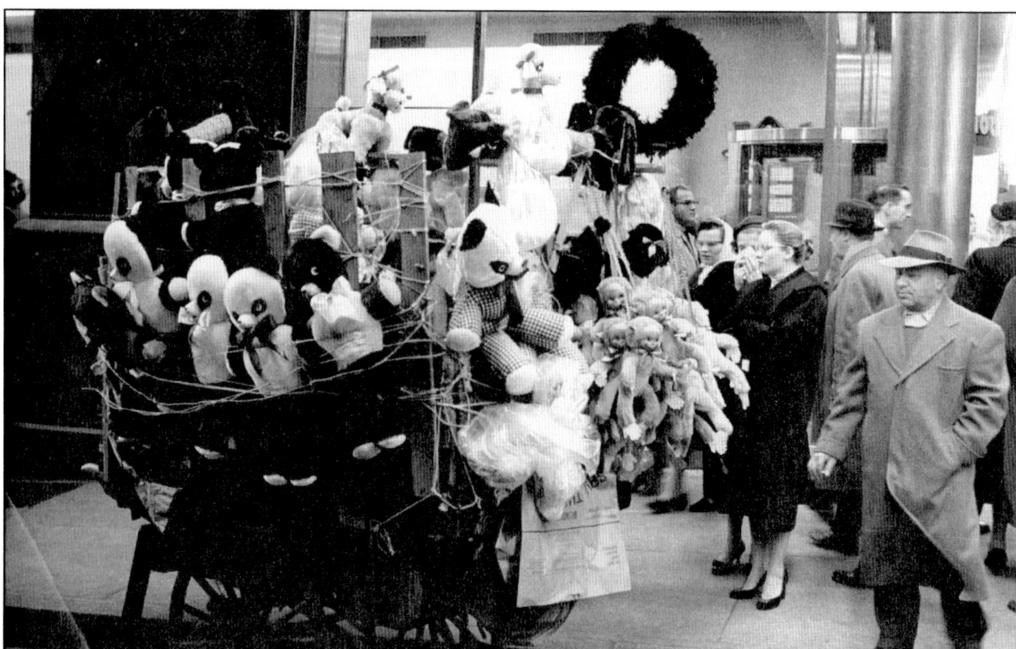

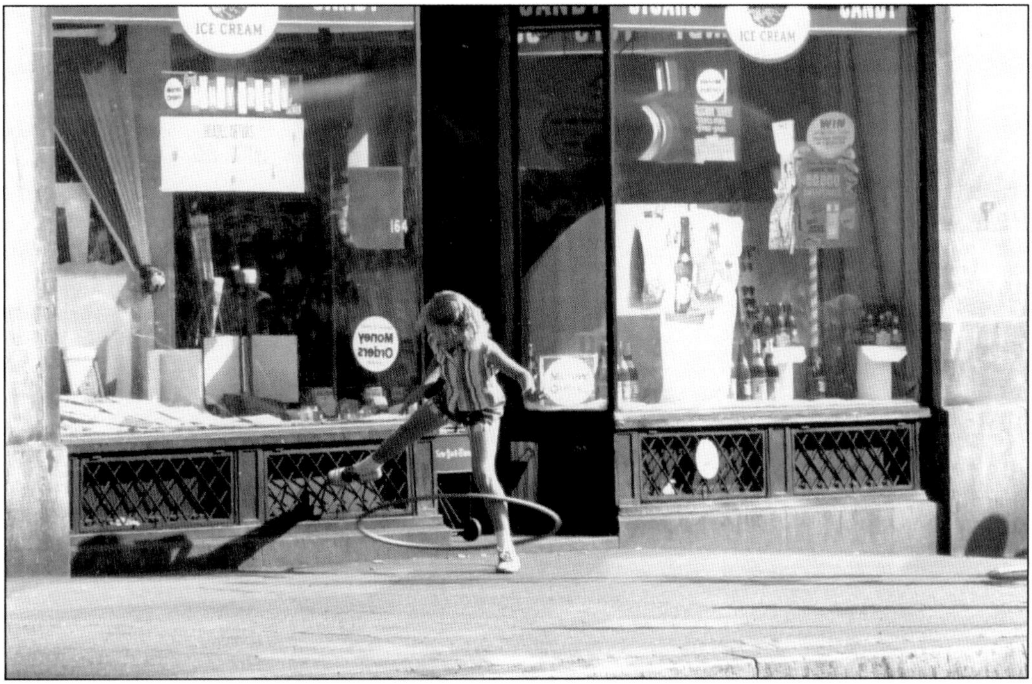


**HULA HOOP CRAZE, 1950S.** Remember the hula hoop? The craze for plastic circles rotating around swaying hips swept the nation in the late 1950s, and New York City youngsters were no exception. Arthur recorded these young girls performing for anyone who would watch on a street in Manhattan.

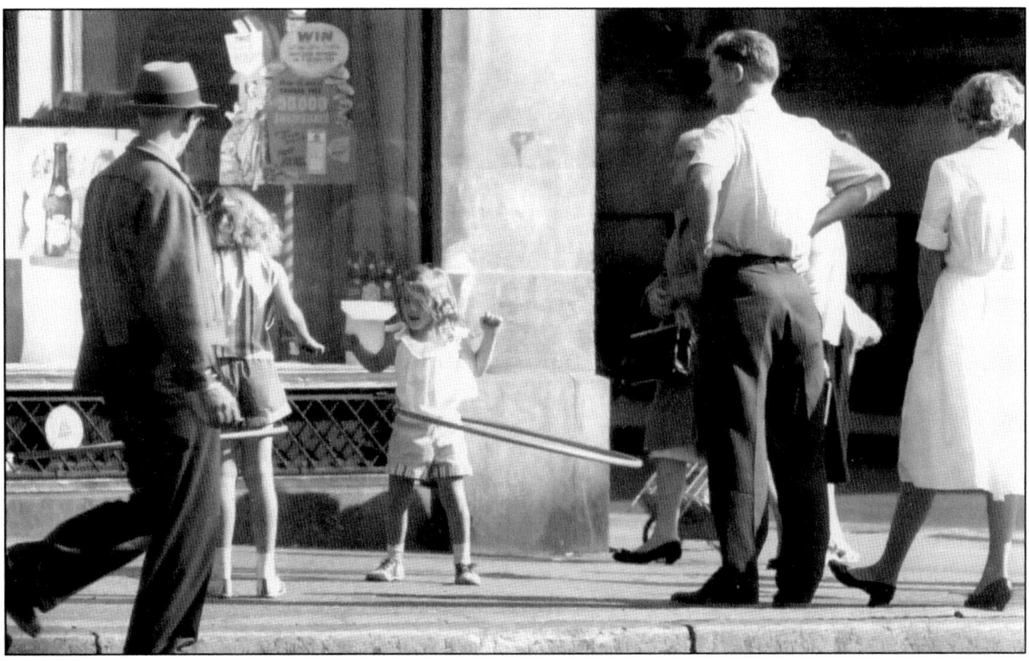

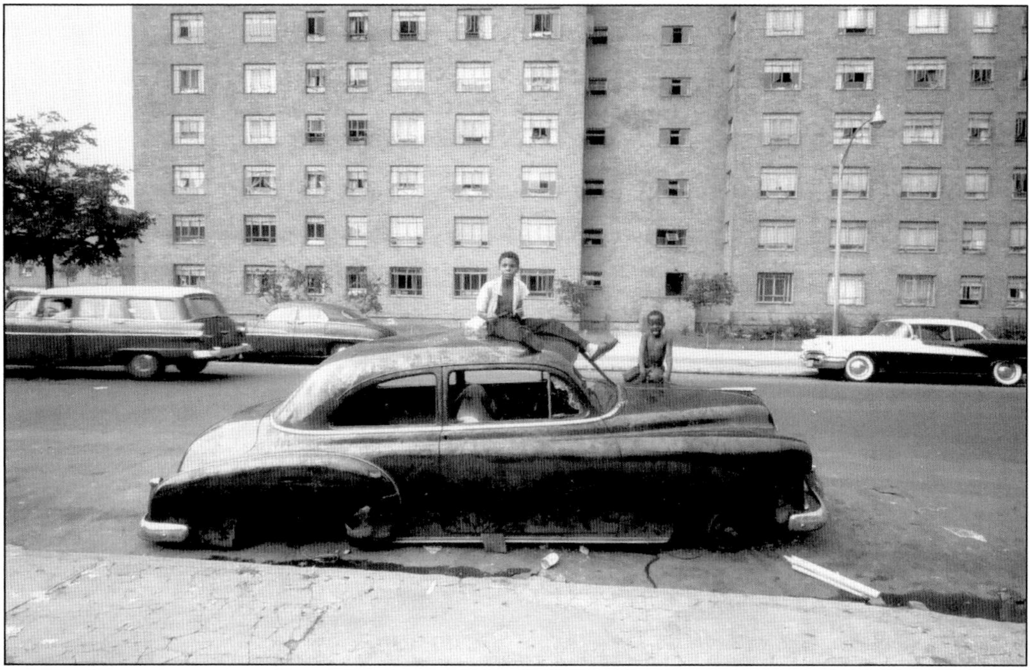

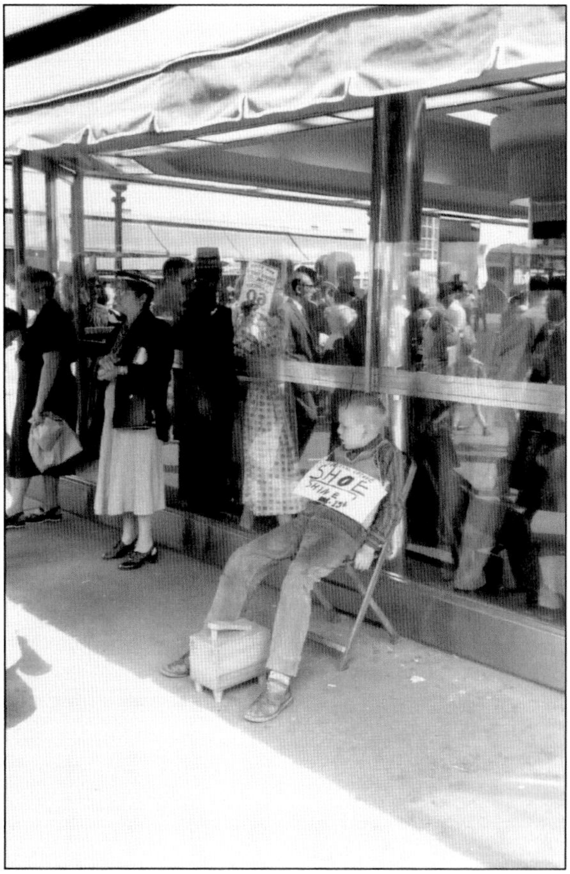


**CITY BOYS, 1950S.** Arthur Rickerby had a keen eye for showing contrasting lifestyles of New York City youngsters. In the photograph above, two young fellows sit atop an abandoned car in the Bronx. The shot to the left features an obviously tired shoe shine boy waiting for his next customer. At 15¢ a shine, it was quite a deal.

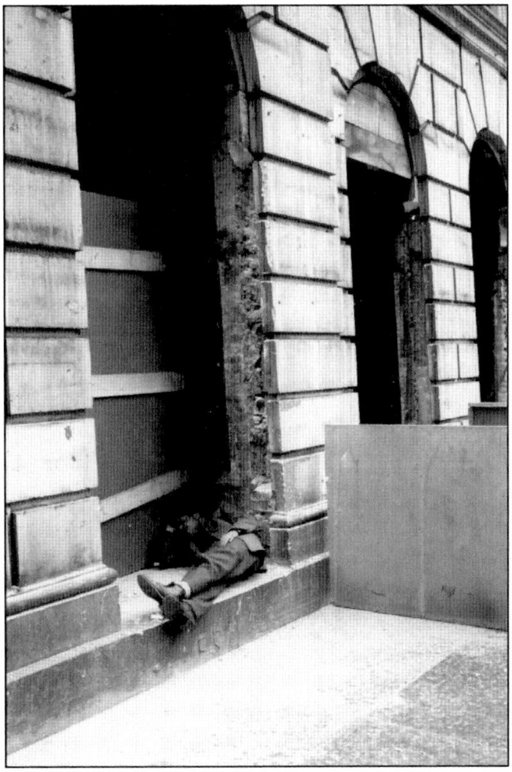

**POVERTY IN THE CITY, 1950S.** Life was not all fun and games during the postwar years. Arthur felt strongly that all city dwellers be represented in his work. Here a homeless man catches a nap on a window ledge, while nearby some workman's overalls are hung out to dry in a tenement building in Brooklyn.

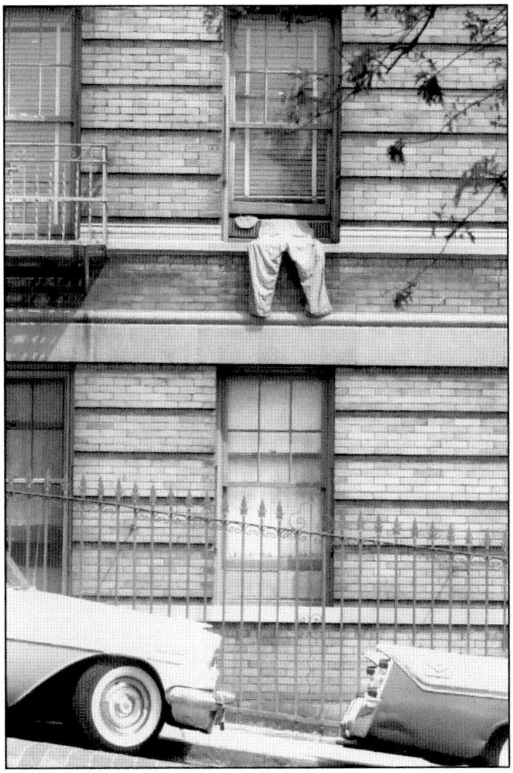

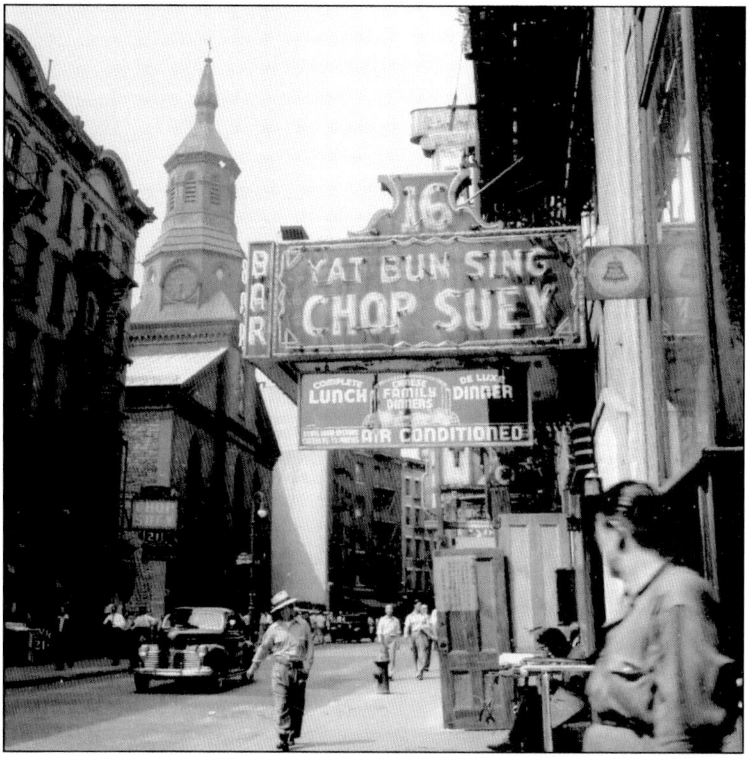


**BUILDINGS HAVE PERSONALITIES TOO, 1950S.** Among the most interesting photographs that Arthur took during the 1950s were those involving the city's buildings. As one who was a student of the way people lived, he knew that the structures folks ate and drank in told volumes about their likes and dislikes. Here he shows two popular establishments, the Yat Bun Sing Chop Suey House in Chinatown and Manhattan's Esquire restaurant.

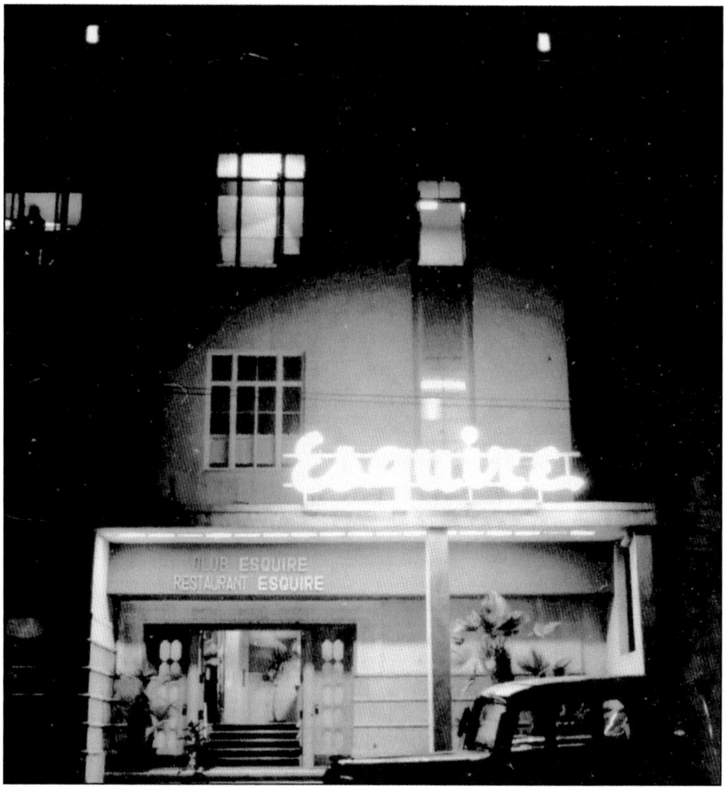

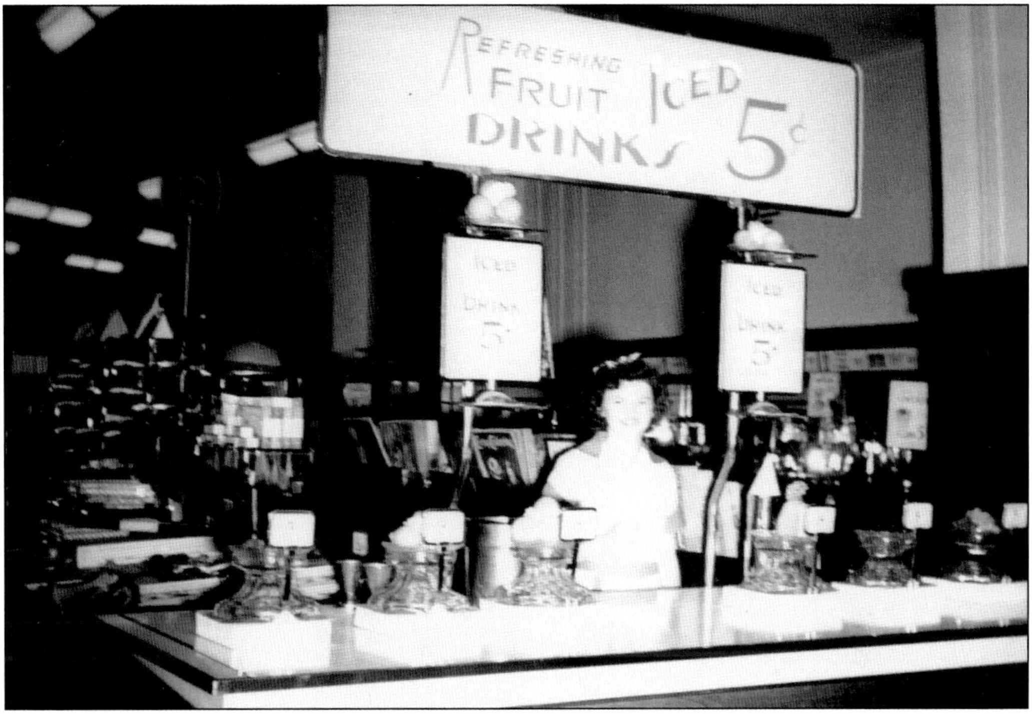


**DINER HEAVEN, 1950S.** During the 1950s, every city had its fair share of diners with classic soda fountains. These photographs feature an interior view showing a smiling waitress and the shiny chrome lunch counter in the famed Woolworth Building in Lower Manhattan.

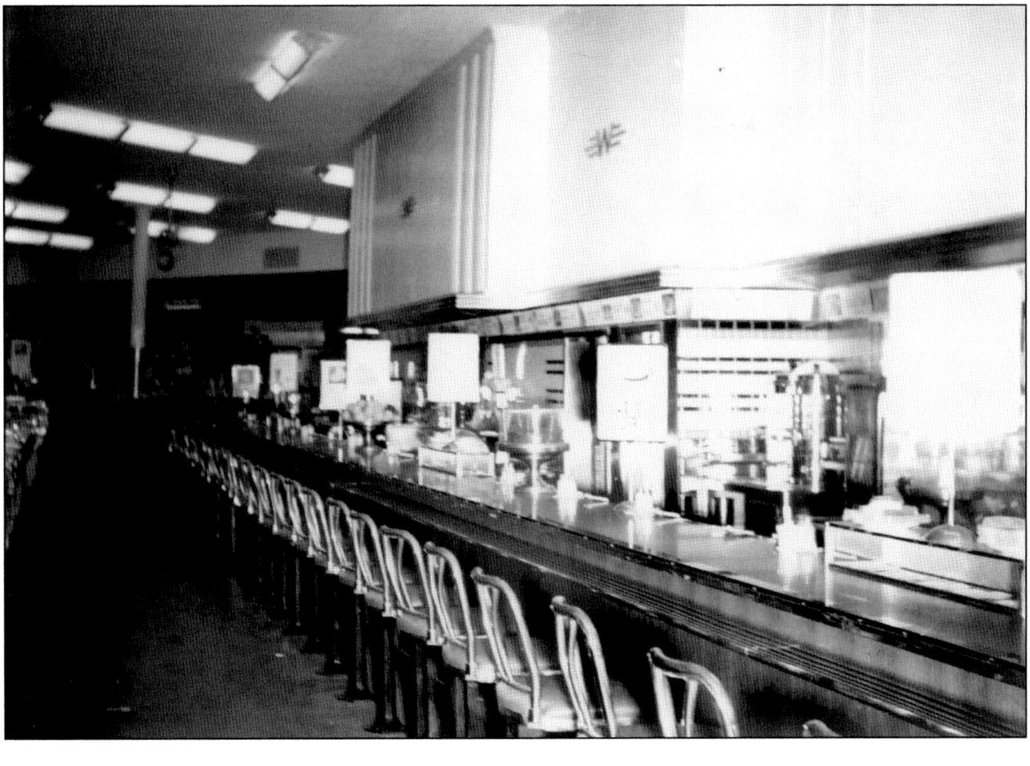

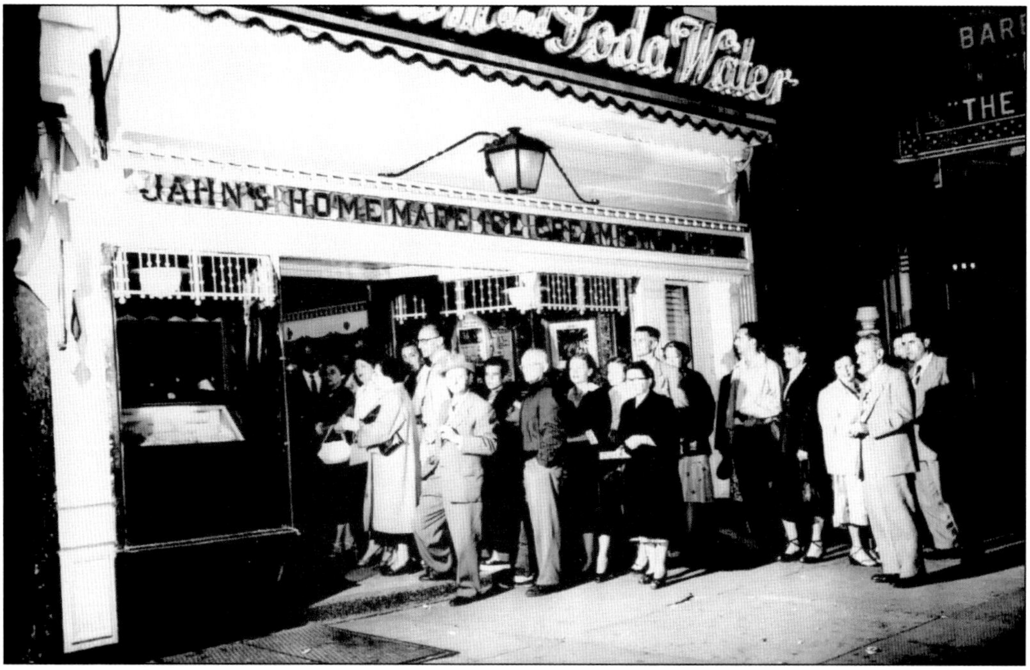


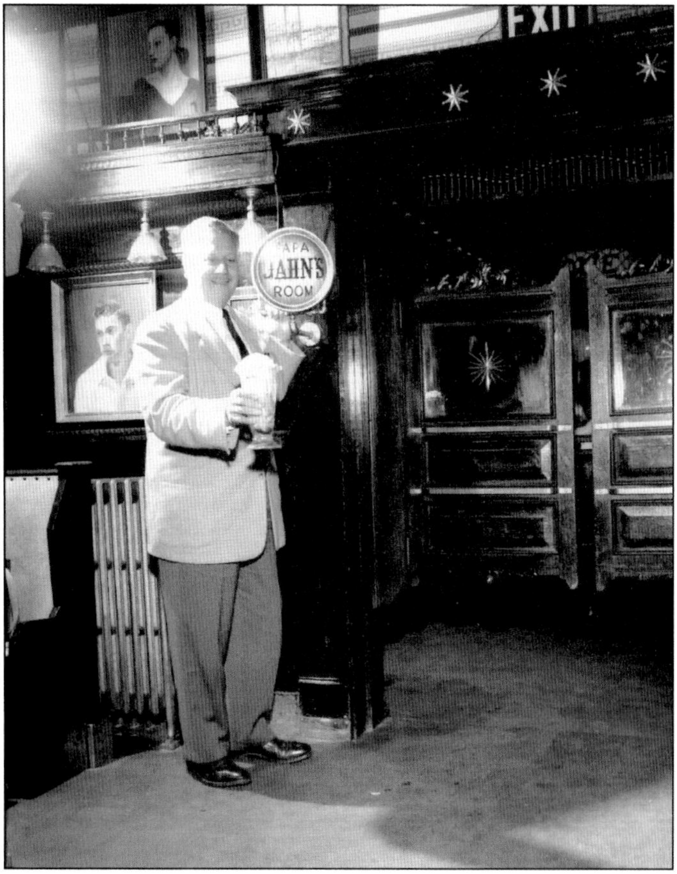


**JAHN'S ICE-CREAM PARLOR, 1950S.** Jahn's Homemade Ice Cream Parlor in the Richmond Hill section of Queens has drawn enthusiastic crowds since 1897. Fifty years after its opening, Arthur decided to celebrate this slice of Americana by featuring the joy of teenagers partaking in the simple pleasures of homemade milk shakes and banana splits. The photograph above shows a crowd gathering at the entrance to Jahn's while the photograph to the left introduces the viewer to the evening manager proudly holding a giant shake.

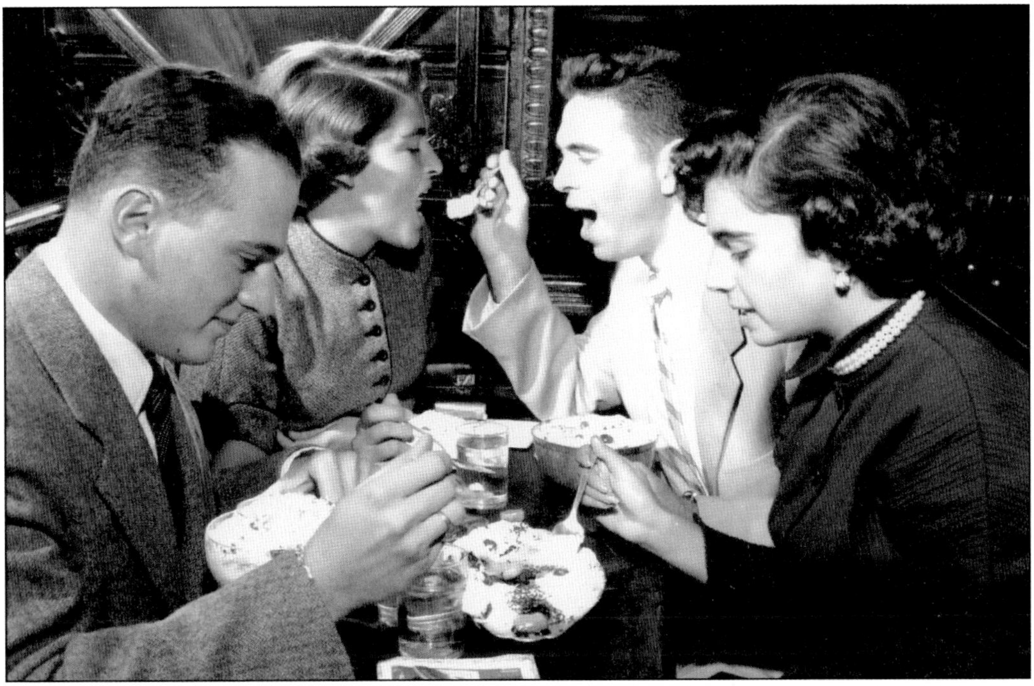

**SHARING IN THE FUN, 1950S.** Once inside Jahn's, the homemade ice cream is cool and delicious. It is impossible not to smile when sharing a sundae with a favorite friend. These photographs tell it all!

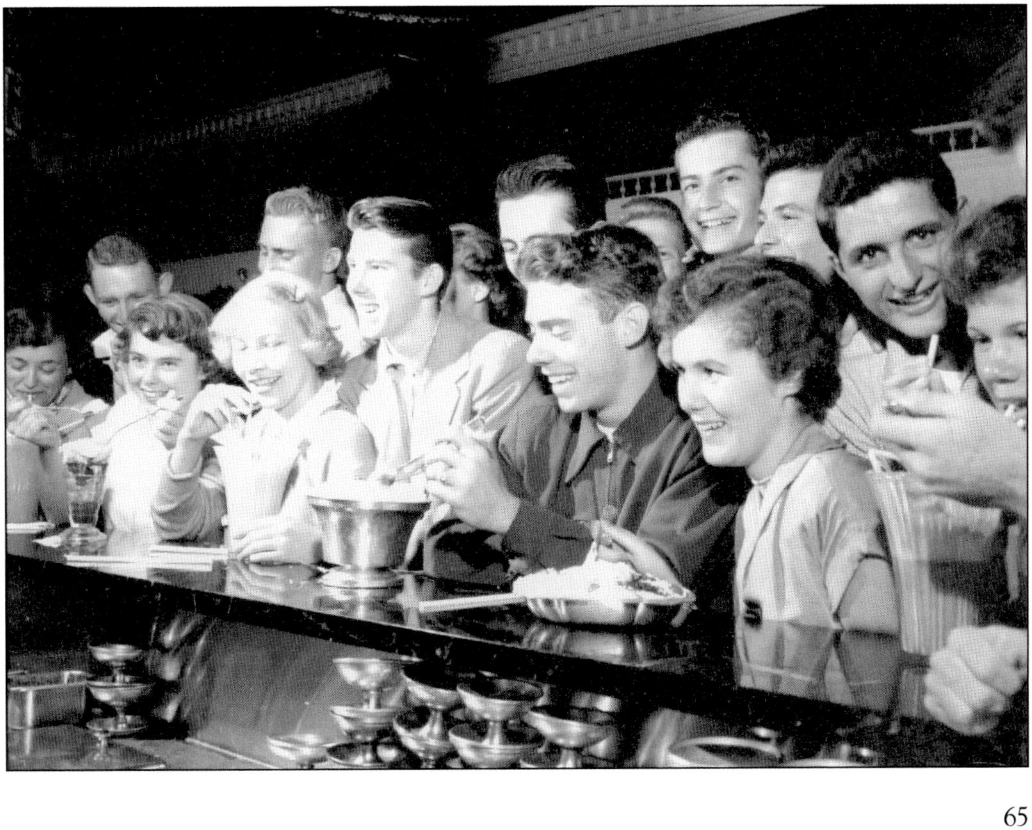

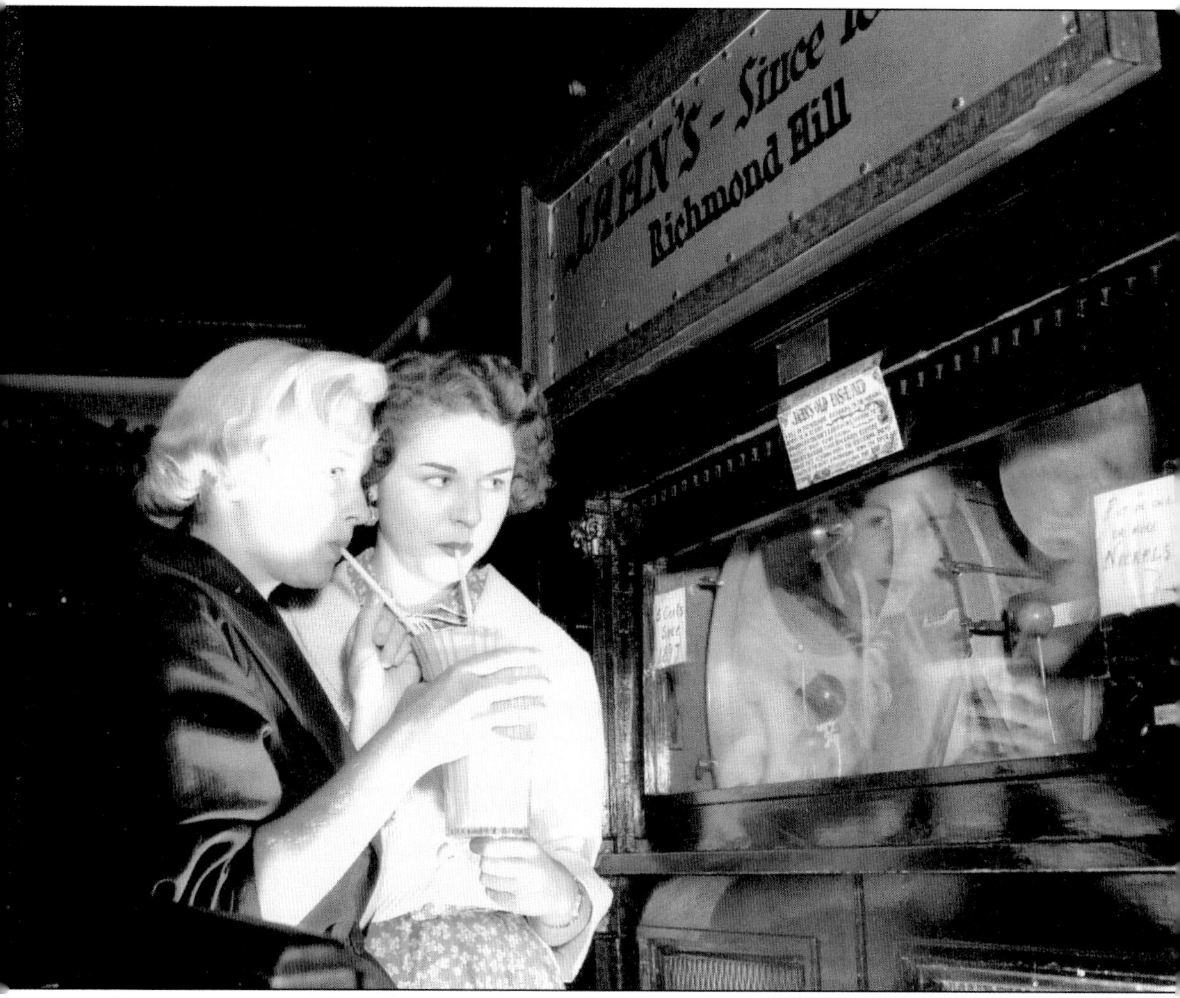


**JUST DESSERTS, 1950S.** Sharing a huge milk shake, these girls enjoy a 19th-century antique music box that costs only a nickel to play. Arthur enjoyed photographing young people, especially teenagers who seemed to relish everything New York.

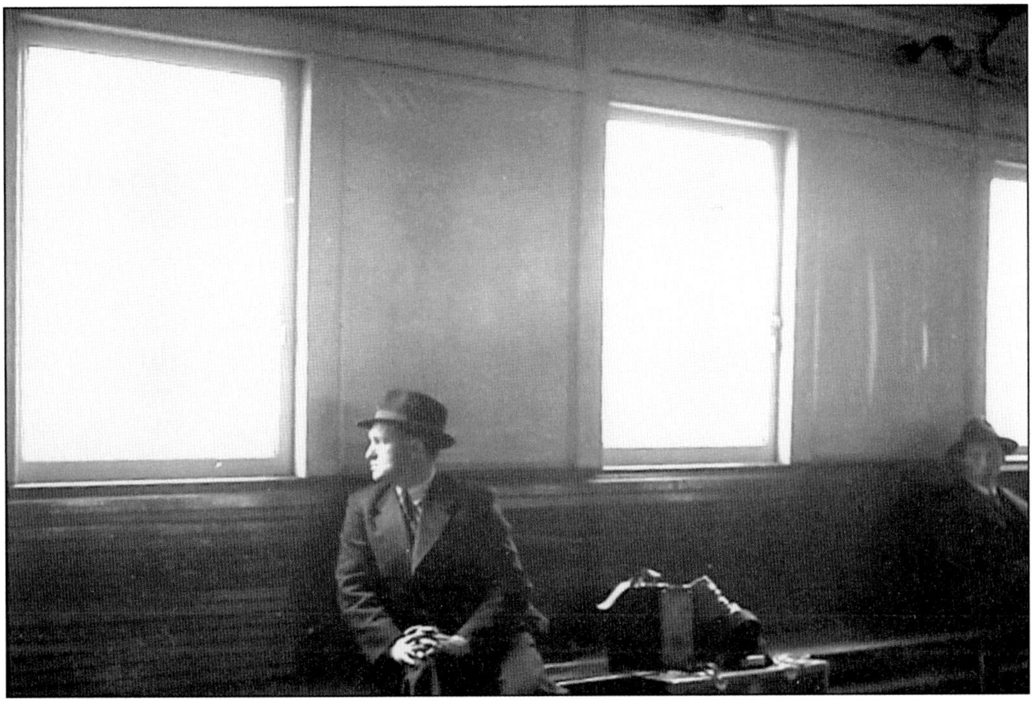

**New York Harbor, 1950s.** In addition to featuring many well-known buildings and landmarks, New York City is also fortunate to have a natural seaport, allowing visitors and residents to come and go. Here Arthur perfectly records the apprehensive expression of a well-dressed man on his way to Ellis Island, the gateway for millions of immigrants hoping to start a new life in a new land, about to embark on his American dream. The photograph below shows another who seems to be lost in thought with the *Mauretania* docked in the background.

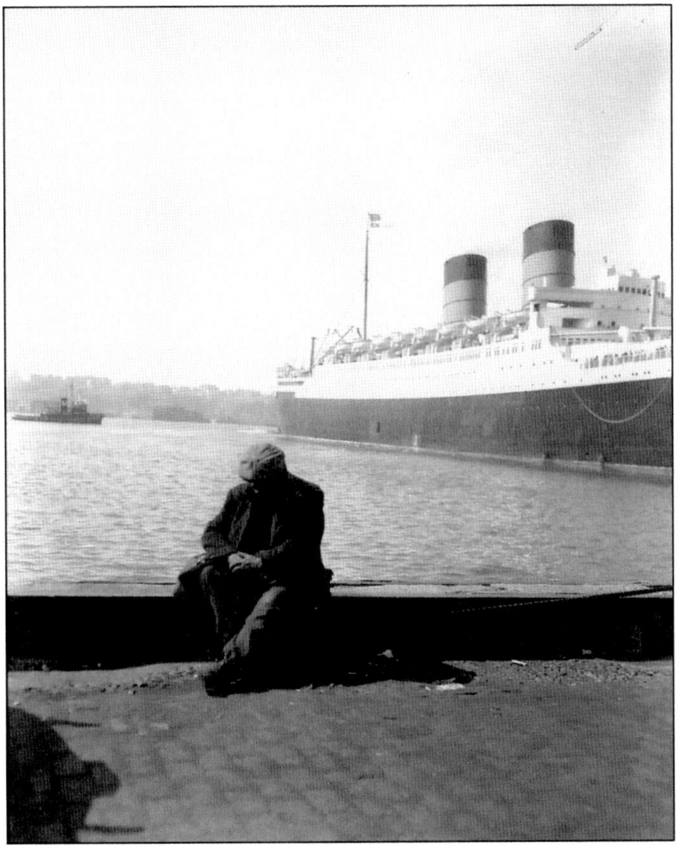

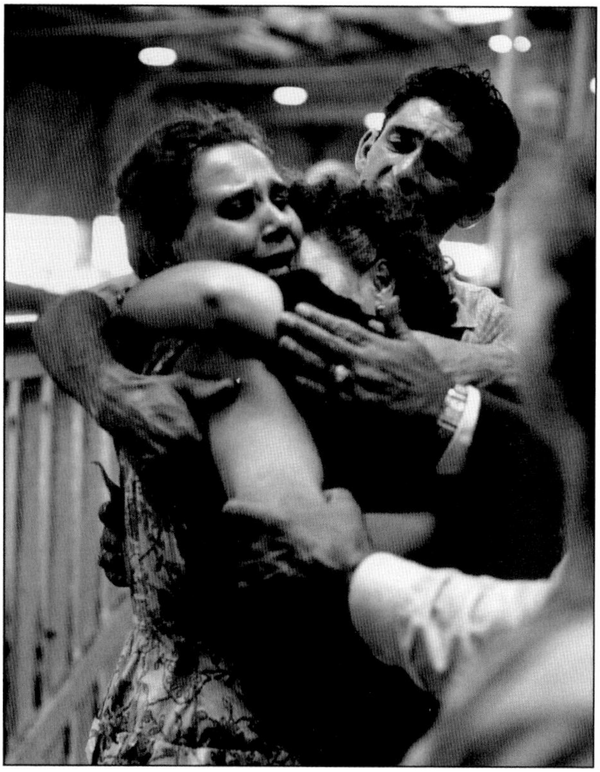

**ANDREA DORIA SURVIVORS, 1956.** In July 1956, the Italian ocean liner the *Andrea Doria* collided with the *Stockholm* and sank off the shores of Nantucket. Hundreds of rescued survivors were brought to a New York City pier. Arthur was there when Jenny Altobelli of Bayonne, New Jersey, was emotionally reunited with her children.

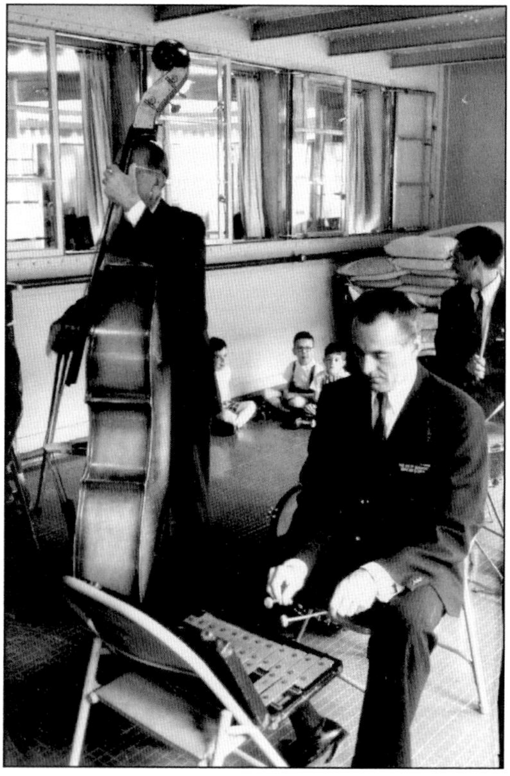

**SEA FEVER, 1958.** Whereas tragedy such as what occurred to the *Andrea Doria* has been part of life as long as folks have ventured out to sea, ships and sailors also tend to ignite one's imagination of journeying to faraway places. Here several youngsters from New York's Peter Cooper Village listen to music and dream on the deck of the SS *America* as the ship's band gives a concert.

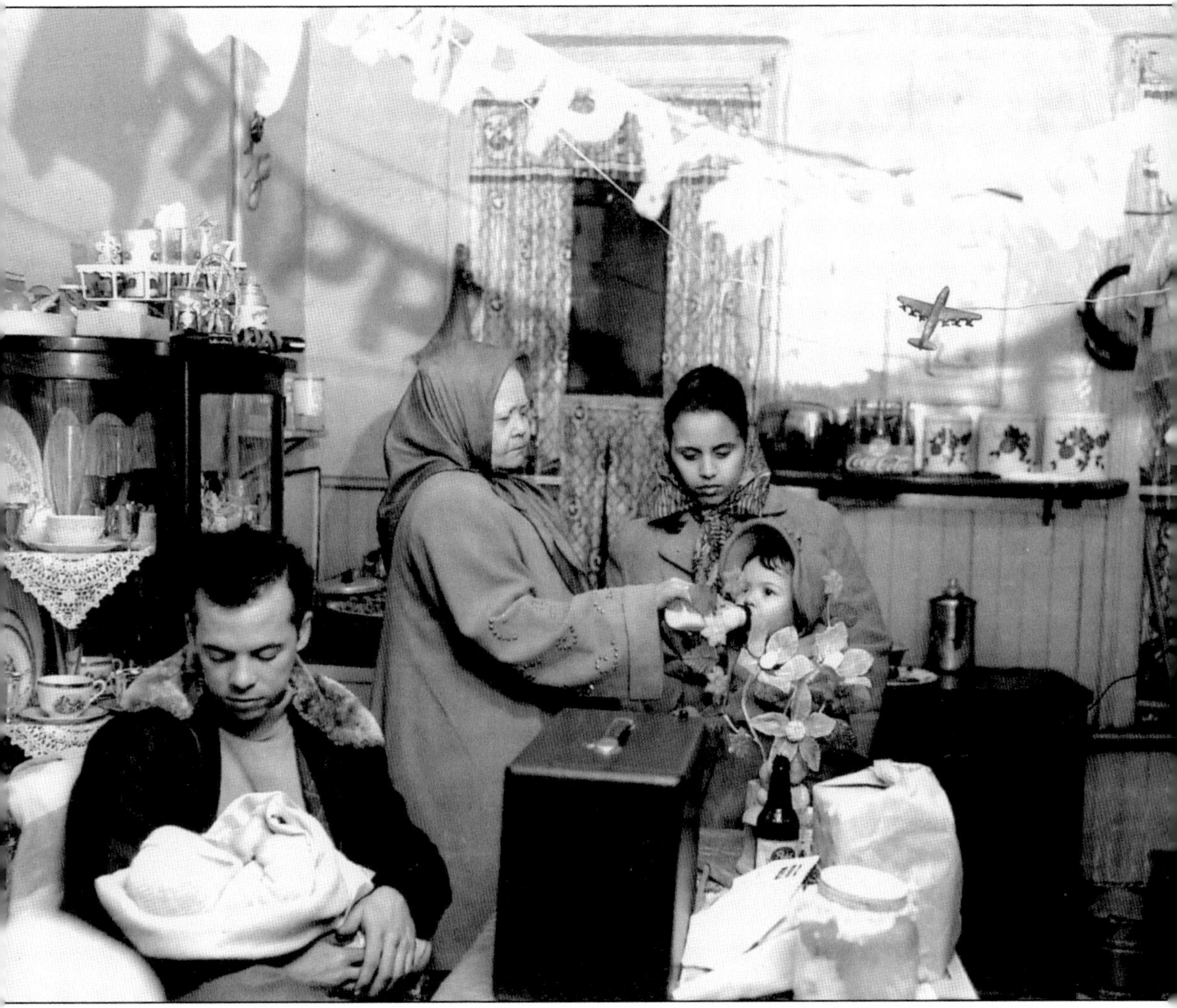

**NEW YEAR TRAGEDY, 1950S.** Although there is a whimsical side to Arthur's work, he was equally adept at covering hard news. What is traditionally one of the happiest days of the year became a time of grim tragedy for members of the Ayala family. They were among dozens of men, women, and children left homeless after a New Year's Eve fire gutted their tenement dwelling in Brooklyn. A Happy New Year streamer glitters ironically in a room with no heat or electricity.

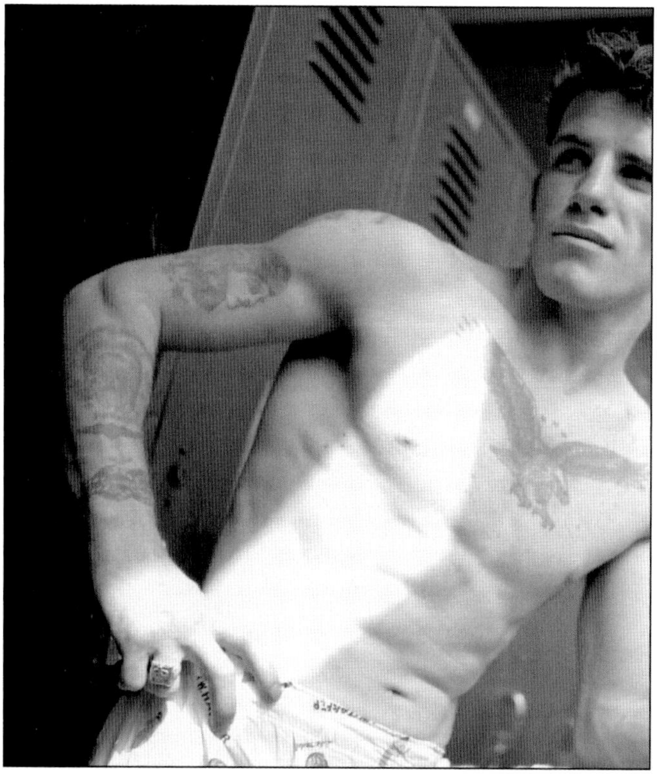

**ODD CHARACTERS, 1950S.** Part of the uniqueness of the city is its diversity and acceptance of all people. New York offers comfortable refuge for even the most bizarre men and women. Here Arthur photographed a tattooed muscle man as well as Gilda the Burlesque Queen.

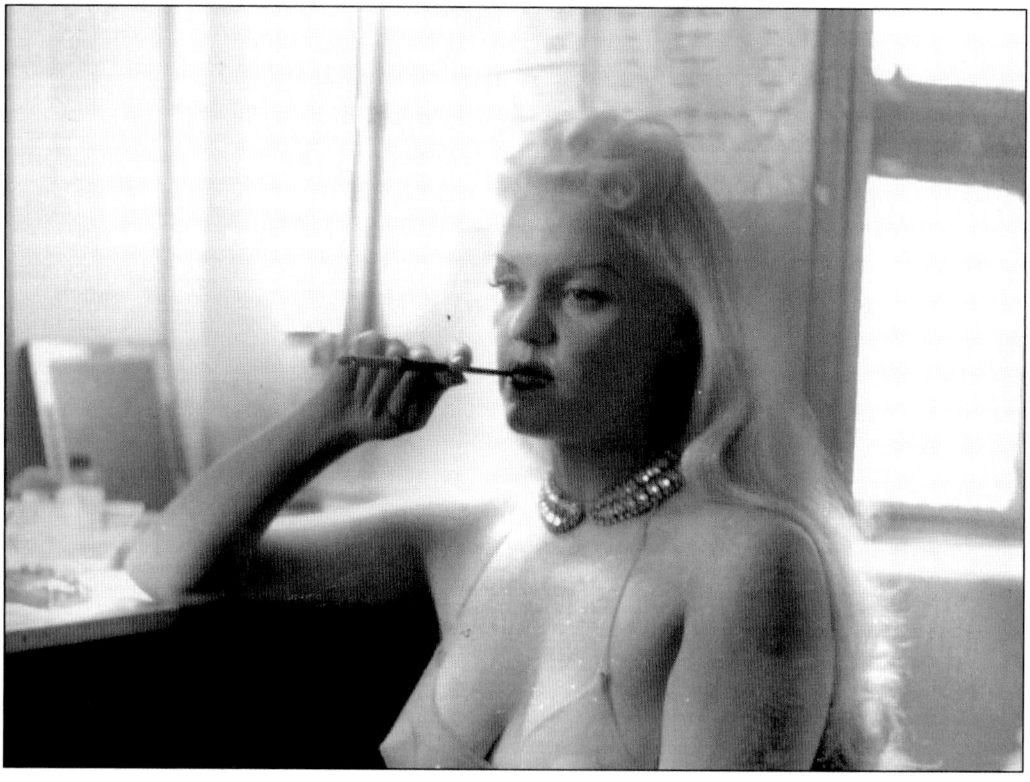

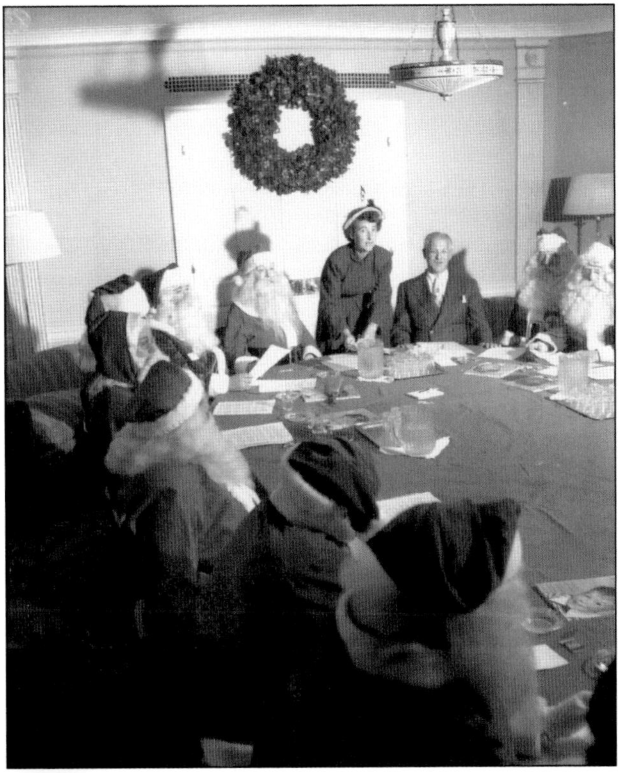

**SANTAS IN TRAINING, 1950S.** Who would have thought that even St. Nicholas needed to go to school? Only in New York City would one find a special school that trains men for the upcoming holiday season. These Santas hone their jolly skills with the help of a young boy.

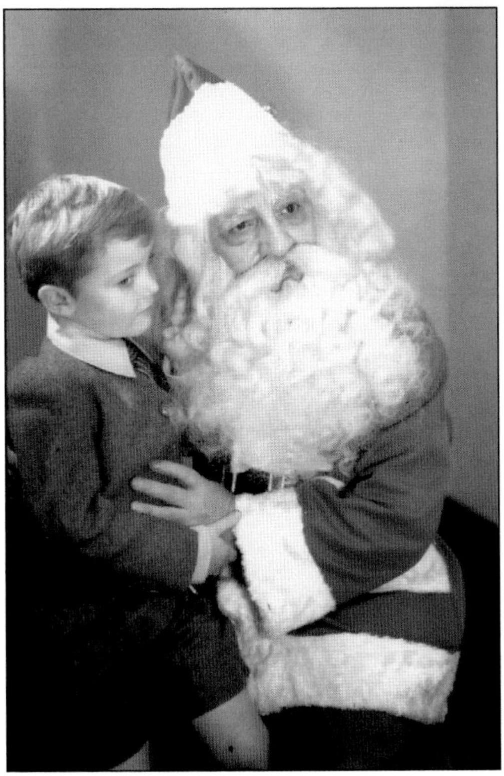

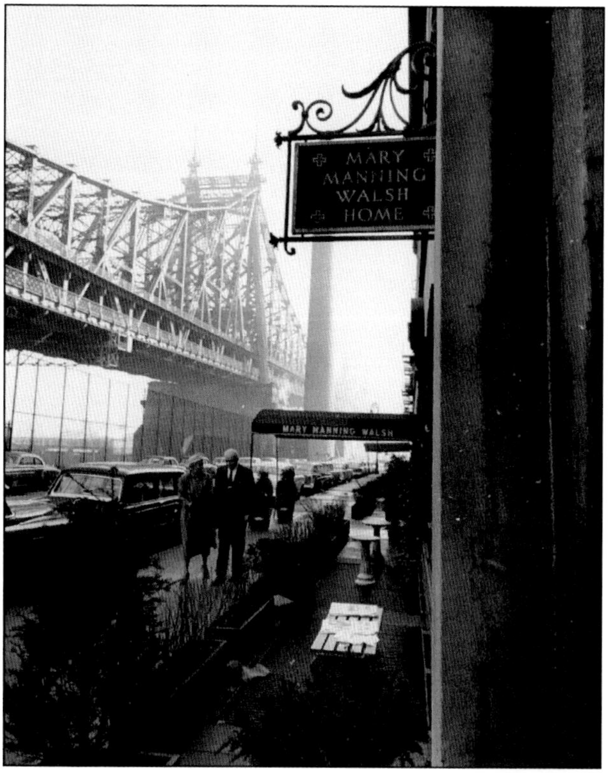


**MARY MANNING WALSH HOME FOR THE AGED, 1956.** Located in the shadow of the Queensboro Bridge, the Mary Manning Walsh Home for the Aged sits close to the heart of the biggest city in the world. Here two residents enjoy a stroll through the street outside the residence. Many of the old folks enjoyed watching the traffic moving on the bridge over the East River and found the view quite exciting.

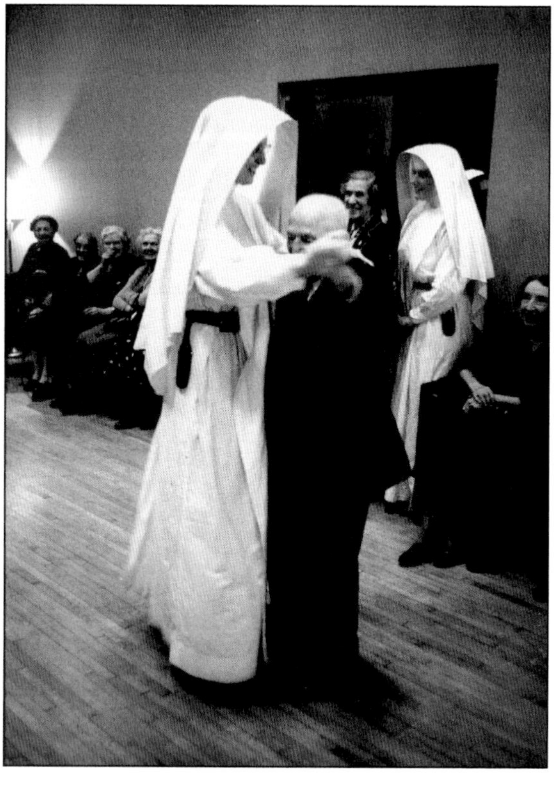

**TWILIGHT GLEAM, 1956.** How do senior citizens in Manhattan fare? Judging by this photograph, old folks greatly enjoy dancing. Arthur, while shooting an essay on the Mary Manning Walsh Home, made this memorable picture of a gentleman resident dancing with one of the nuns in charge of his care.

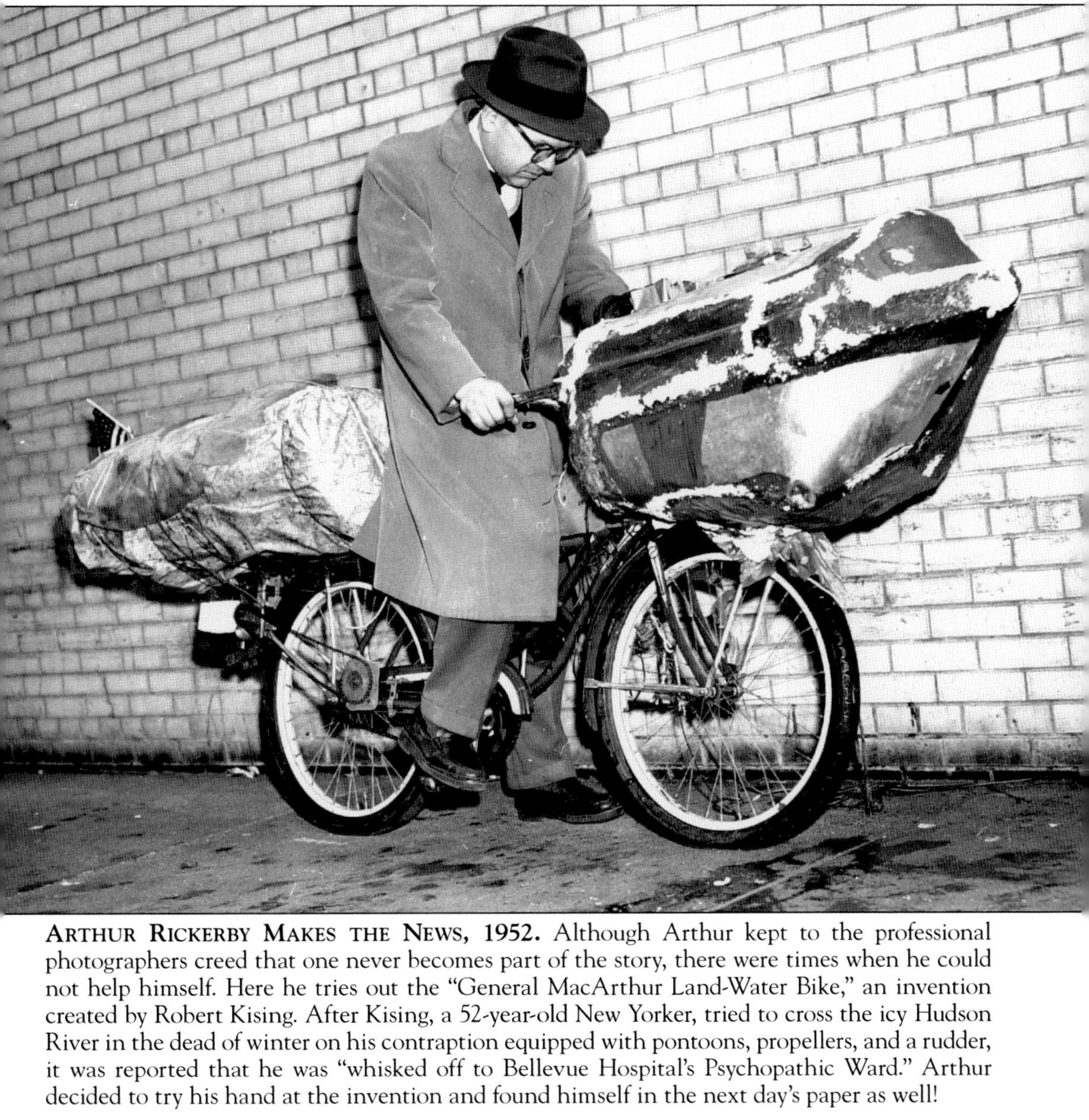

**ARTHUR RICKERBY MAKES THE NEWS, 1952.** Although Arthur kept to the professional photographers creed that one never becomes part of the story, there were times when he could not help himself. Here he tries out the "General MacArthur Land-Water Bike," an invention created by Robert Kising. After Kising, a 52-year-old New Yorker, tried to cross the icy Hudson River in the dead of winter on his contraption equipped with pontoons, propellers, and a rudder, it was reported that he was "whisked off to Bellevue Hospital's Psychopathic Ward." Arthur decided to try his hand at the invention and found himself in the next day's paper as well!

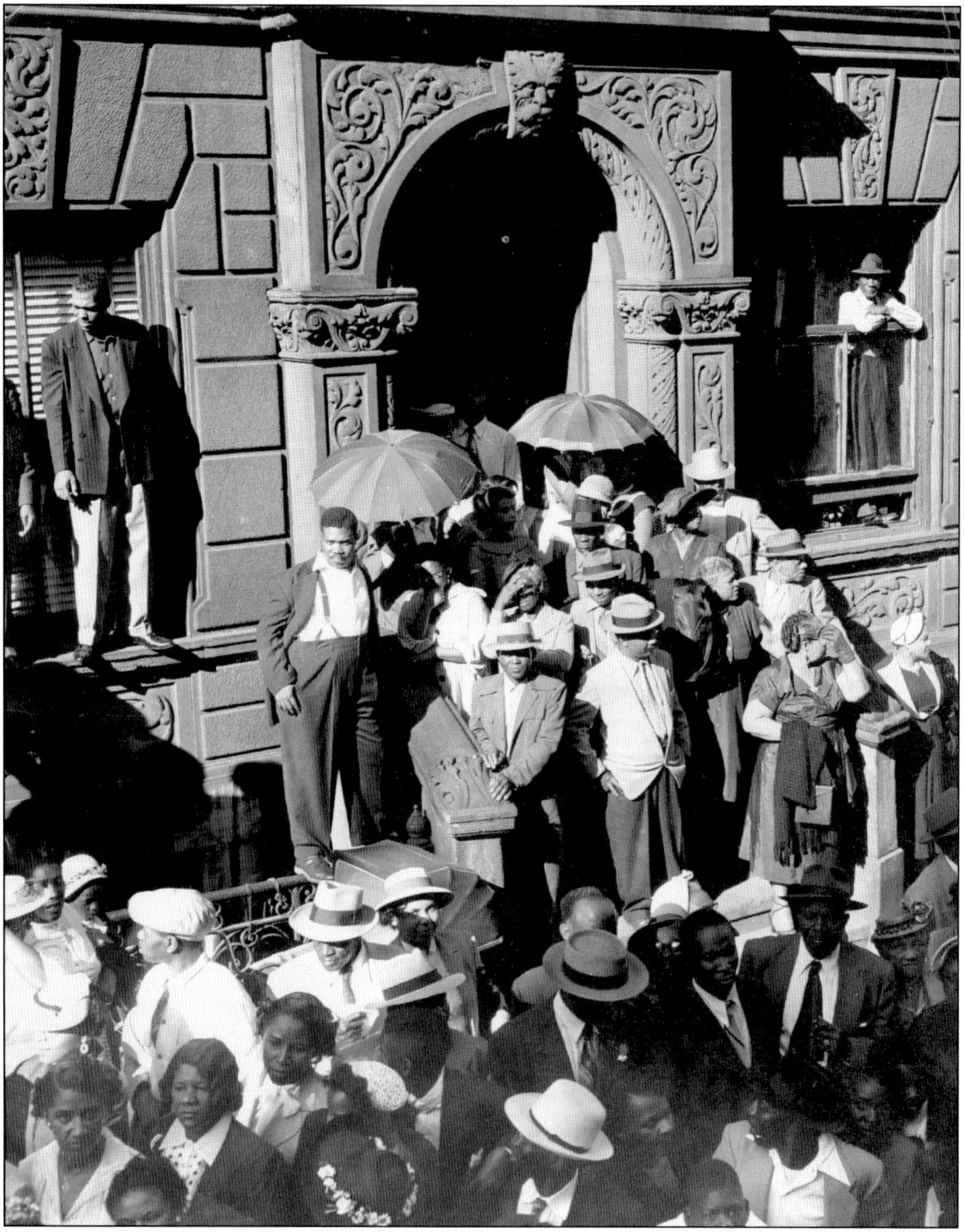

**HARLEM, 1950S.** An entire book can be written about Harlem, a mecca for music, art, and literature, which is well known around the world. However, it is the men and women of Harlem that give the neighborhood its vibrancy and color. In this photograph, Arthur shows a well-dressed crowd leaving a community gathering to face the midday sun.

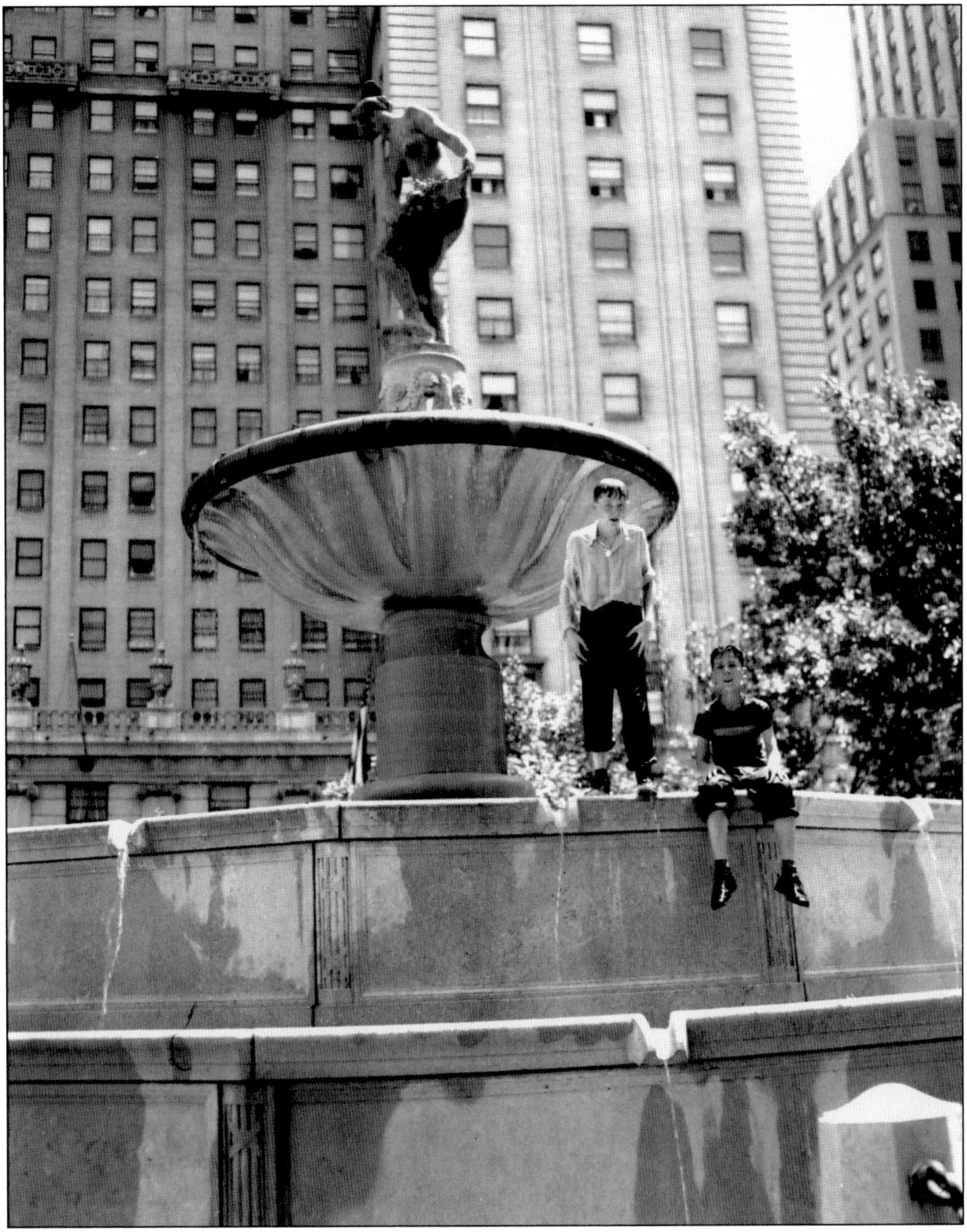

**KEEPING COOL ON FIFTH AVENUE, 1950S.** Arthur spotted these two young boys cooling off at a fountain during the summertime. The fully clad youngsters had been wading and playing in the pool at 59th Street and Fifth Avenue in front of the Hotel Plaza.

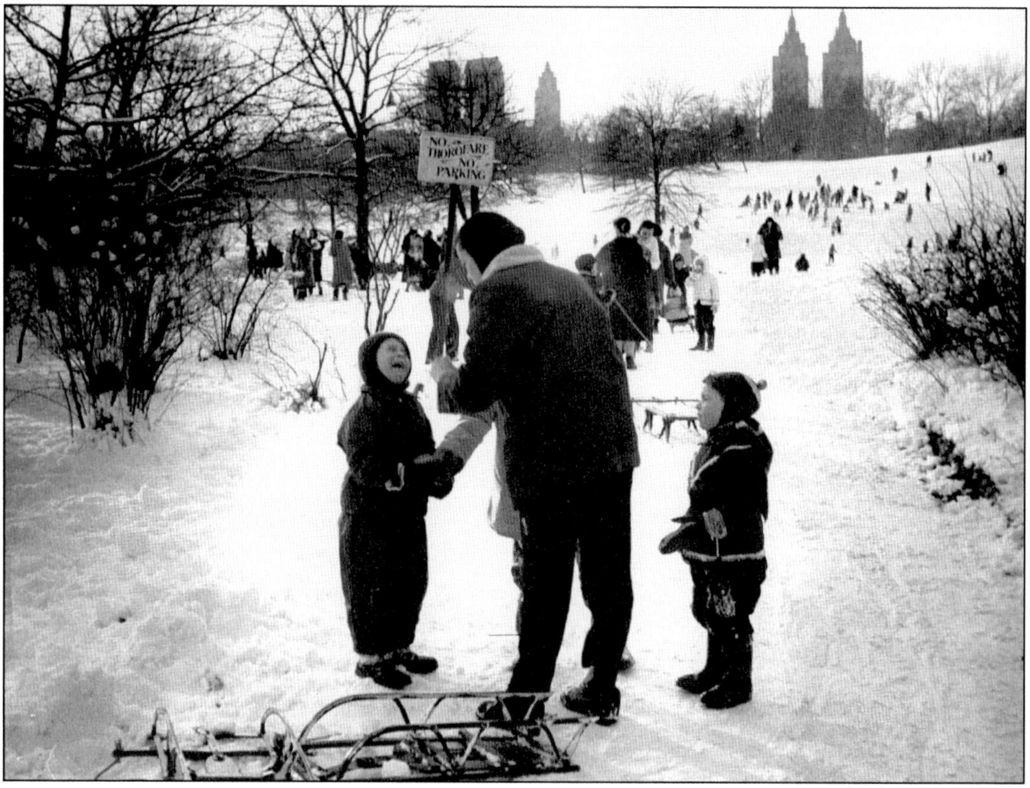


**Central Park, 1950s.** Central Park is perhaps the most famous city park in the world. At any time of the day or night, one will find families, baby strollers, or simply those out for a brisk walk taking in the great outdoors. These images show children who are enjoying sledding, snowball fights, and building snowmen after a snowfall turned the park into a winter wonderland.

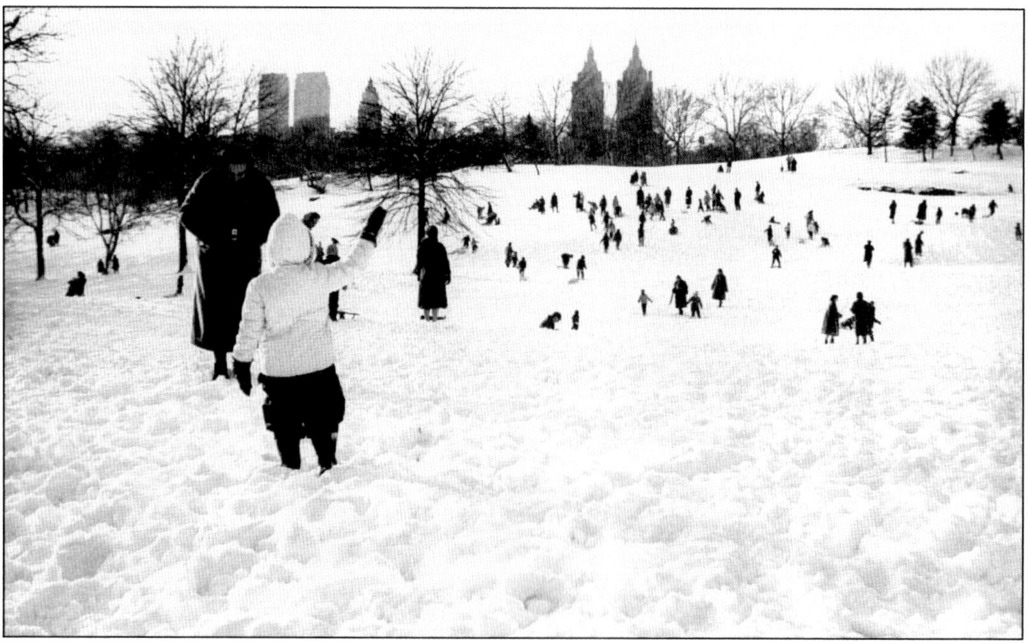

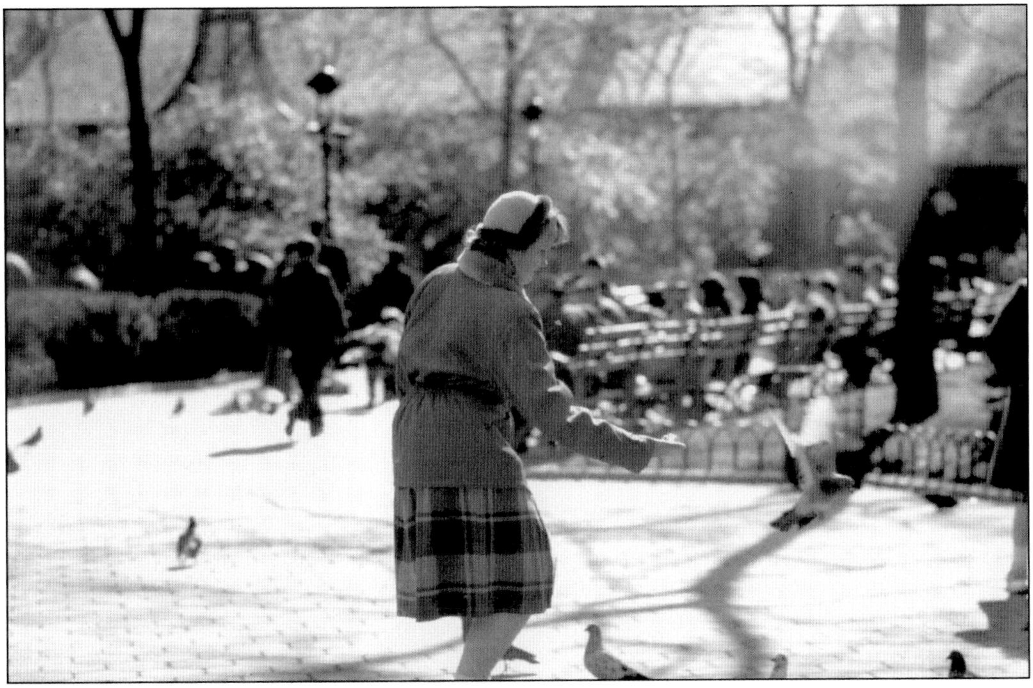

**PEANUTS FOR ALL, 1950S.** The photograph on the right shows a peanut vendor roaming Central Park in search of his next customer. The image above features a young lady feeding her new friends, the omnipresent pigeons.

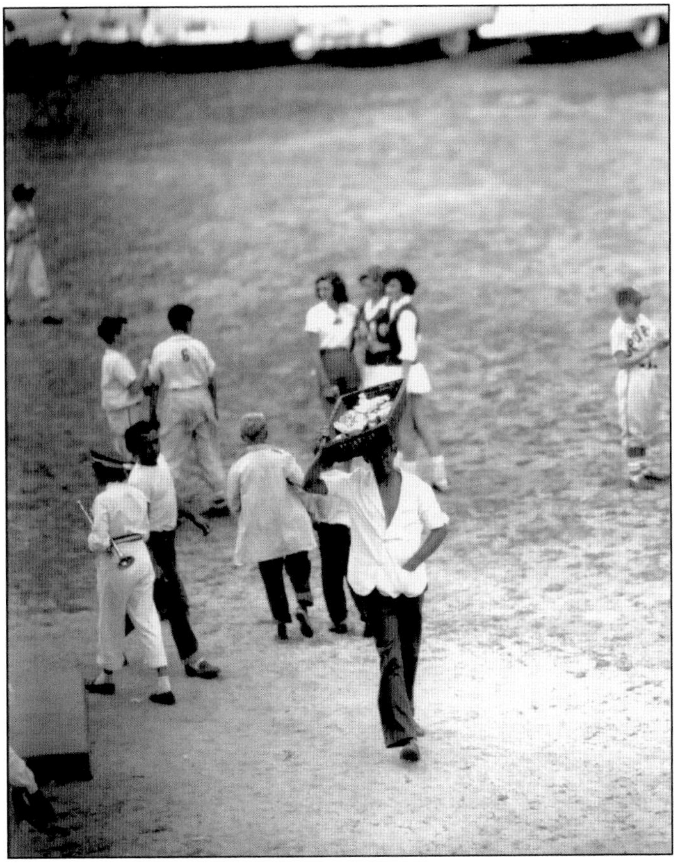

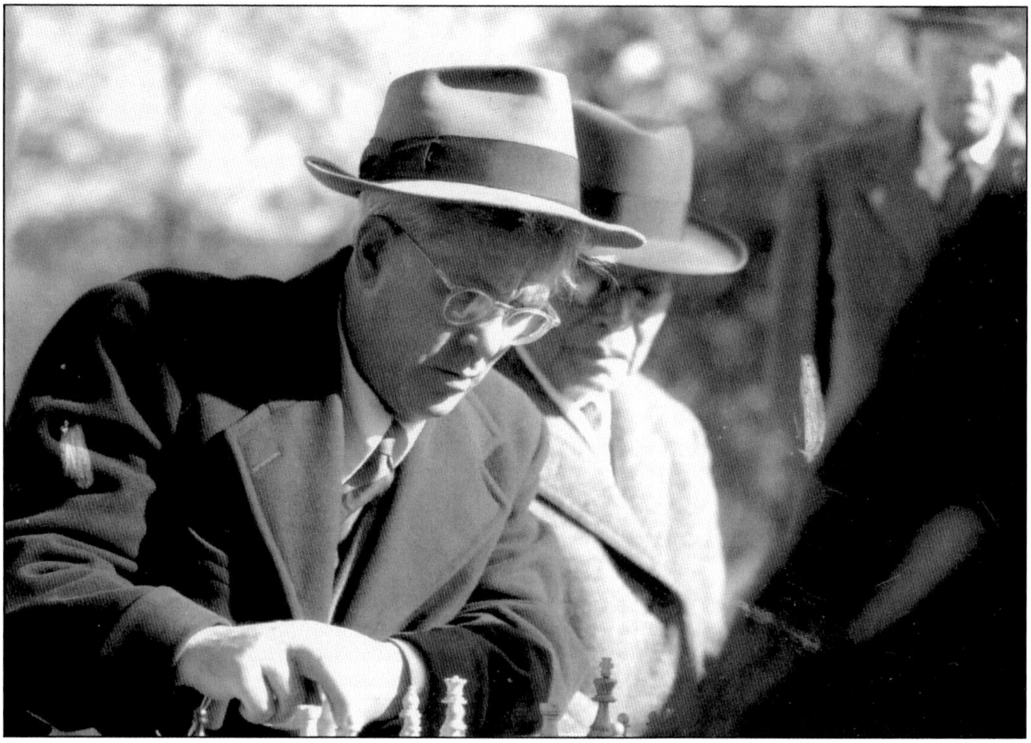

**CHECKMATE, 1950S.** Bryant Park, in the shadow of the New York Public Library, has for decades been a haven for anyone interested in testing their chess skills. Arthur caught these men doing battle and attracting an audience.

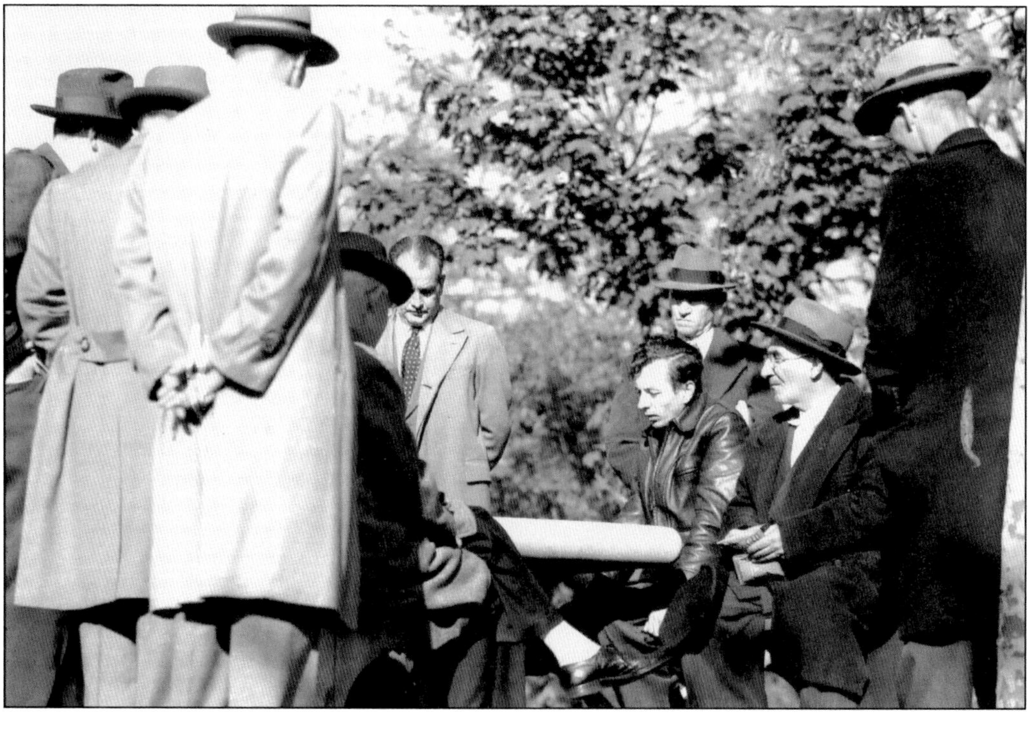

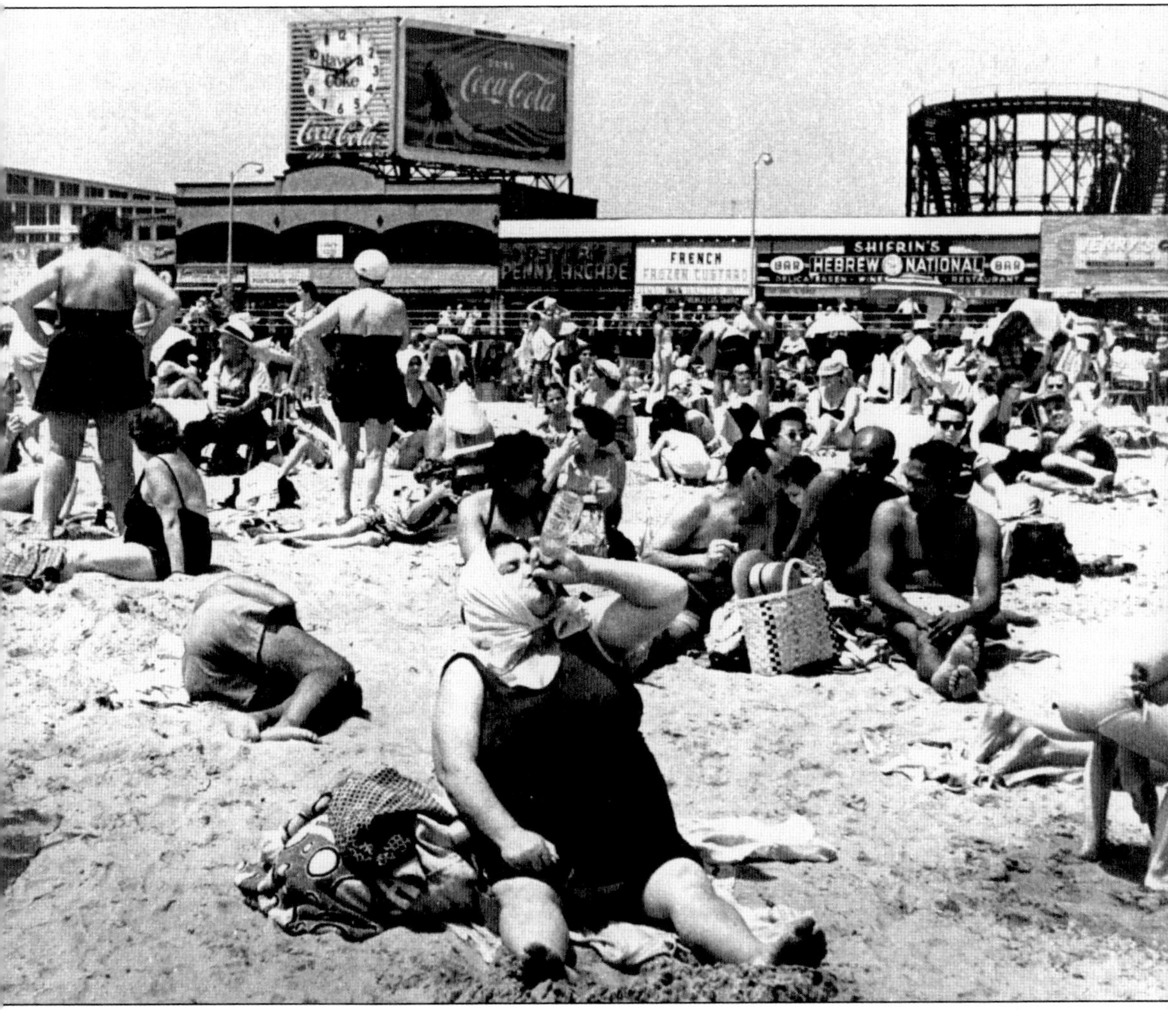


**CONEY ISLAND, 1950S.** When the summer heat takes hold, New Yorkers of all shapes and sizes have for years found their way to Coney Island, often called the "world's largest playground." It is the city's own six-mile stretch of beach on the Atlantic Ocean, well known as a haven for fun in the sun.

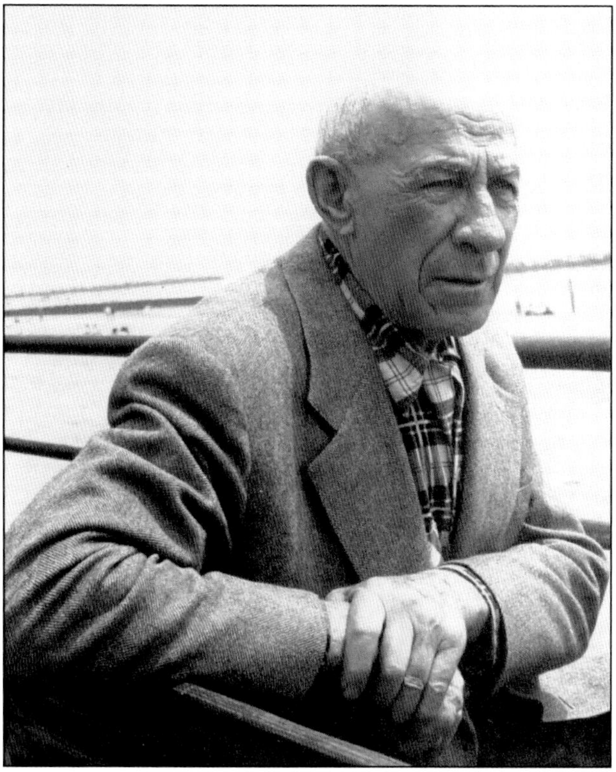

**ON THE BOARDWALK, 1950S.** Even as a child, Arthur enjoyed the sights, sounds, and people found at Coney Island. He loved to record the beach crowd. The photograph on the left shows an elderly gentleman pensively gazing out into the Atlantic Ocean. Below, two children, clutching their sand bucket and toys, impatiently stare at the camera before darting onto the waiting warm beach.

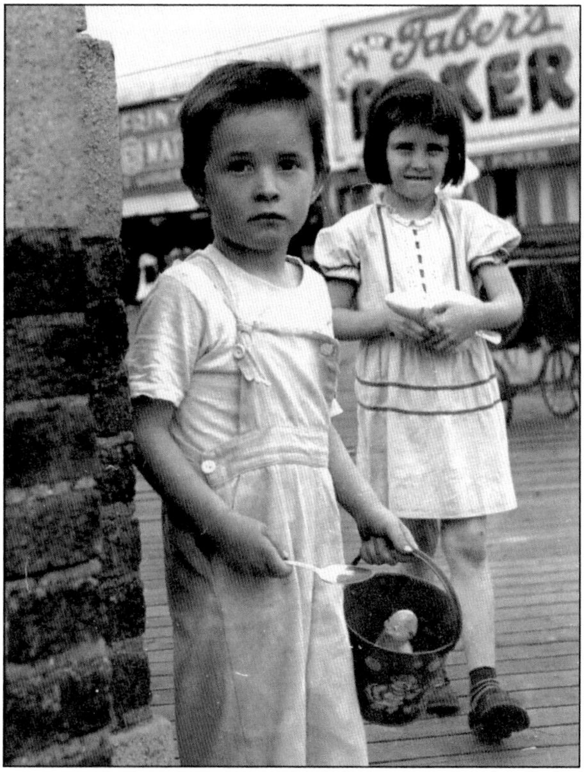

# *Five*

# The Place to See and Be Seen

"Where we find the people, celebrities are born," one historian of 20th-century popular culture mused, "and where there are celebrities, people congregate." In a sense, as magazines were found in racks on the corner of every town in America and as the television age of the 1950s enveloped the entire country, the very sighting of a celebrity became an event. As such, the sighting became news that got the attention of the press. There was no place in the world in the mid-20th century that seemed to attract personalities from all walks of life, whether they were politicians, poets, musicians, or Hollywood stars, like New York City.

And why not? Gotham was, after all, a mecca for the arts, theater, literature, and popular culture. What other city could boast of Times Square, Broadway, Fifth Avenue, Madison Avenue, Wall Street, and even the United Nations? Fifty years before the word *paparazzi* became a household term, the celebrities of a simpler time actually enjoyed and craved the attention they received. New York City seemed to be a magnet for the rich and the famous as they came, saw, and sometimes conquered. Each time they did, it seemed there was a curious and adoring crowd, and always positioned just outside of the congregating crowd, in a clever way to take just the right kind of photograph, was the ubiquitous Arthur Rickerby. By the 1950s, Arthur became such a familiar face around town that everyone of any stature whatsoever either knew or recognized him, especially those personalities and celebrities whom his lens captured perfectly.

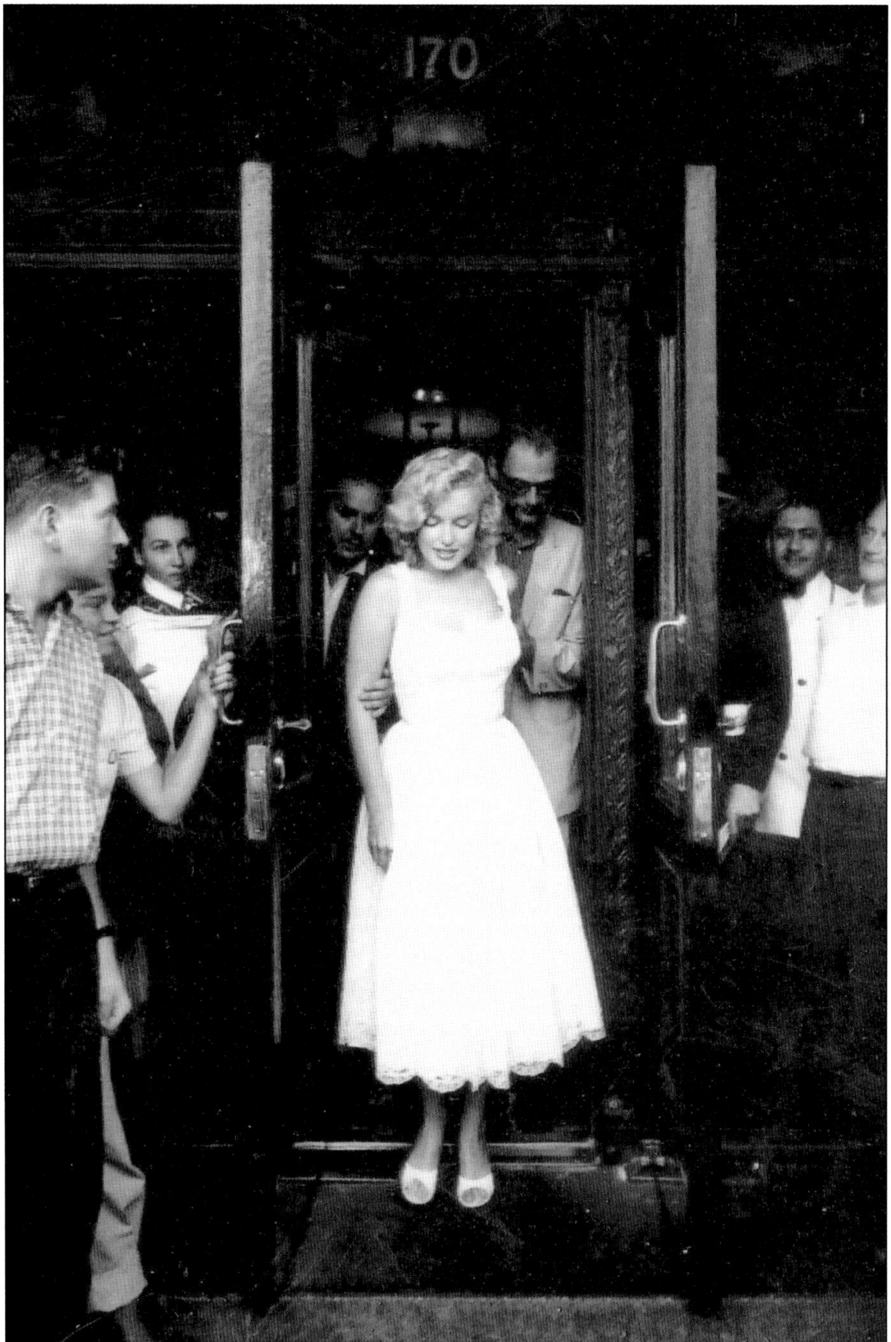


**MARILYN MONROE, 1950S.** Celebrities—from movie stars and politicians to musicians and world leaders—seemed to flock to New York City almost daily during the 1950s, and Arthur recorded many of them on film. There was none bigger than actress Marilyn Monroe, perhaps the one person who captured the country's "new direction" better than all others. When she visited the Big Apple with her husband, playwright Arthur Miller, their image appeared in newspapers everywhere.

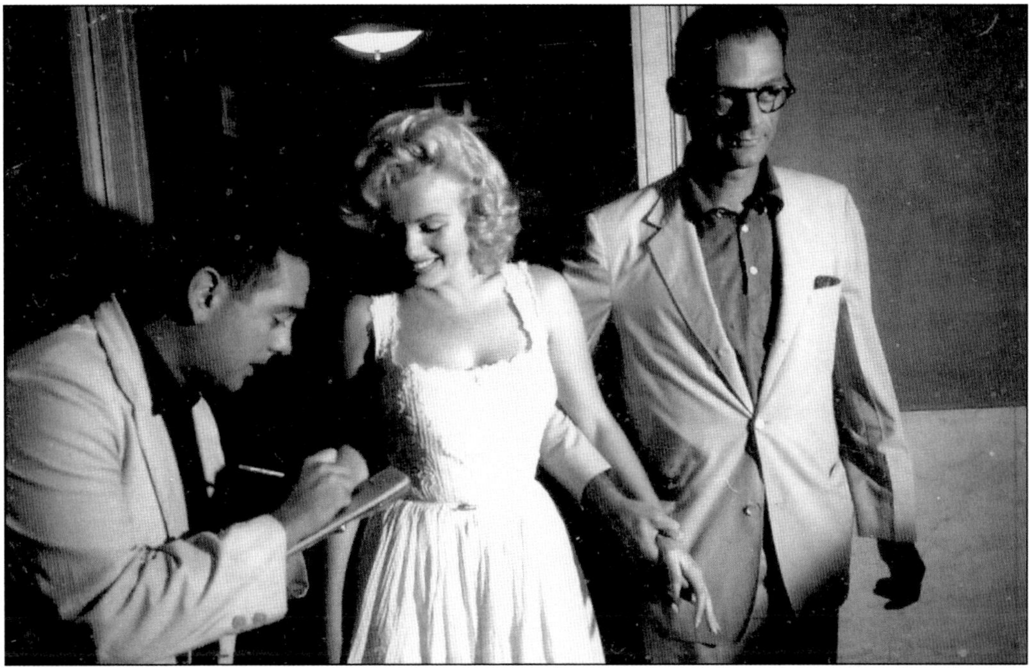

**MARILYN MONROE AND PLAYWRIGHT ARTHUR MILLER, 1950S.** In January 1954, Marilyn Monroe married former New York Yankee great Joe DiMaggio. By October, "America's couple" had separated, and within a year and a half, Monroe had met and married the celebrated playwright Arthur Miller. By 1961, that marriage ended in divorce as well, but during their time together, every move they made was breathlessly covered by the ever-present press. Here Monroe, while chatting with a reporter, is shown leaving a New York City hospital among the flashing camera bulbs.

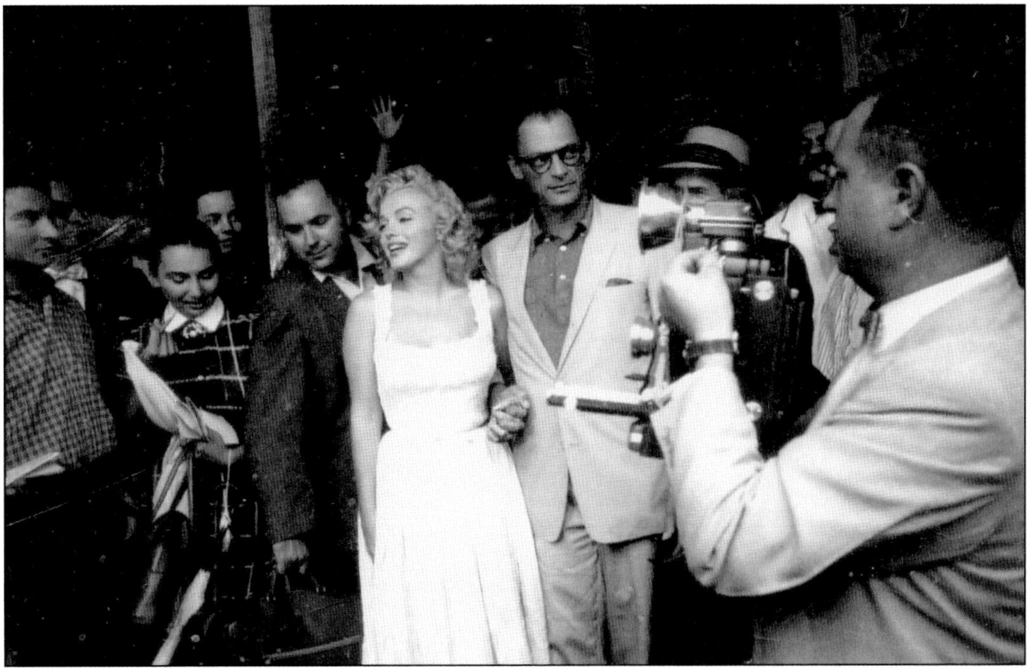

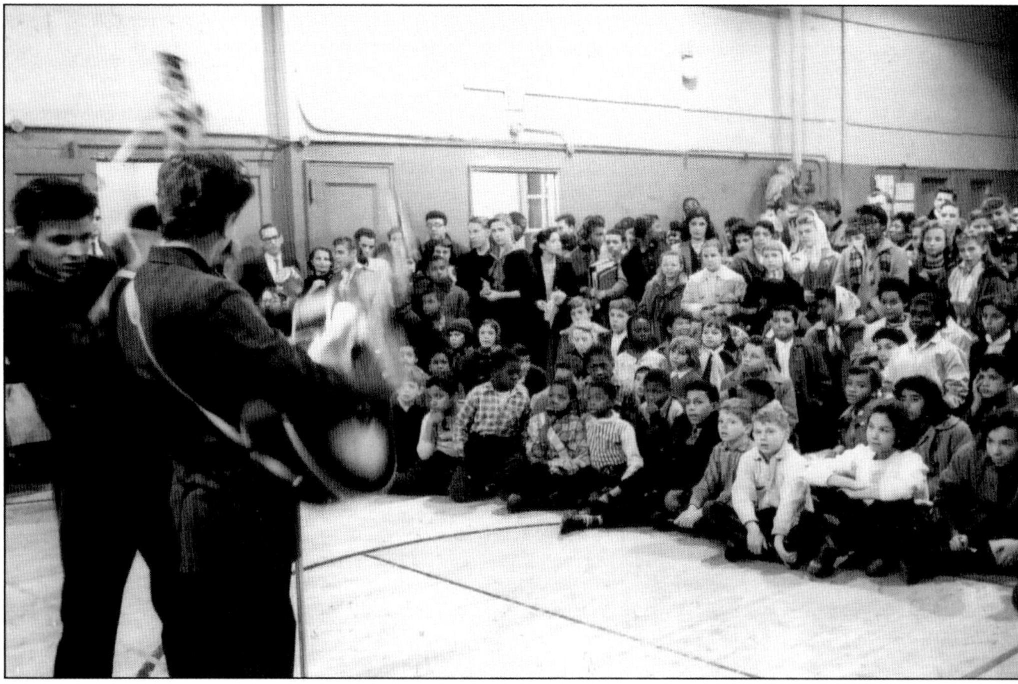

**THE EVERLY BROTHERS, C. 1953.** In the early 1940s, eight-year-old Don Everly and his six-year-old brother Phil performed as signers on their parents' radio show on KMA in Shenandoah, Iowa. A decade later, "Little Donnie" and "Baby Boy Phil," as they were called, were at the forefront of the rock and roll revolution that swept America and the world. Here Arthur perfectly photographed gleeful teenagers at a New York City high school when the duo sang "Bye Bye Love" just for them.

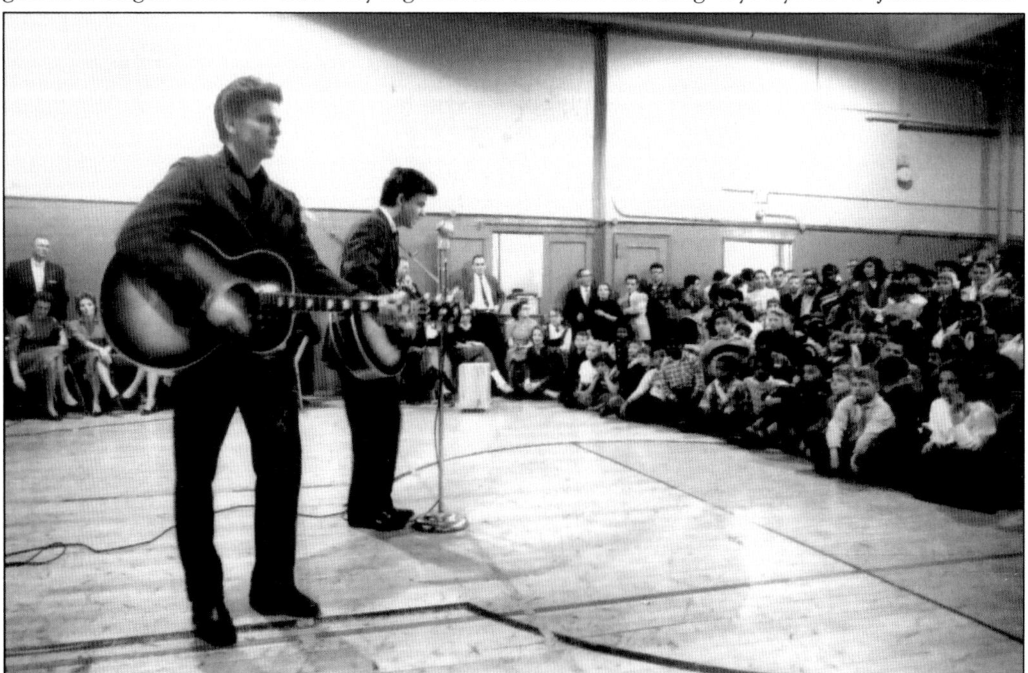

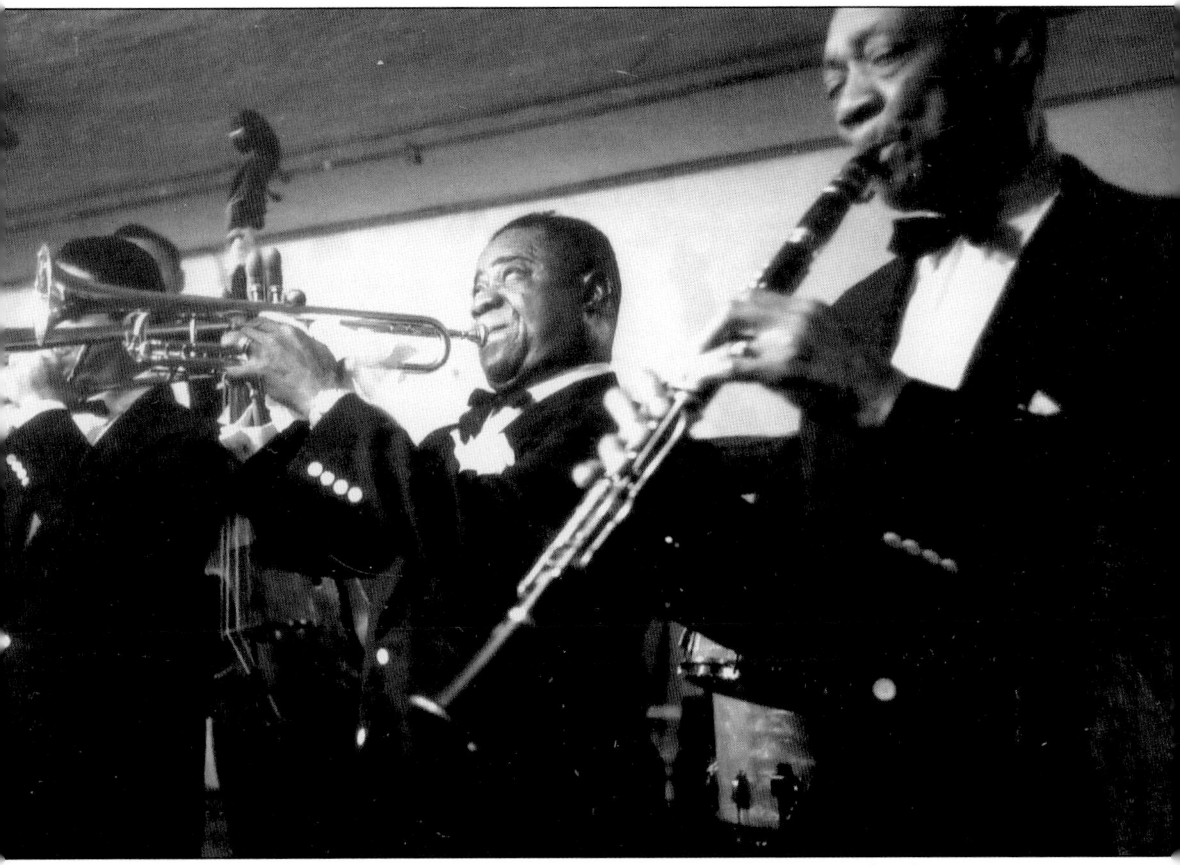

**LOUIS "SATCHMO" ARMSTRONG, 1950S.** Louis Armstrong was, quite simply, the greatest jazz musician who ever lived. His trumpet playing was technically superb but also spontaneous and clever. He was a treat to watch whether he sang, played solo, or blew with his band. Arthur took these rare previously unpublished photographs of the amazing performer while on stage at a small club in the Big Apple.

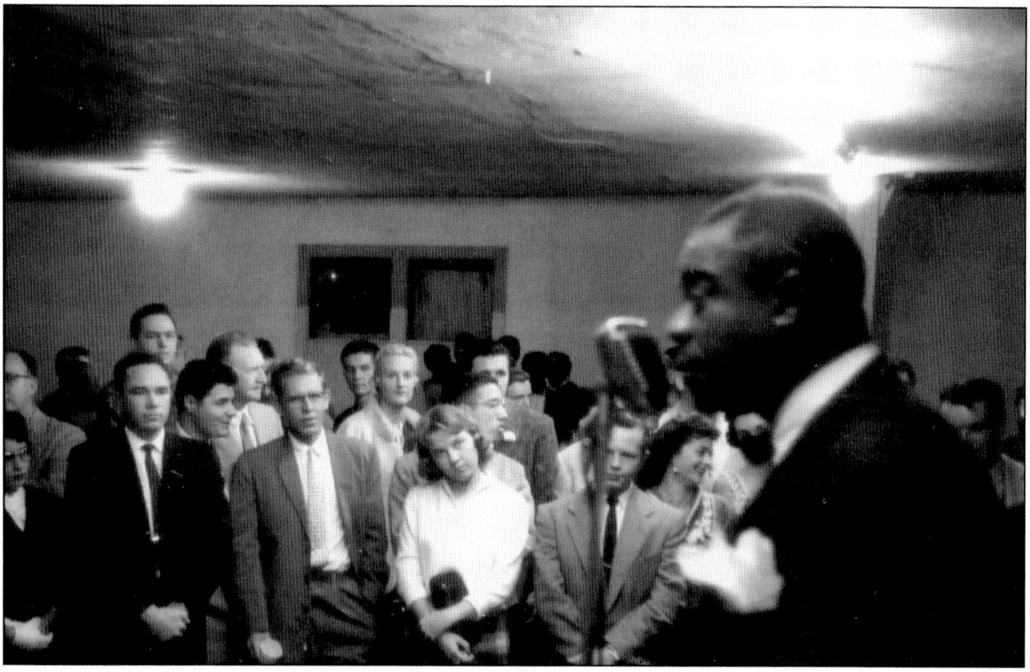

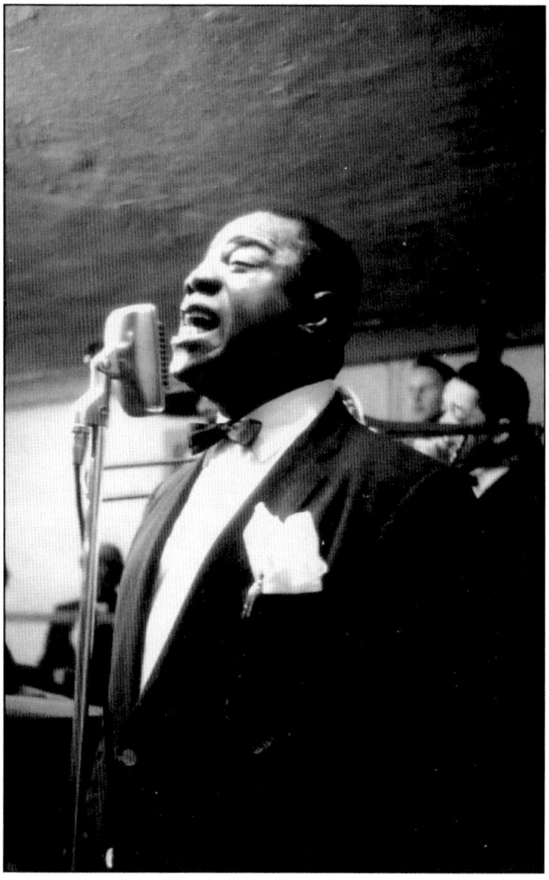

**A Joy to Watch, 1950s.** New Yorkers have a particular love affair with America's greatest musicians, among them Louis Armstrong. For one whose photographs reveal an artistic quality on their own, Arthur Rickerby felt a particular kinship when he shot the jazz great during a performance in the city in the early 1950s. By the time these photographs were taken, Armstrong had played in New York City literally hundreds of times beginning in the early 1920s when he, fresh from New Orleans and Chicago, joined Harlem's Fletcher Henderson Orchestra, the top African American band of his day.

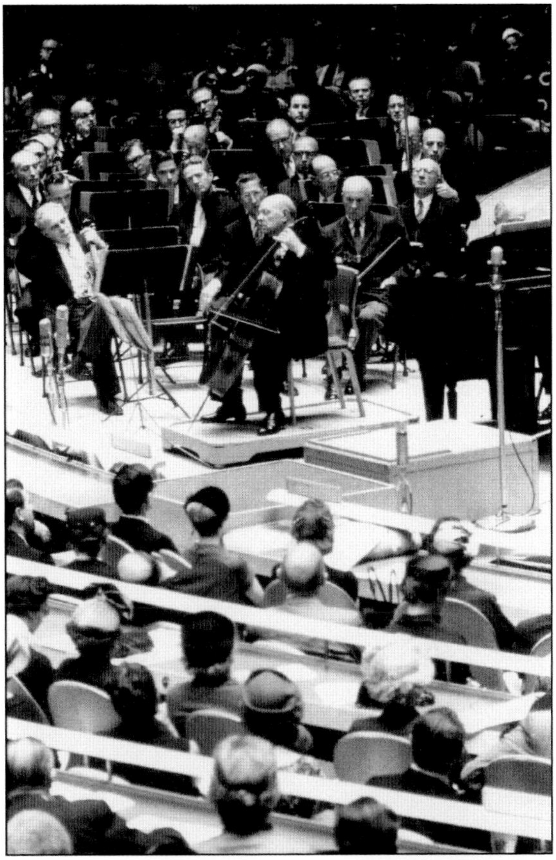

**WORLD-CLASS MUSICIAN PABLO CASALS, 1950S.** Renown cellist and conductor Pablo Casals first toured the United States as a young man in 1901 when he accompanied a 21-year-old vocalist. Over 50 years later in the mid-1950s, Casals thrilled New York audiences with several performances at Carnegie Hall. On December 6, 1963, Pres. John F. Kennedy awarded Casals the Presidential Medal of Freedom. The medal is inscribed, "With the cello under his fingers, he has touched the heart of the world."

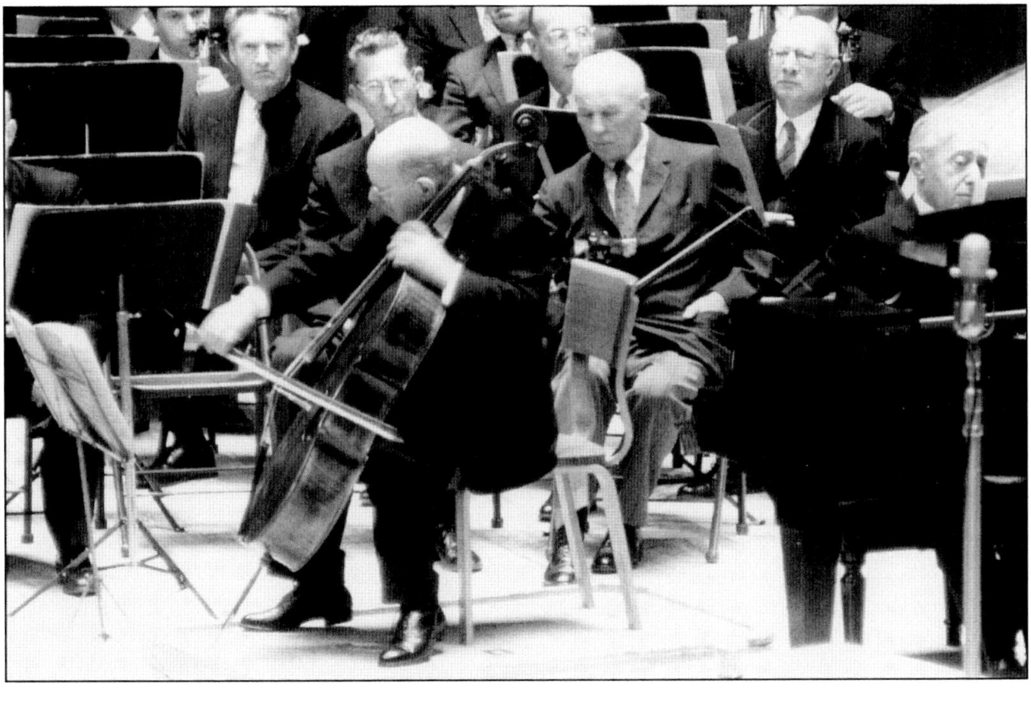

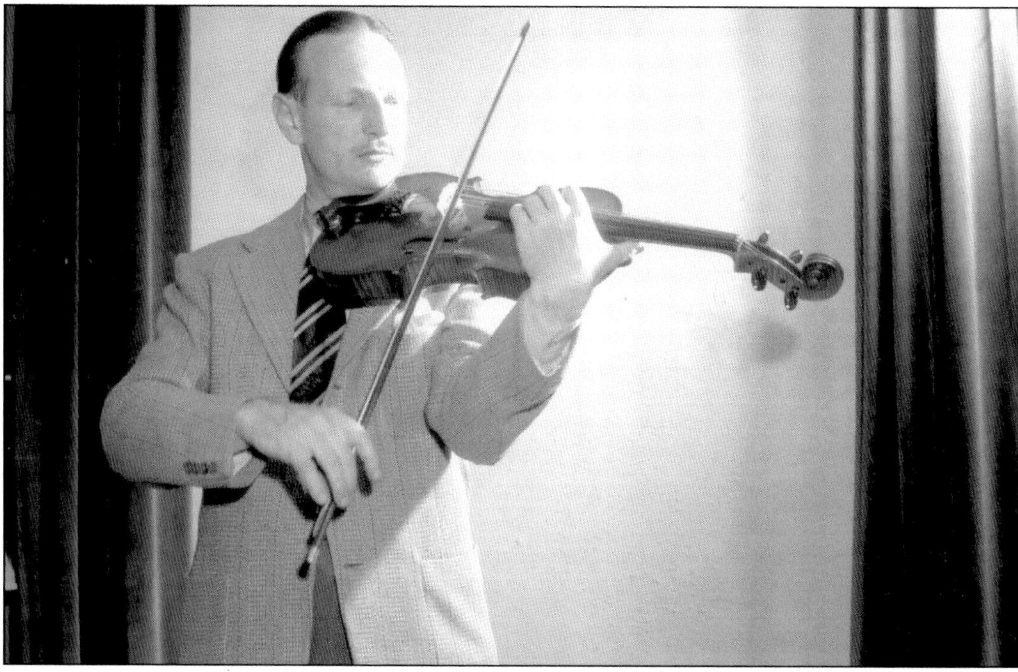

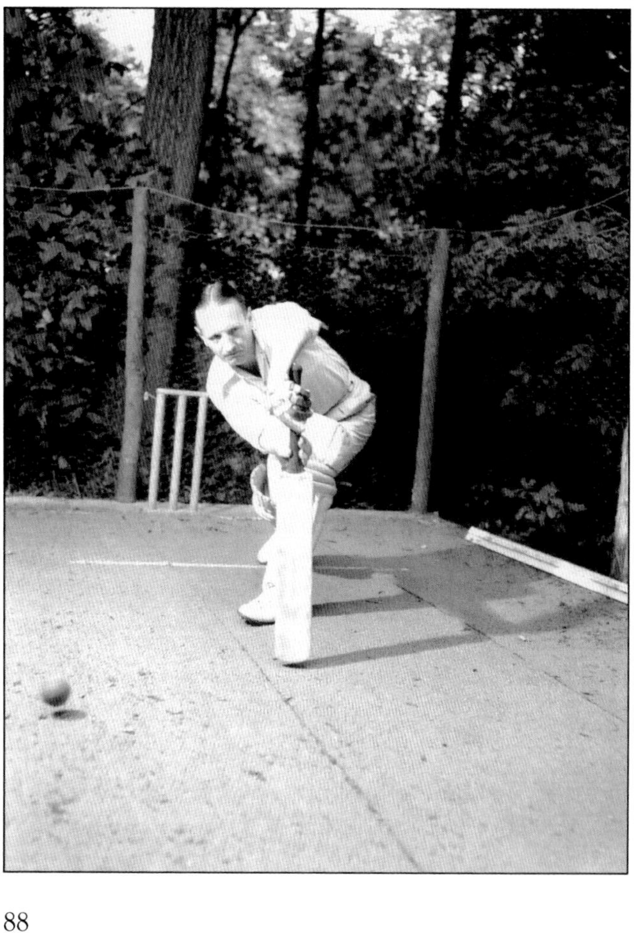

**WILLIAM PRIMROSE, 1949.** Scotland's William Primrose was one of the world's premier violists. Primrose was schooled in the 1930s under the tutelage of the great Arturo Toscanini when he played for the NBC Symphony in New York City. Here Arthur caught up with the musician enjoying some time away from the symphony hall with his beloved violin. The Scotsman also showed Arthur his form as a pretty fair cricket player.

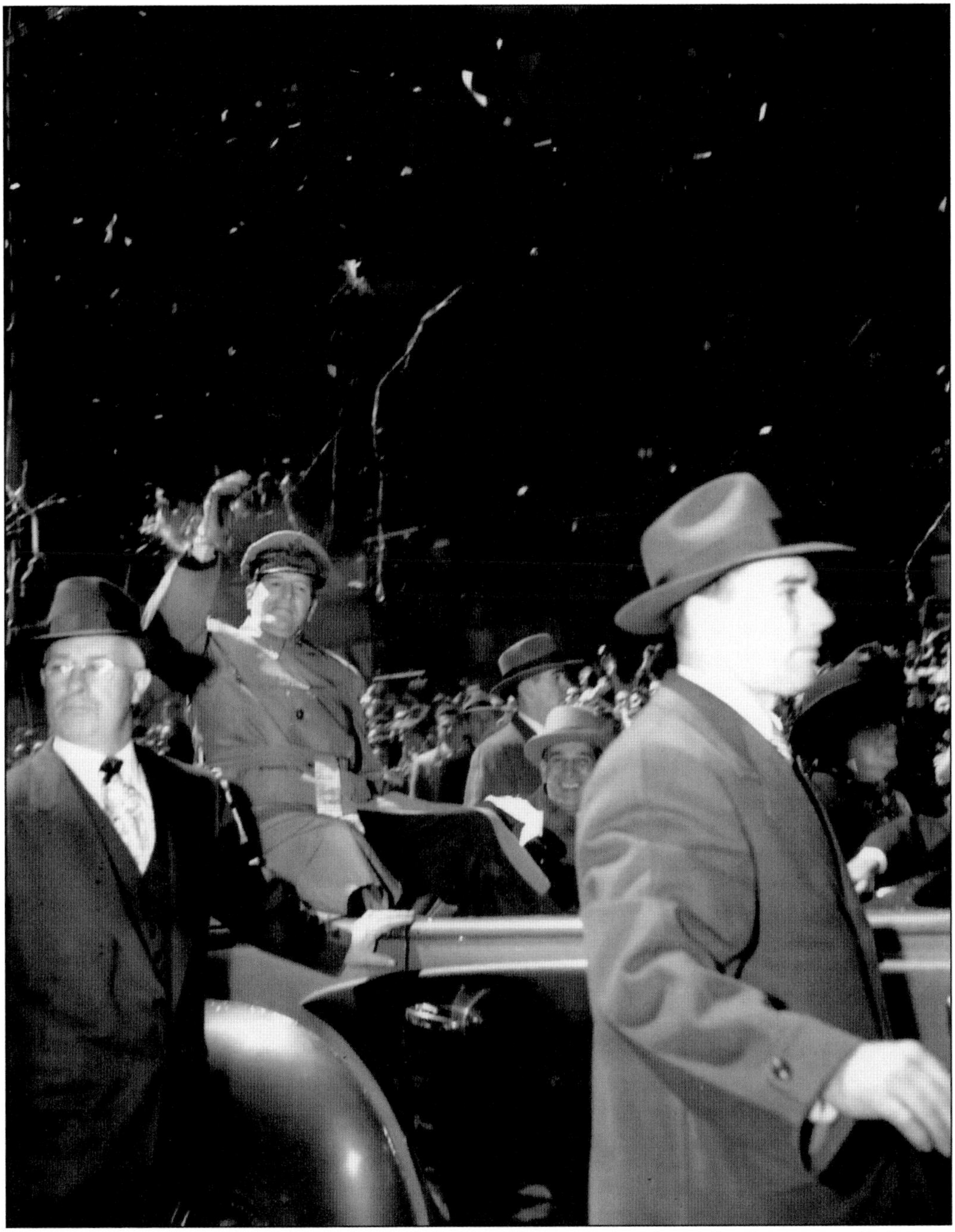

**A HERO'S WELCOME FOR GEN. DOUGLAS MACARTHUR, 1951.** After being recalled from Korea by Pres. Harry S. Truman in 1951, the ticker-tape parade in the heart of Manhattan for the wartime hero Gen. Douglas MacArthur was among the most elaborate and exciting ever staged. Naturally Arthur was present with his trusty camera and perfectly recorded the general acknowledging the throngs who greeted him with enthusiasm.

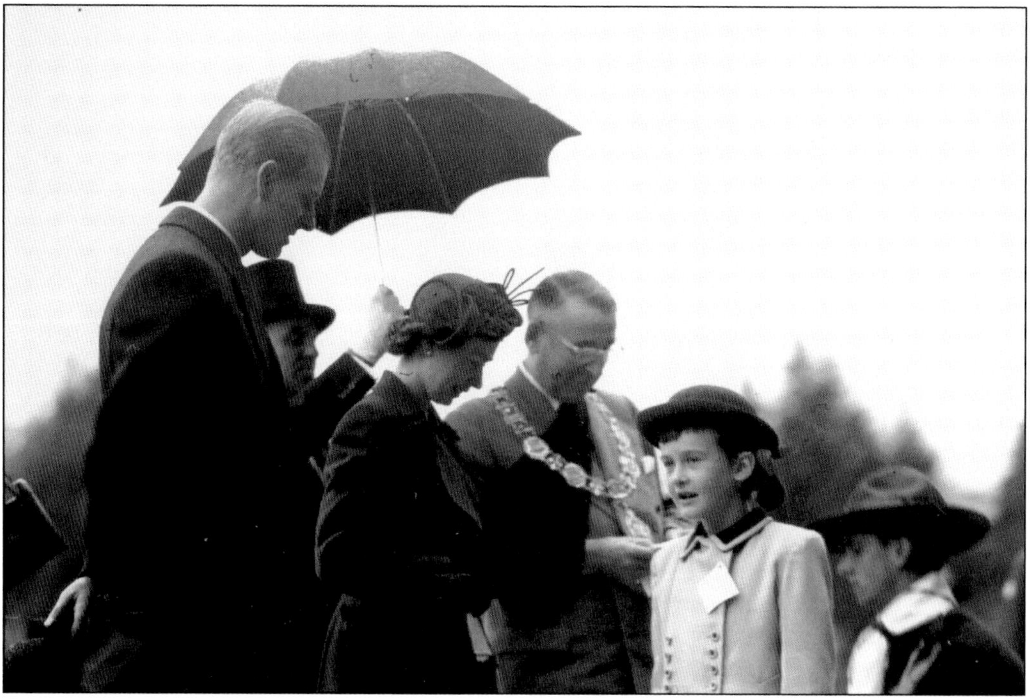

**THE BRITISH ROYAL TOUR, 1951.** During the year of the Gen. Douglas MacArthur parade, with the overwhelming number of spectators who attended, a much more genteel and sedate crowd greeted Princess Elizabeth (presently Queen Elizabeth II) and her husband Philip, the Duke of Edinburgh, when they visited North America. Adoring spectators traveled hundreds of miles to catch a glimpse of the future queen.

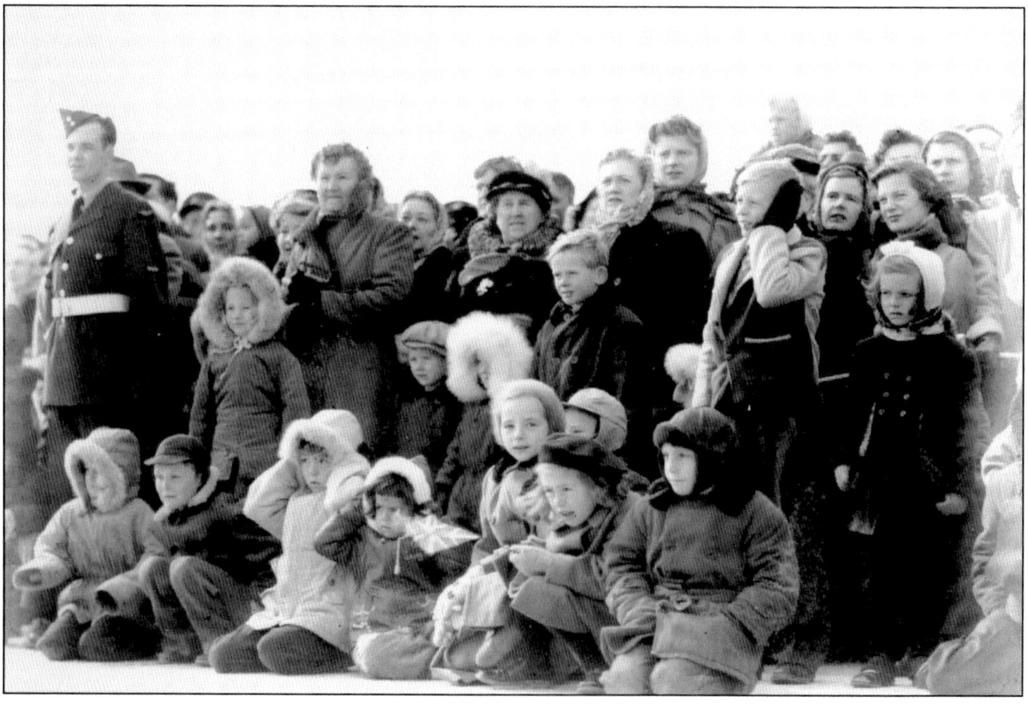

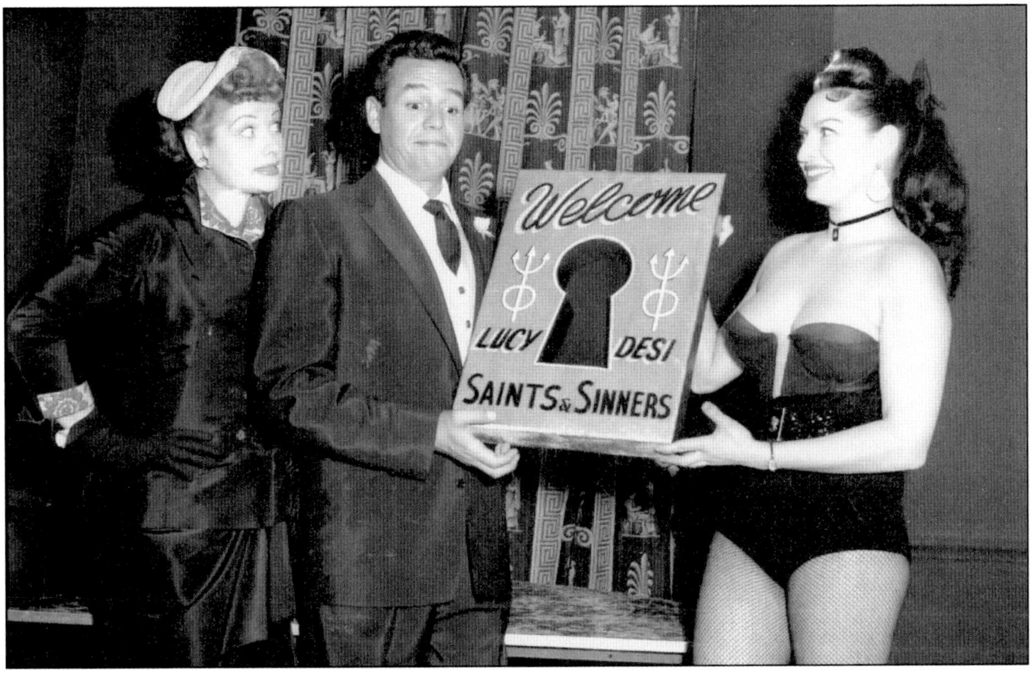


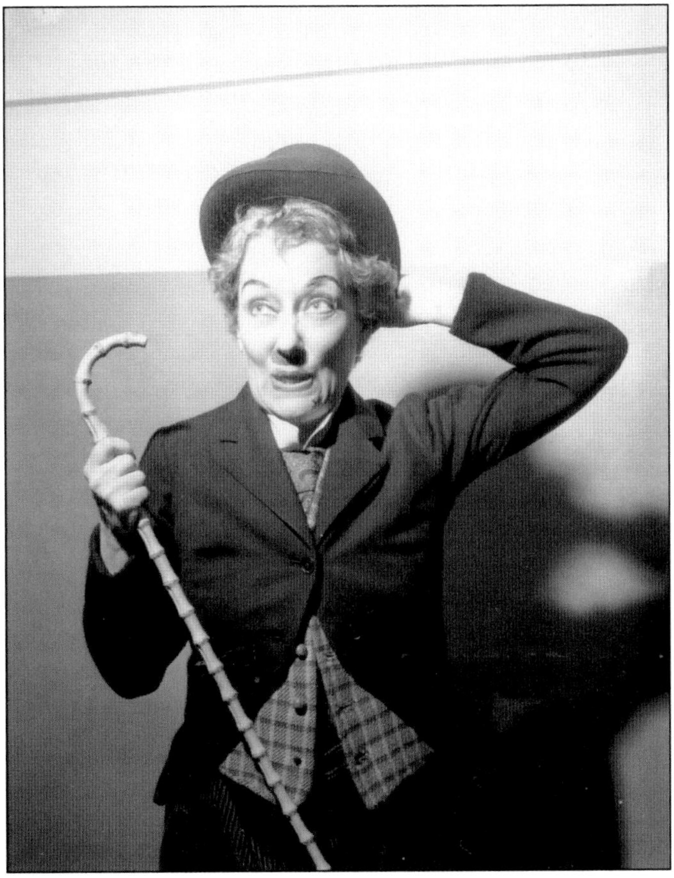

**LEGENDARY COMEDIANS, 1954.** When the television age mushroomed across the United States in the early 1950s, that little box found in every living room in America created a "new" kind of star. The *I Love Lucy* show starring Lucille Ball and her husband Desi Arnez debuted in 1951 and became an instant hit. Here Arthur photographed the "first couple of comedy" when they were honored at the famous Circus Saints and Sinners luncheon in New York City. That same year, Arthur caught up with a star of a different era, screen actress Gloria Swanson, whose comedic roles in silent films brought her worldwide fame.

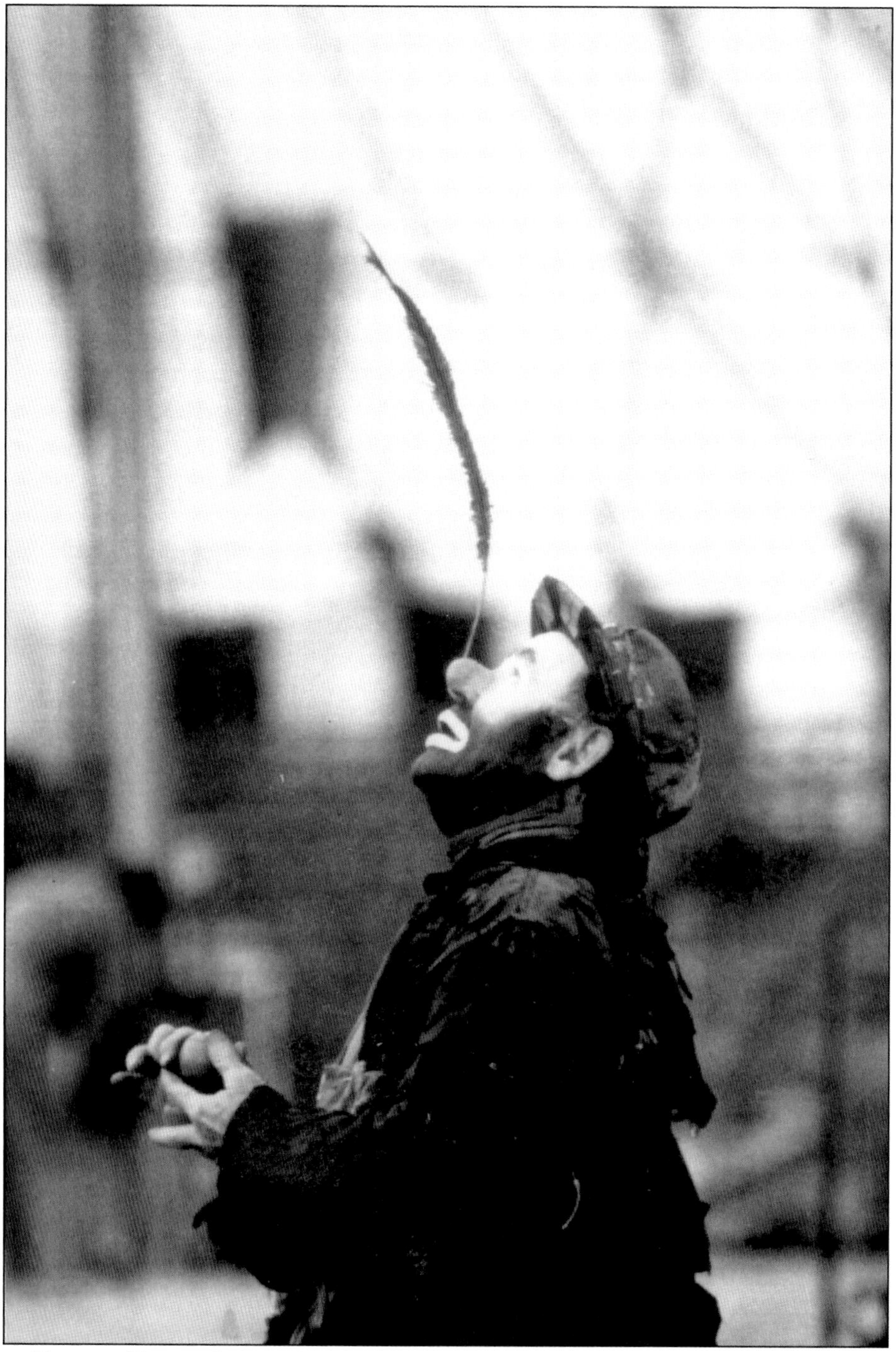

**WORLD-FAMOUS TRAMP CLOWN EMMETT KELLY, 1950S.** During the 1950s, after performing in front of circus audiences around the world for decades, Emmett Kelly settled in New York City, not only performing off Broadway but also entertaining as a traveling mascot for the Brooklyn Dodgers baseball team. Arthur took this poignant photograph of Kelly in character as "Weary Willie" balancing a giant feather on his nose. Of all the photographs that Arthur took, this was his favorite.

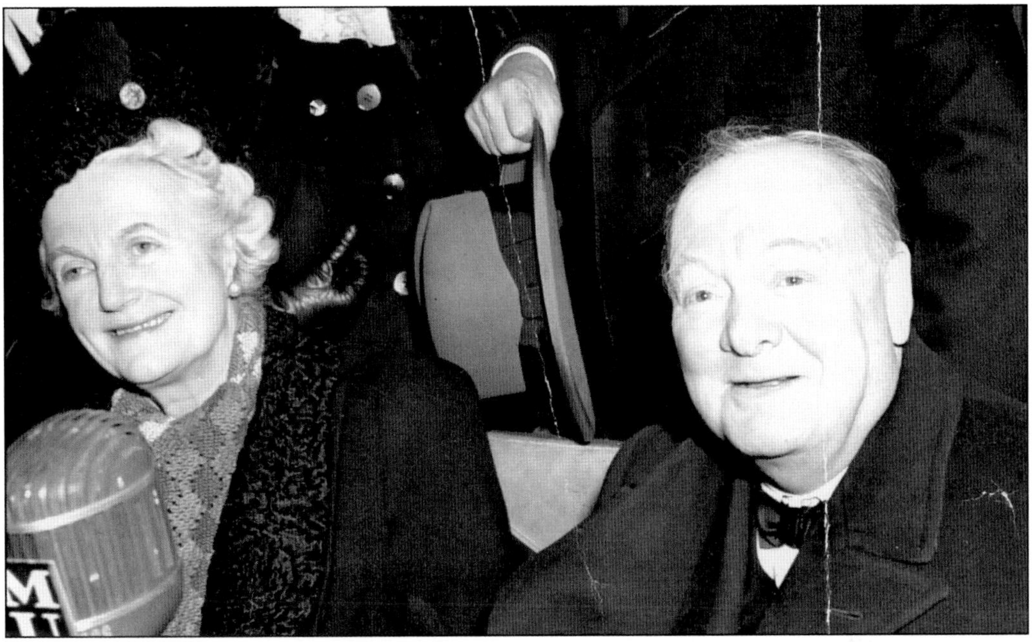

**WINSTON CHURCHILL, 1946.** When former British prime minister and private citizen Winston Churchill vacationed in New York City in January 1946, it was rumored that he would be named the first secretary general of the United Nations. He was not, but here Arthur photographed the British icon as he and his wife joked with reporters about his chances for the position.

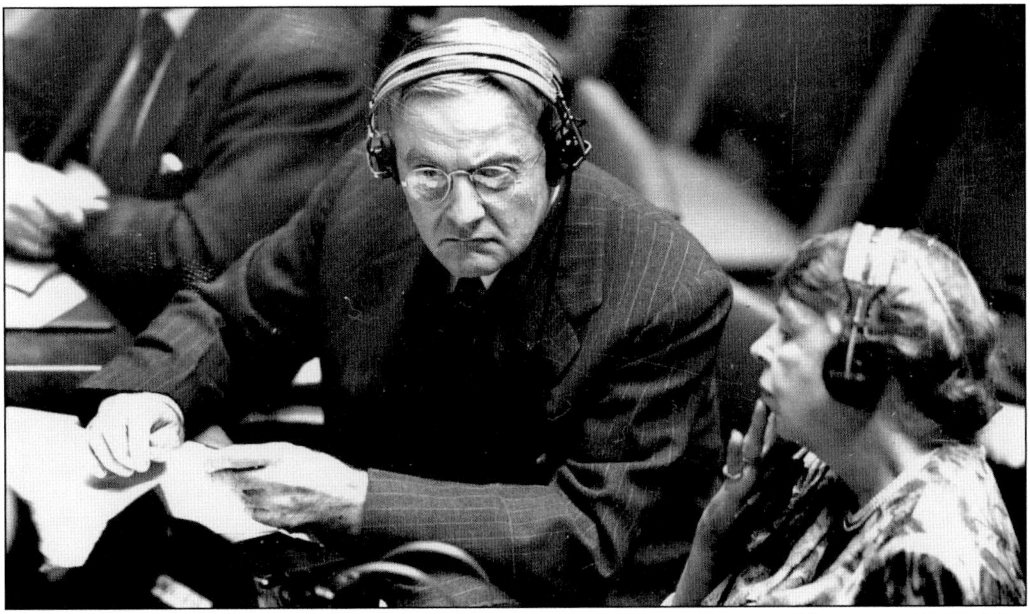

**ELEANOR ROOSEVELT AND JOHN FOSTER DOUGLAS AT THE UNITED NATIONS, 1947.** The United Nations and international politics gave Arthur many interesting opportunities to take historic photographs that would define the tension that developed between Russia and the United States directly after World War II. Here a very serious Eleanor Roosevelt is shown seated with Secretary of State John Foster Douglas as Soviet delegate Andrei Gromyko called Douglas a "warmonger."

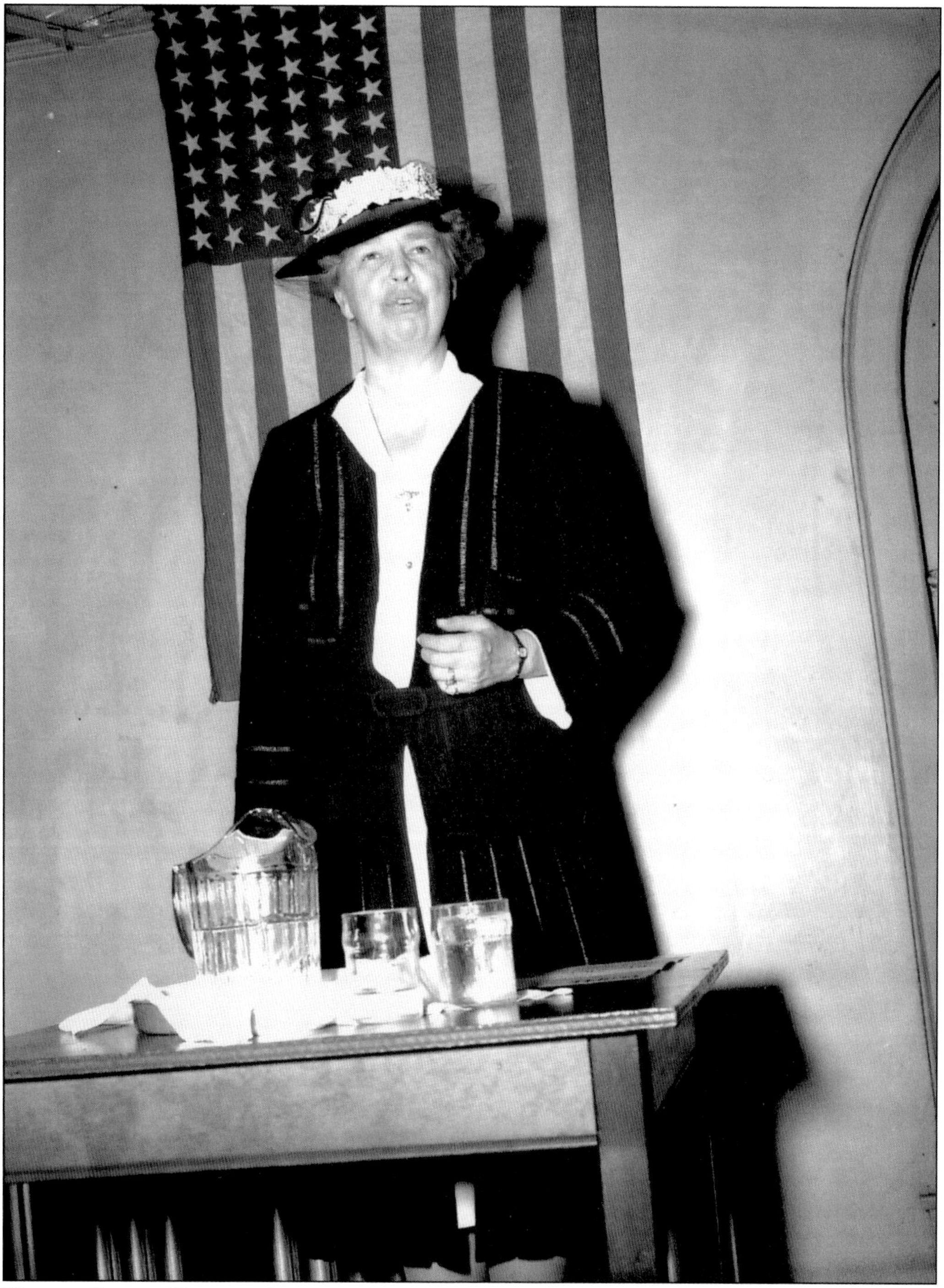

**HUMAN RIGHTS PIONEER ELEANOR ROOSEVELT, C. 1947.** Eleanor Roosevelt used her position as first lady to promote the New Deal of her husband, Pres. Franklin D. Roosevelt, as well as civil rights. After FDR's death in 1945, Eleanor created a new career as an author and spokesperson for the United Nations. One of the 20th century's most influential women, Pres. Harry Truman called her the "First Lady of the World" in honor of her extensive travels to promote human rights.

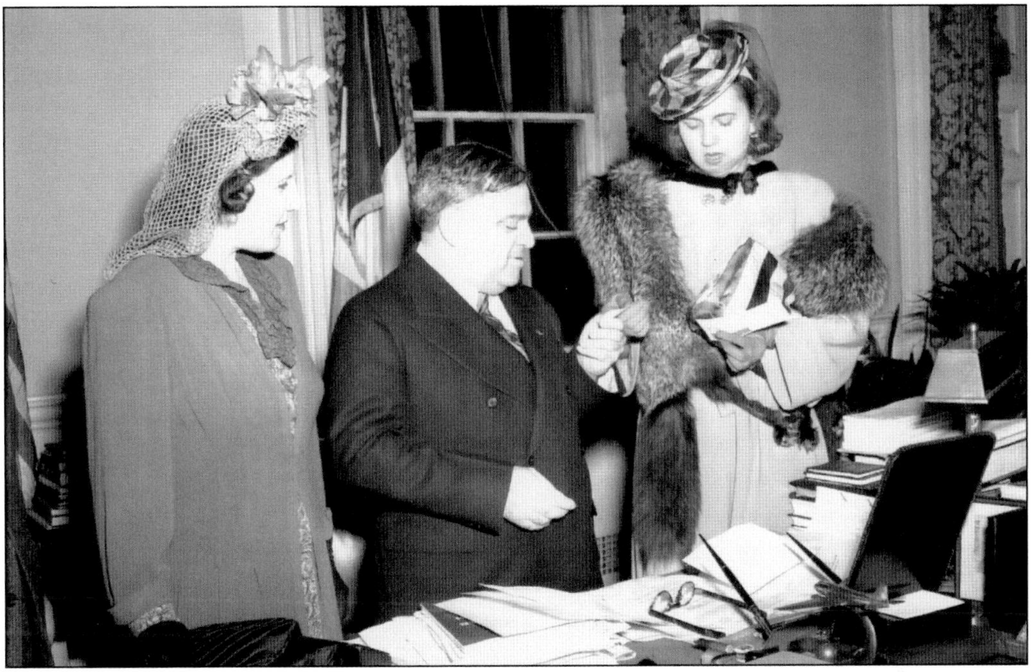

**Mayor Fiorello H. LaGuardia, 1940s.** When Arthur returned from World War II, he caught up with the mayor of his home city, Fiorello H. LaGuardia, a little man with few pretensions but who had a keen sense of the pulse of New York City. LaGuardia is considered one of New York City's greatest mayors because of his role in leading New York during the Great Depression.

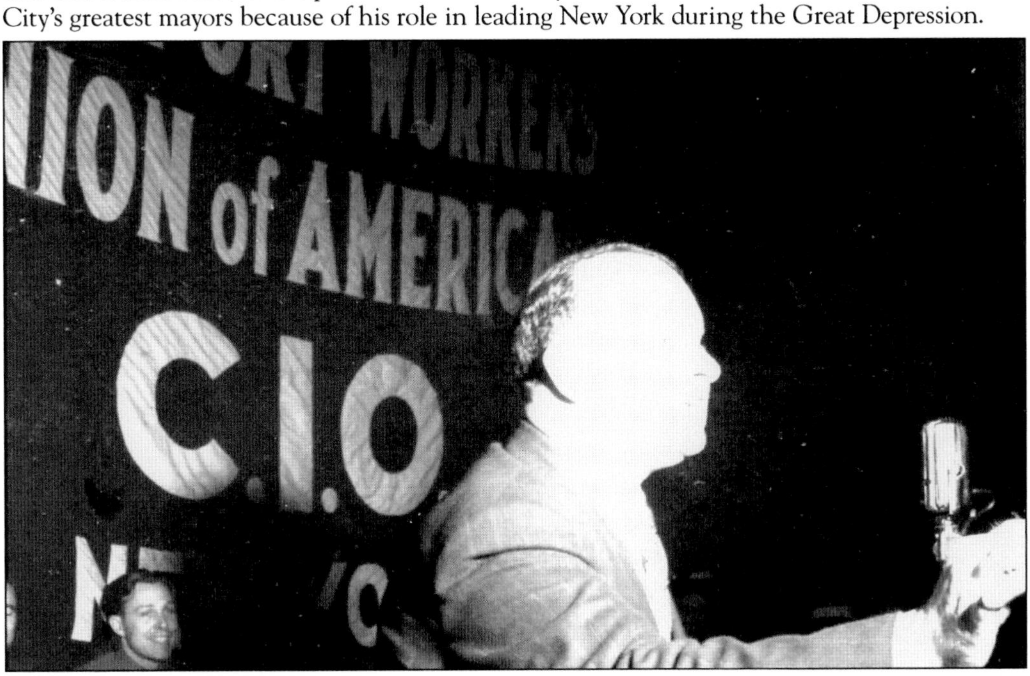


**Union Boss Mike Quill, c. 1947.** If one talked politics in Gotham after the war, they also talked union intrigue and power. This photograph features Mike Quill, one of Manhattan's most powerful labor leaders, addressing his members and urging them to vote Democrat in the upcoming election.

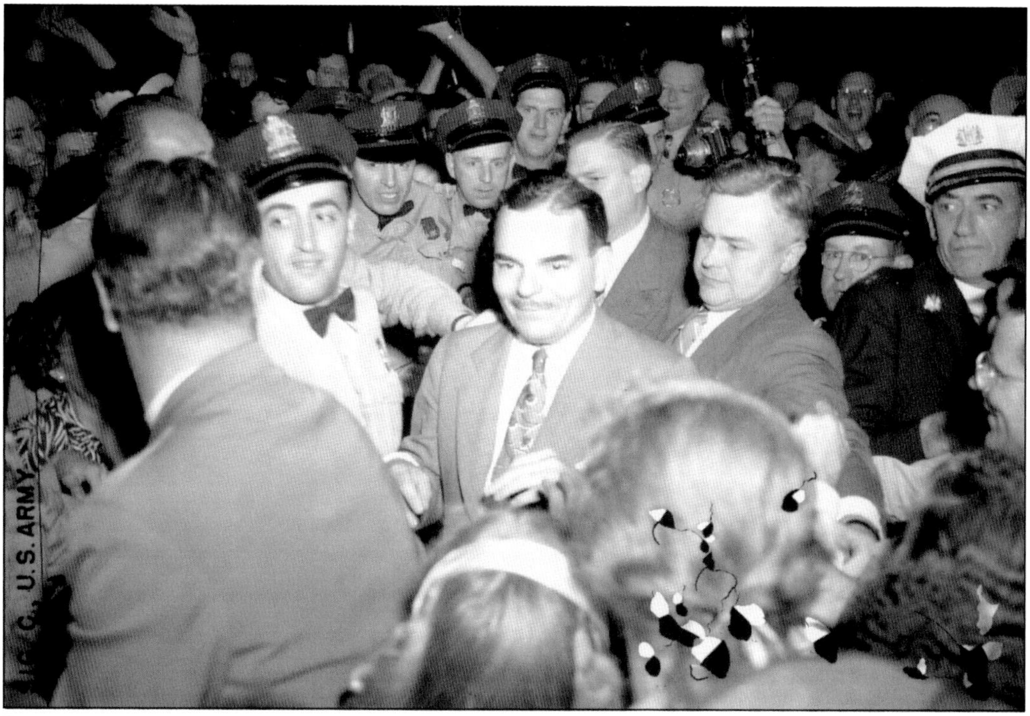


**PRESIDENTIAL POLITICS, 1948.** Being from New York, the most populated state in the union in 1948, meant that national office might take center stage for any politician. Here New York's own Gov. Thomas Dewey is escorted by police from his hotel room to the waiting conventioneers on the floor. Below, Dewey gives a rousing nomination speech in front of a giant photograph of Abraham Lincoln. Arthur Rickerby was there to record history.

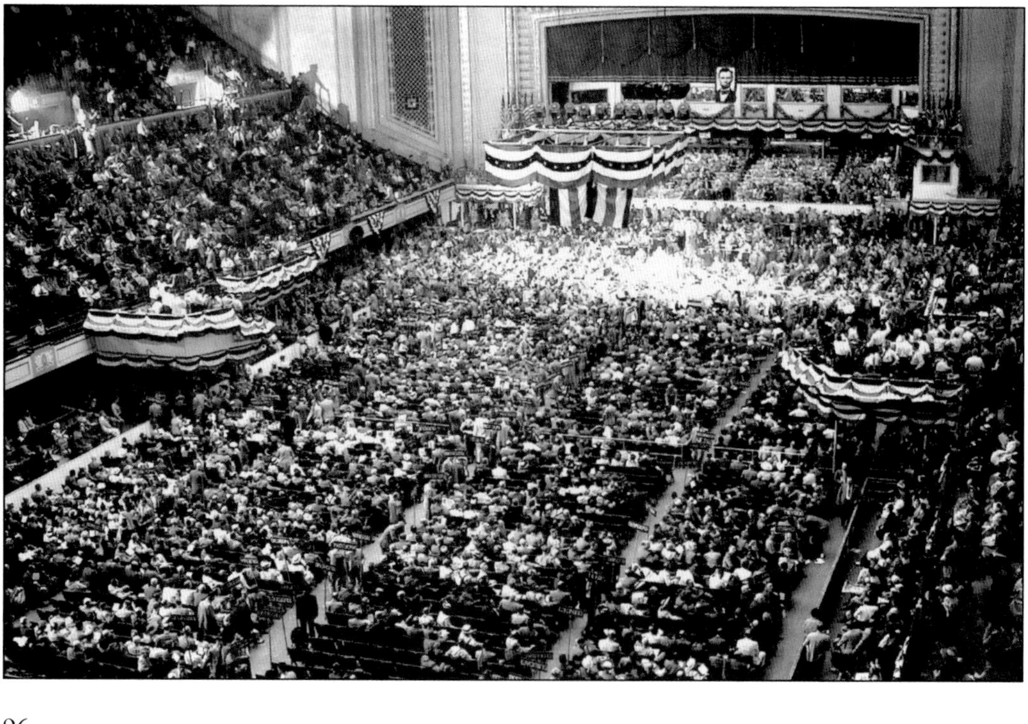

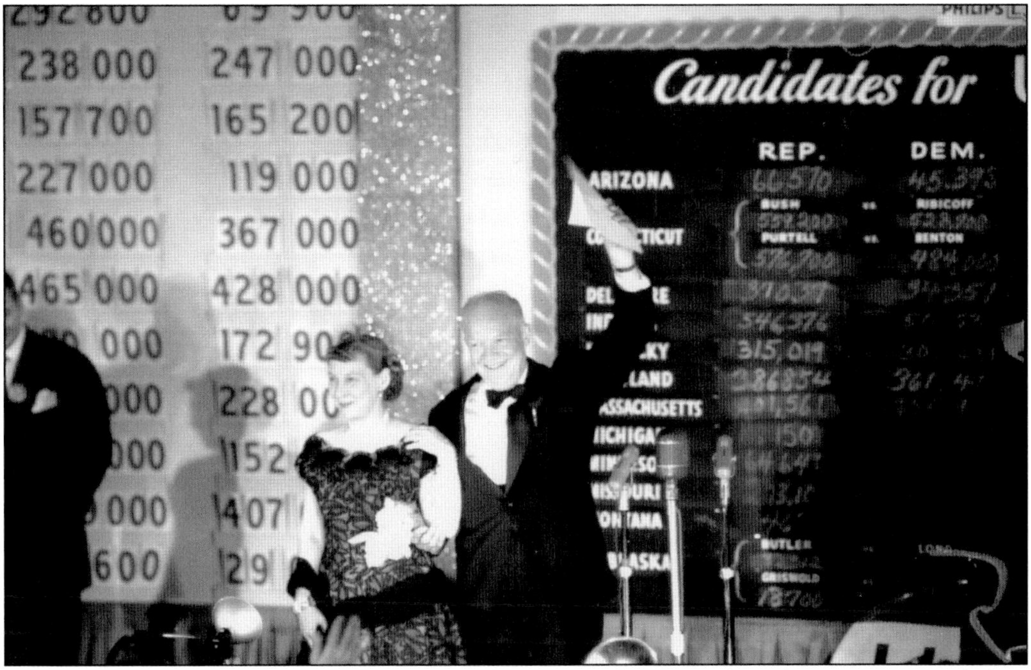


**PRES. DWIGHT D. EISENHOWER, 1952.** Arthur covered many political campaigns, including the presidential election of 1952. In these photographs, Arthur captured the beaming face of newly elected Pres. Dwight D. Eisenhower along with wife Mamie at the GOP headquarters in New York's Commodore Hotel on election night. In his victory speech to the party faithful, Eisenhower asked the country to unite behind him.

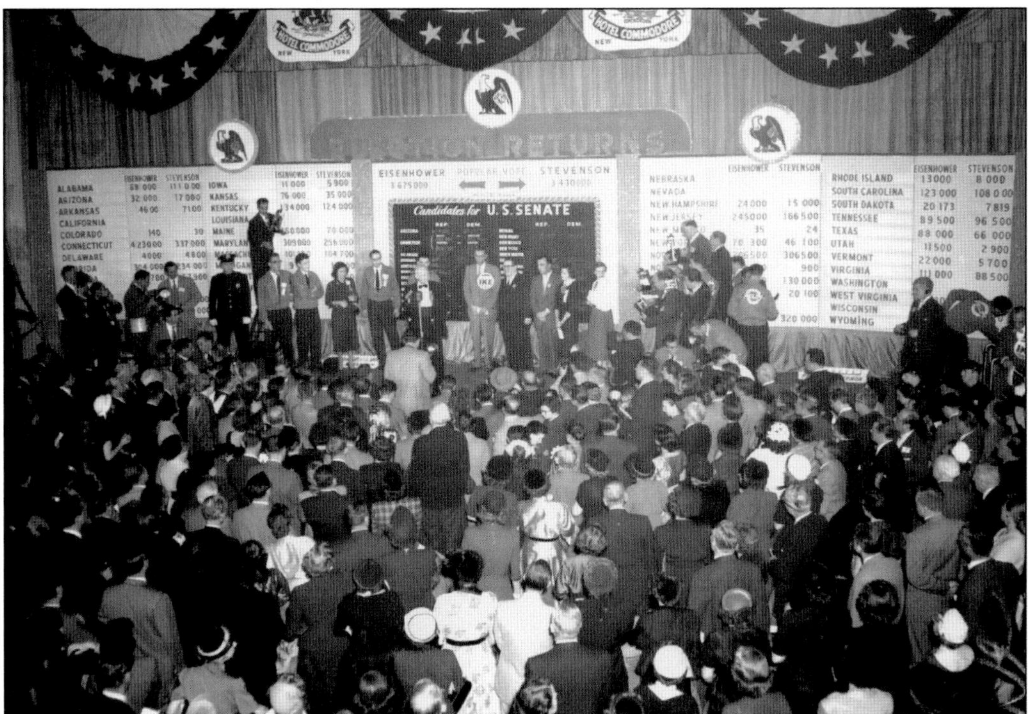

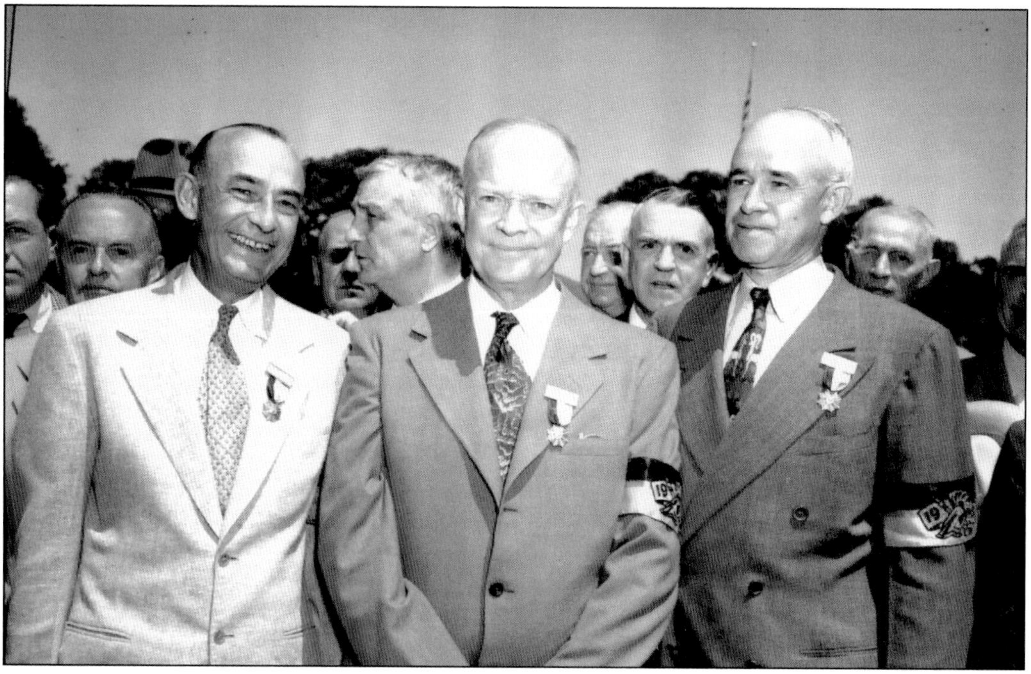

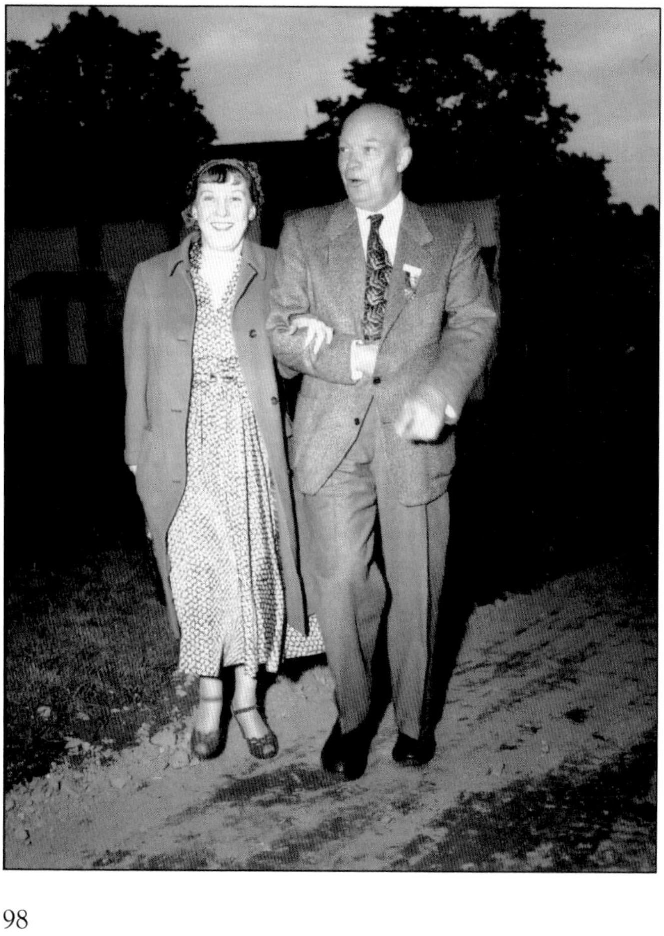

**RELAXING BEFORE THE CAMPAIGN, 1956.** A short time after Pres. Dwight D. Eisenhower received the nomination for a second term, he took some time off to relax and catch up with friends. These photographs feature the president with his old friend Gen. Omar Bradley (above) and out for a stroll with Mamie.

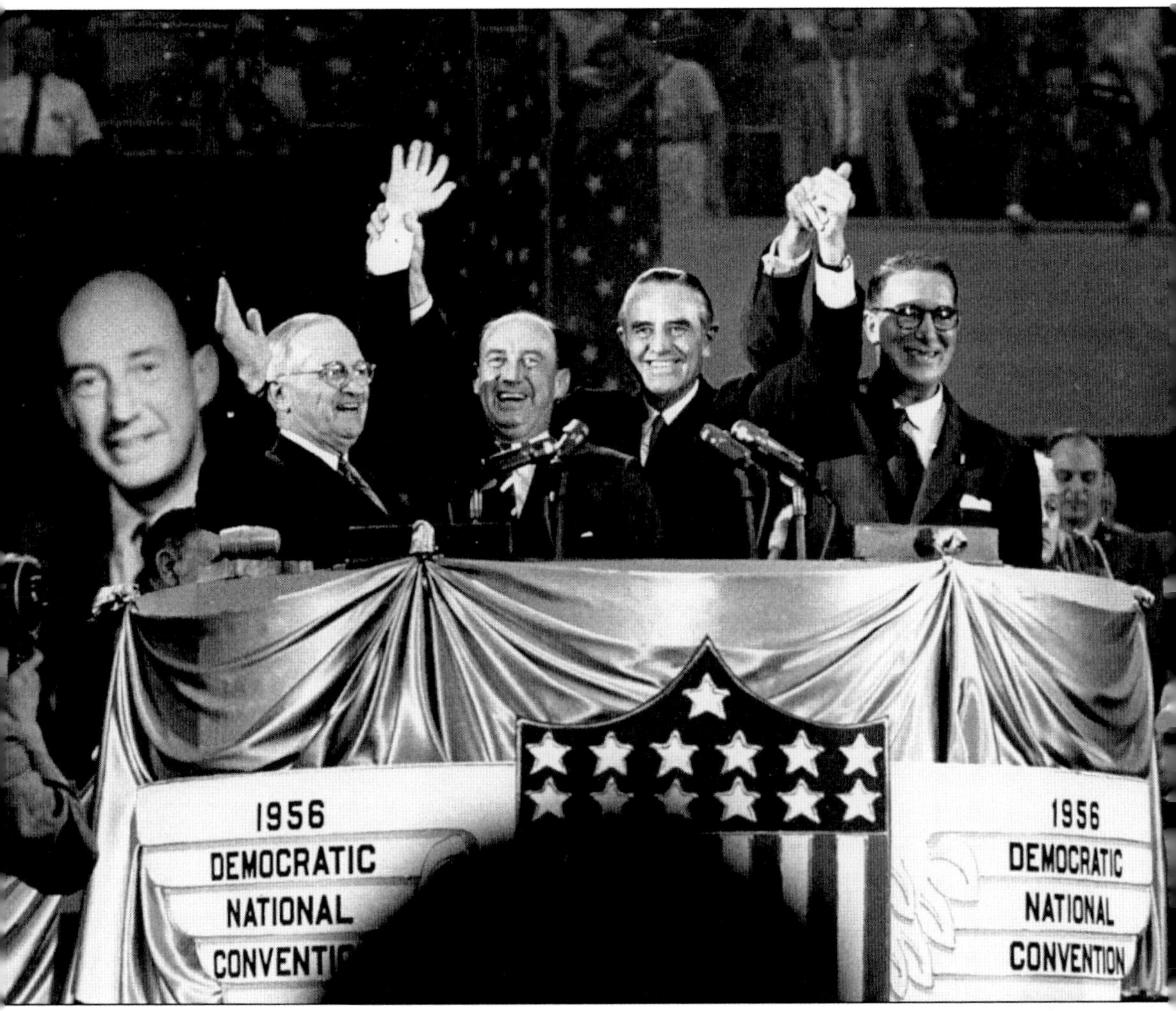


**DEMOCRATIC NOMINEE ADLAI STEVENSON, 1956.** Following his acceptance speech at the 1956 Democratic National Convention, Adlai Stevenson, the former governor of Illinois, was all smiles after defeating Sen. John F. Kennedy and others for the presidential nomination. Arthur Rickerby attended several national political conventions and seemed to always snap the right photograph at the right time. Here Stevenson stands with former president Harry S. Truman (left) and his running mate, vice presidential candidate Abraham Ribicoff (far right).

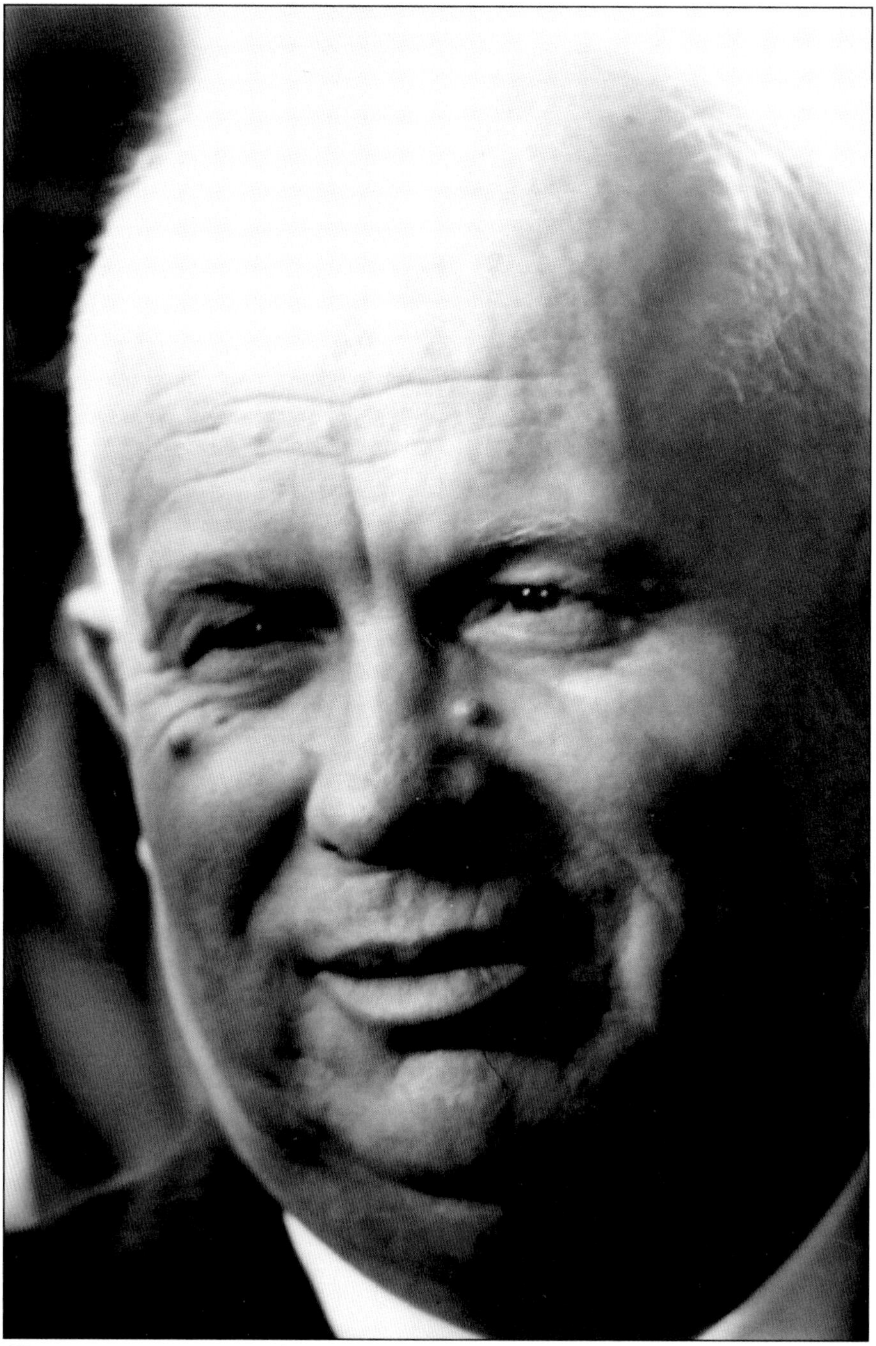

**NIKITA KHRUSHCHEV, 1960.** As the 1950s came to a close, the cold war between the United States and Russia was still in full swing. In fact, many say that Pres. John F. Kennedy defeated Richard Nixon in the 1960 election because he argued that the outgoing Eisenhower administration created a "missile gap" that allowed the Soviets to become "dangerously" powerful. A few days after the presidential election, on November 10, 1960, Soviet president Nikita Khrushchev visited New York City when he addressed the United Nations General Assembly. Arthur took this portrait of the visiting Russian.

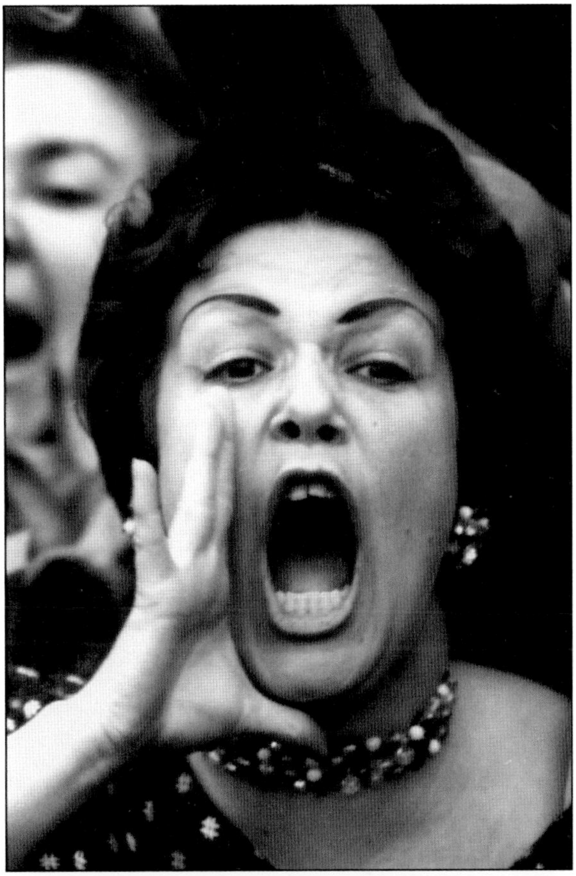

**SOVIET PRESIDENT GETS BOOED, 1960.** It was reported that Soviet President Nikita Khrushchev repeatedly interrupted the United Nations General Assembly in the fall of 1960 by pounding his fists on the desk and shouting in Russian. When the proceedings ended, Arthur was on hand as New Yorkers let their view of the visiting dignitary and his antics be known.

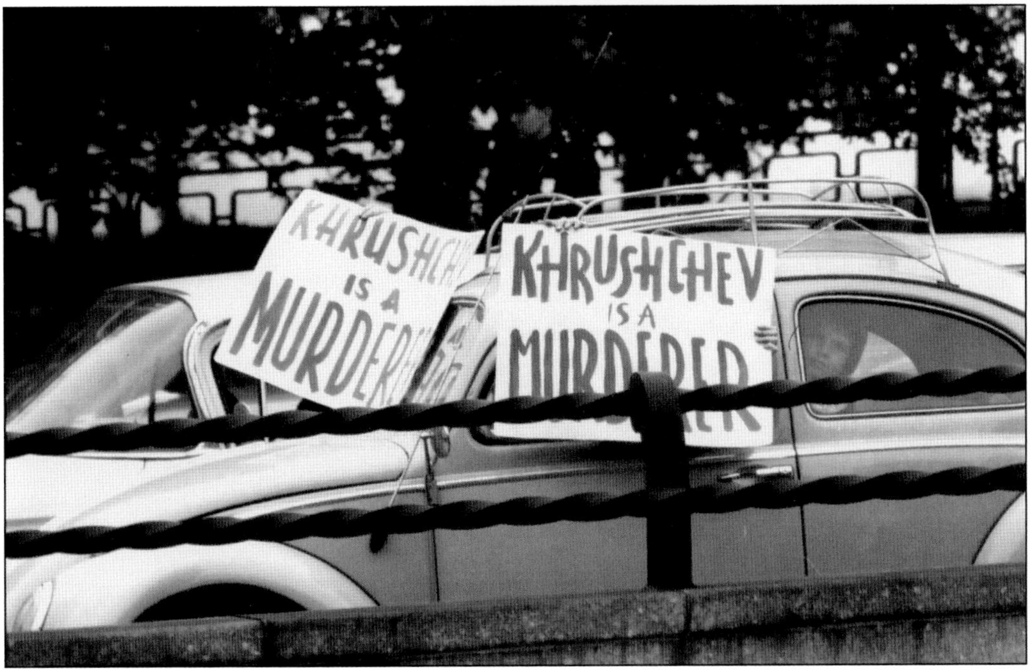

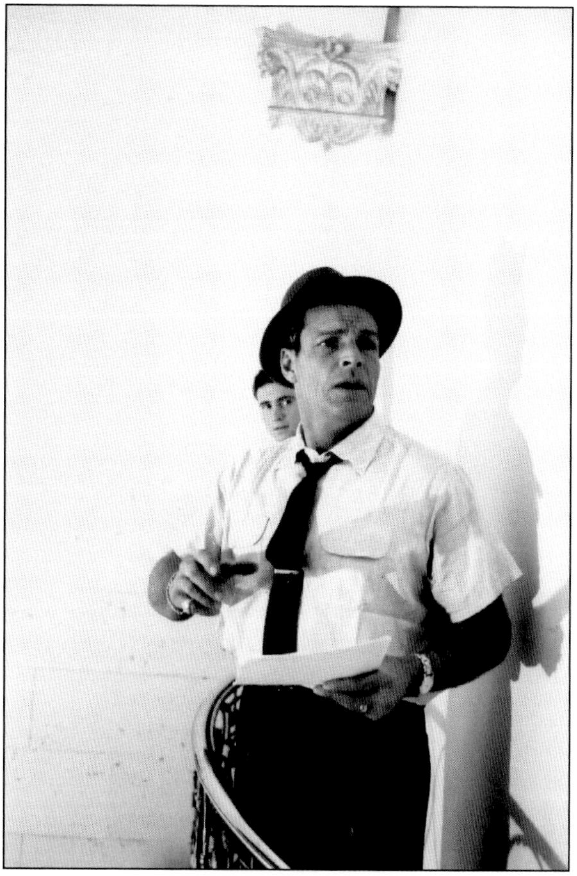

**KING OF SERIALS BUSTER CRABBE, 1950s.** Hollywood's Buster Crabbe played Tarzan, Flash Gordon, and Buck Rogers in countless movies in the 1930s and then starred in westerns and pirate flicks during the 1940s and 1950s. In fact, baby boomers well remember that during the 1950s Crabbe appeared on television on Monday nights on WOR-TV (Channel 9) in New York City, hosting one of his many films each and every week. Arthur caught up with the actor affectionately known as the "King of Serials" working out in a city gym. Today's Hollywood moguls Steven Spielberg and George Lucas credit Crabbe as being an inspiration for movies such as the Indiana Jones series, as well as Spielberg's *E.T.* and Lucas's Star Wars films.

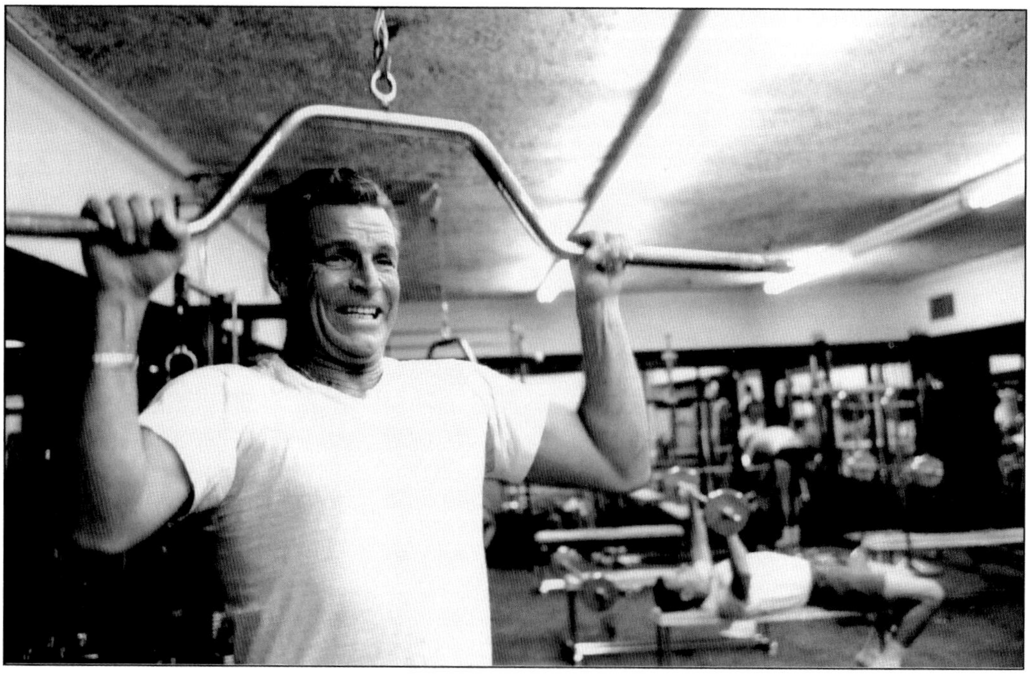

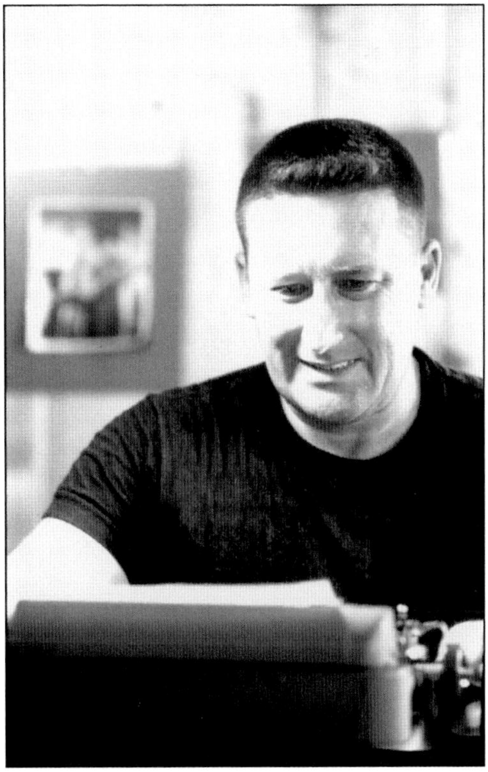

**PAPERBACK WRITER MICKEY SPILLANE, LATE 1950S.** Who better to define the gritty streets of New York City than the hugely popular author Mickey Spillane? The New York native created detective Mike Hammer in his 1947 classic book *I, The Jury*. That book took off after being released in paperback, and dozens more were to come. Today nearly 200 million Hammer books have been sold worldwide. On the right, Arthur shows Spillane at the typewriter, pounding out a story for his next book. Below, Spillane, seemingly always in character as Mike Hammer, dons his hat and trench coat and steps out onto a New York City street. Spillane made Arthur immortal by naming a character after him in one of his books—an FBI agent named Arthur Rickerby in *The Girl Hunters*.

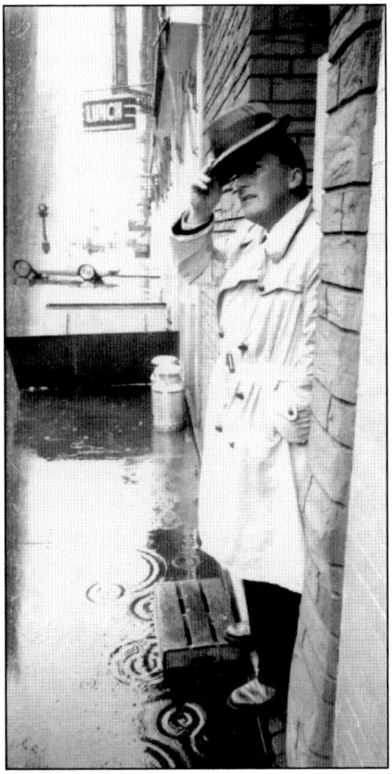

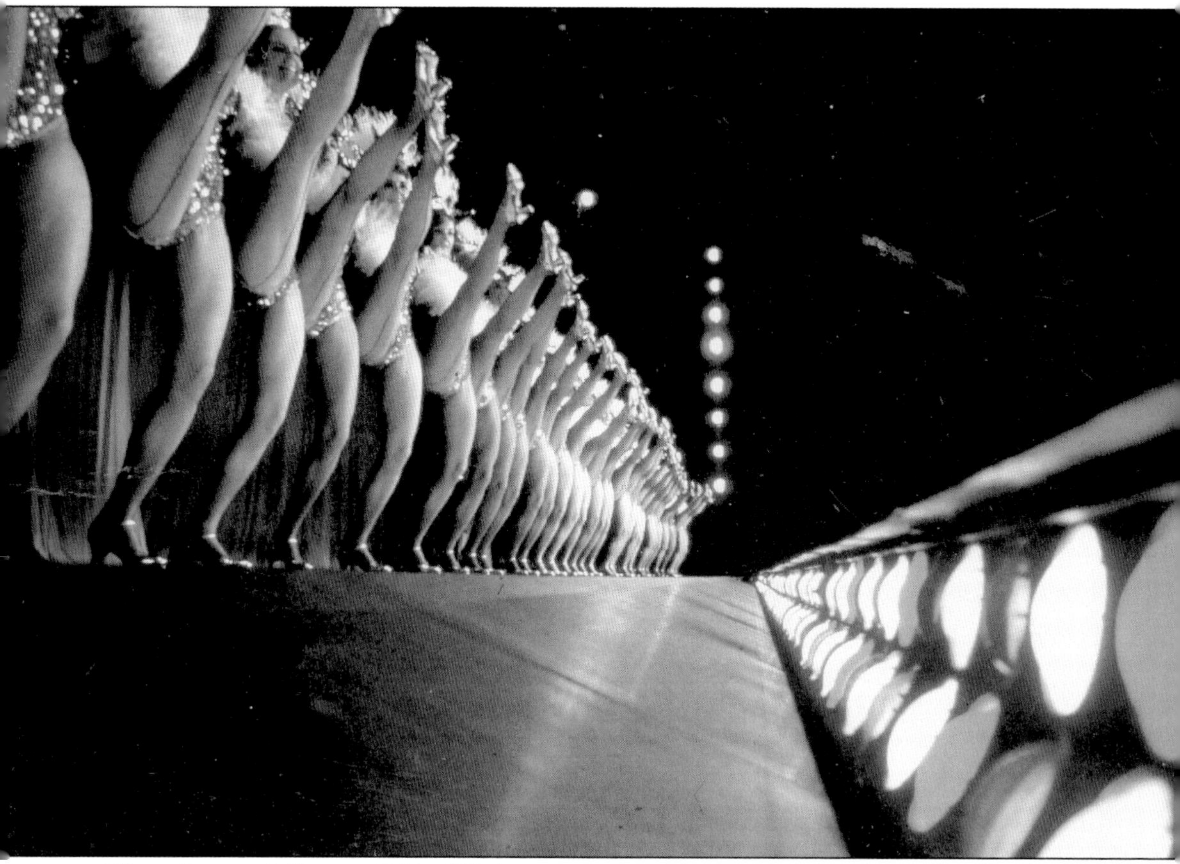

**HIGH STEPPIN', EARLY 1960S.** Working on a feature story for *Life* magazine, Arthur Rickerby shot hundreds of photographs of the world-famous Radio City Music Hall Rockettes. He recorded this memorable image of them doing their fabled high kick during the finale of the most famous dance routine in all entertainment.

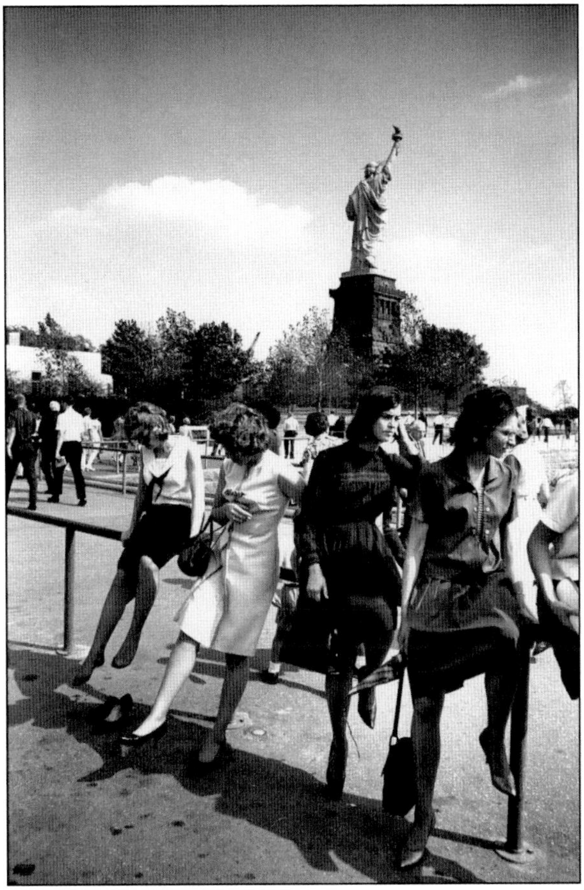

**FROM PLAY TO WORK, EARLY 1960S.** Arthur was interested in featuring the Rockettes away from their grueling four-a-day, seven-days-a-week performances. Several of the girls are shown here relaxing and sightseeing with Lady Liberty in the background, while the photograph below shows them hard at work on their dance routine.

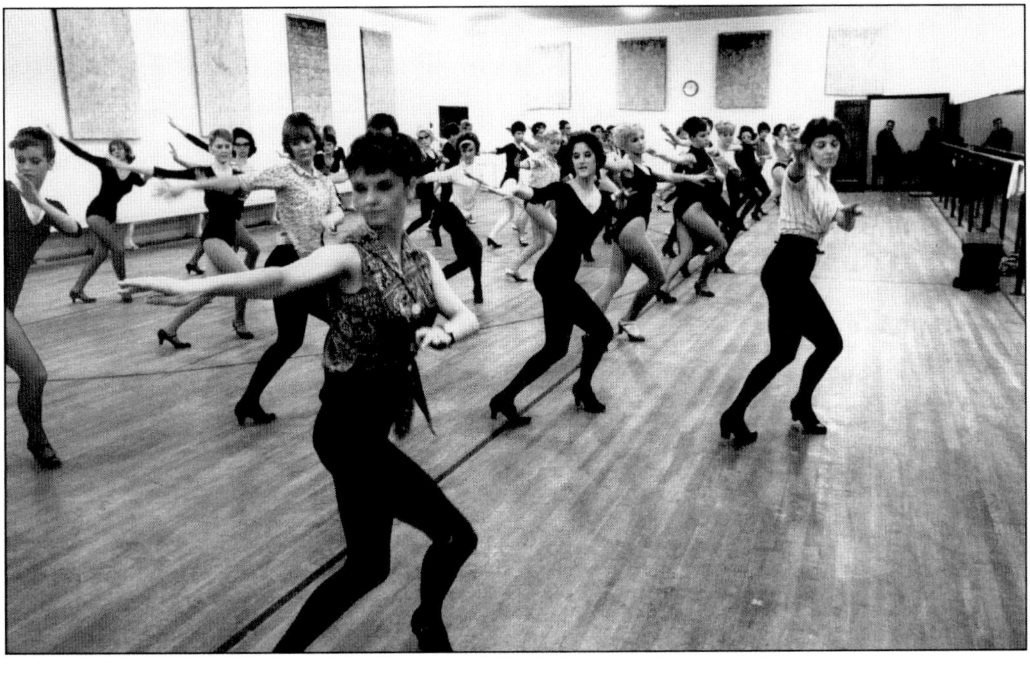

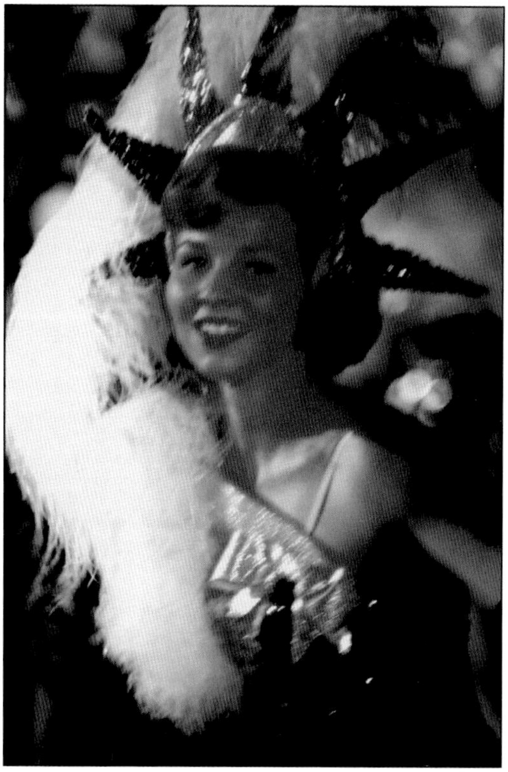

**The Bright Lights of the Big City, Early 1960s.** It has been said that more people see the famous Rockettes annually on the stage of Radio City Music Hall than vote for the New York City mayor! Each performer, groomed to dance and entertain, becomes a celebrity in her own right. While backstage, Arthur was able to catch the attention of one Rockette, adorned with a head piece resembling the Statue of Liberty, as she prepared to perform. In the photograph below, three Rockettes soak up the audience applause.

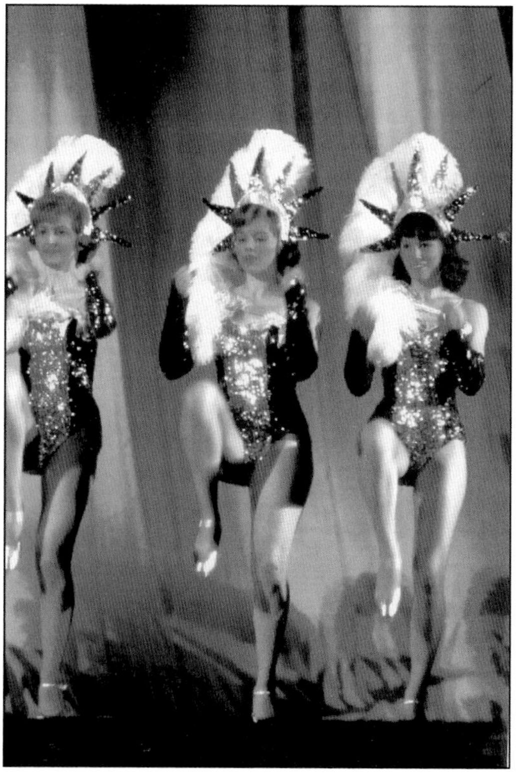

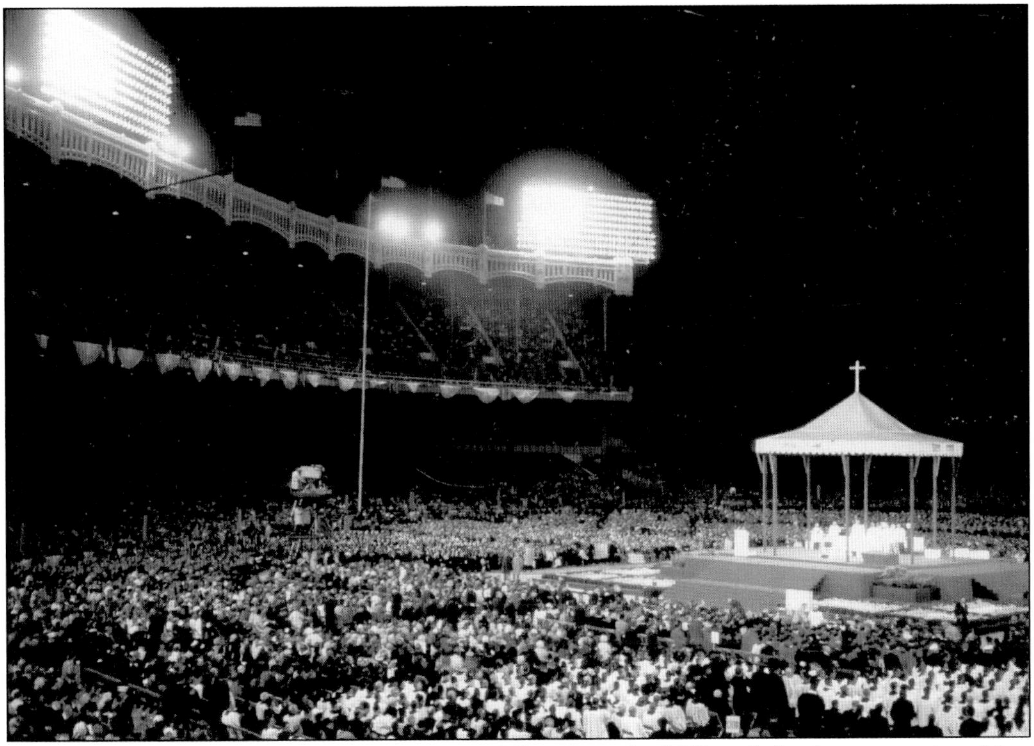

**POPE PAUL VI AT YANKEE STADIUM, 1965.** When Pope Paul VI made his historic visit to New York City, the only venue that could accommodate the expected crowds was Yankee Stadium. Arthur snapped these photographs of the Catholic leader celebrating mass in front of a crowd of over 80,000 as well as a worldwide television audience.

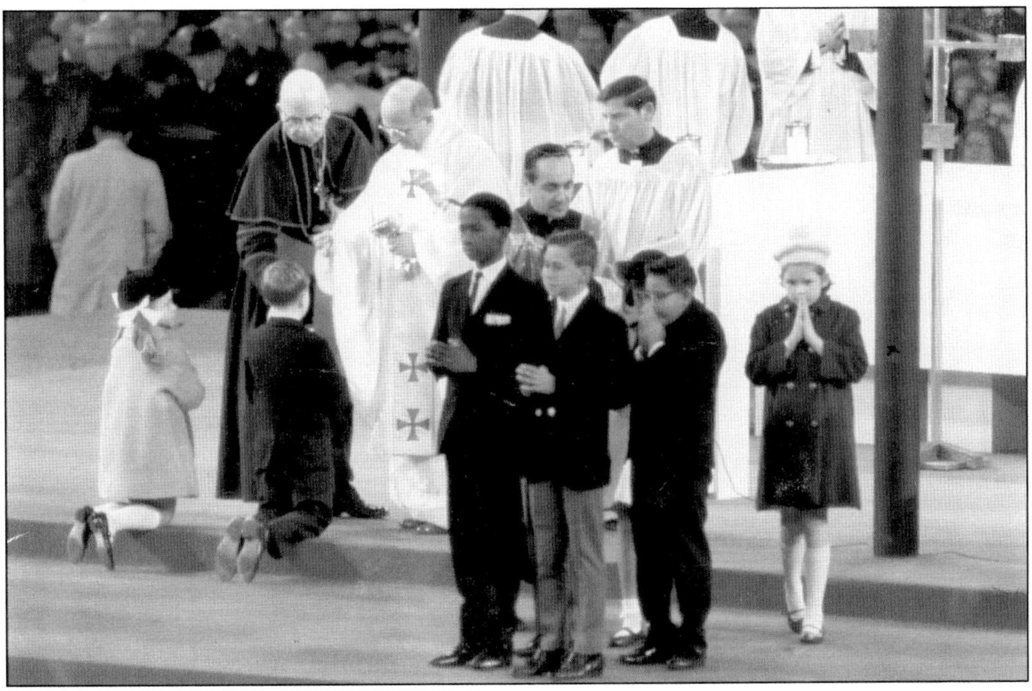

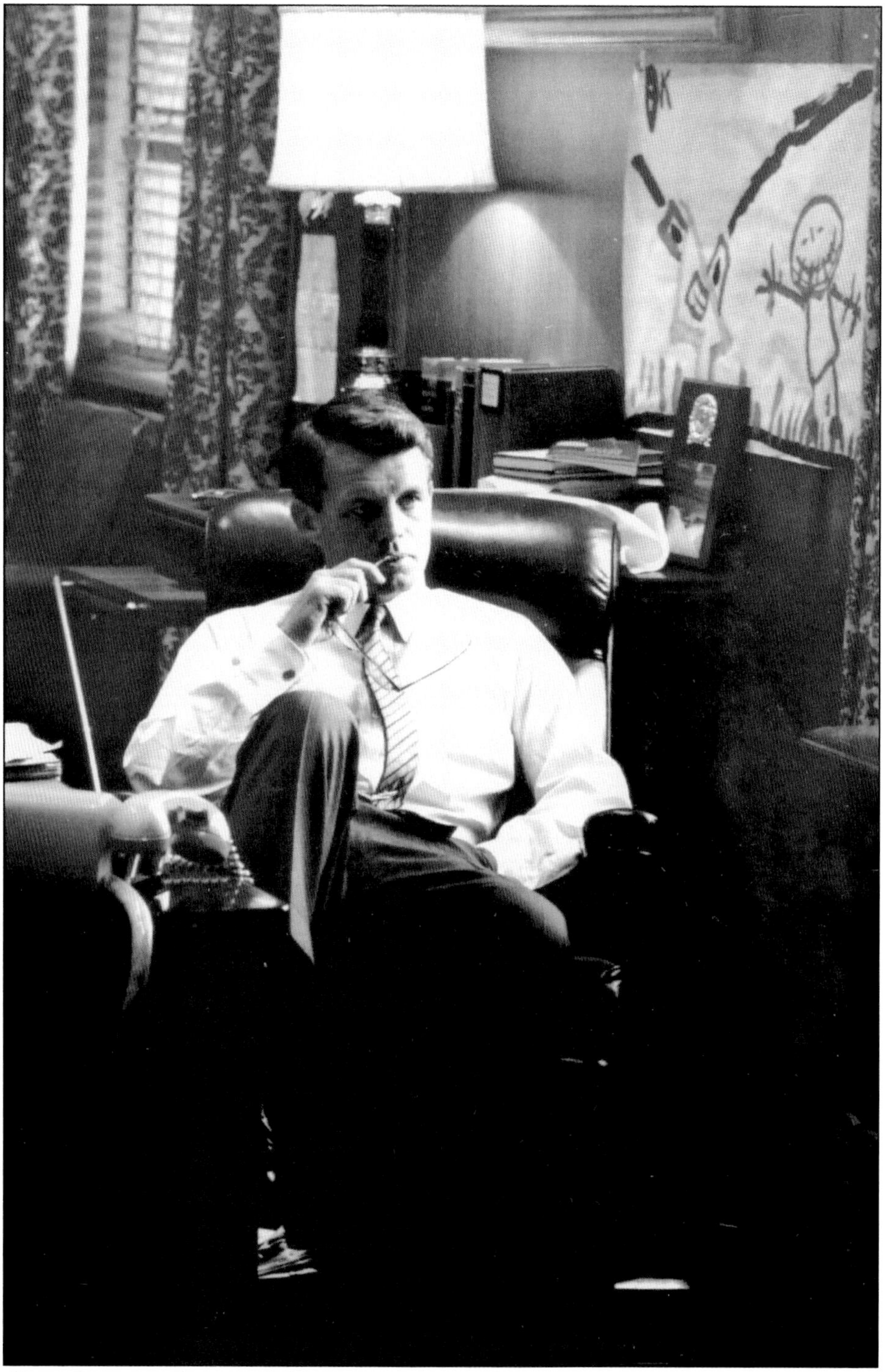

**NEW YORK SENATOR ROBERT F. KENNEDY, 1965.** After Pres. John F. Kennedy was assassinated in 1963, his brother Robert readied himself for a run at the presidency a short time after becoming a United States senator representing the Empire State. Arthur snapped this photograph of the Kennedy icon during a pensive moment in his office adorned with his children's artwork.

# *Six*

# Sports Capital of the World

Early in life, before his passion for the camera took full flight, Arthur Rickerby had wanted to become a Broadway dancer. His spouse, Wanda, recalled that as a young man, Arthur could move "swiftly and gracefully" and that it was his agility on his feet that allowed him to be at the right place at the exact right time to capture the perfect shot. Even during his college years at Duke University in the early 1940s, Arthur had a knack for taking creative game action and other sports photographs.

What was it about sports that interested the developing lensman? First, Arthur knew that the very excitement that sports created for the spectator would be a natural vehicle for what he wanted to convey with his camera. After all, sports have universal appeal. It awakens passions and creates bonds between people from every walk of life. The second reason is more practical. Arthur was, after all, trying to support his family by working with his camera. His avocation, in a sense, was his vocation. Arthur knew that as a source of entertainment and inspiration, his sports photographs would find a wide audience and hoped that he would be able to carve out a comfortable living.

New York City, with its major venues dedicated to all professional sports, gave Arthur much to work with. Whether taking an action shot of a college basketball game at Madison Square Garden or simply documenting the close relationship apparent between New York Yankees teammates Mickey Mantle and Roger Maris, Arthur's images evoke the excitement and drama of sport during the mid-20th century. This chapter presents several of the most famous and interesting sports images that Arthur recorded on film during his extraordinary career.

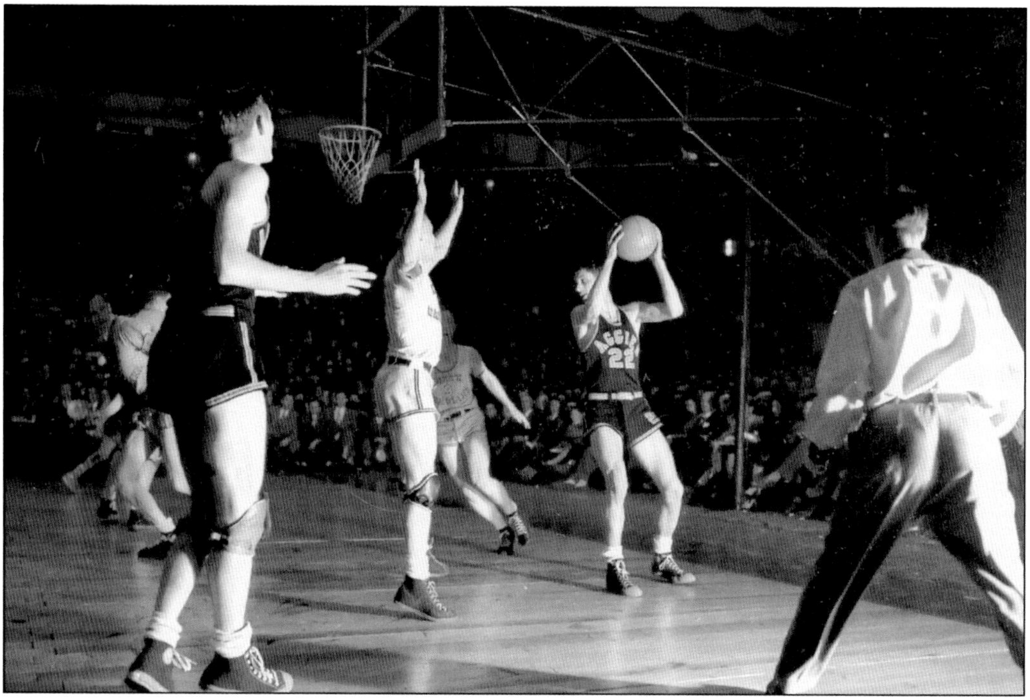


**PITCHED BATTLES ON THE BASKETBALL COURT, 1946.** New York's Madison Square Garden is known around the world as America's chief indoor sports and entertainment arena. On a good night, patrons eat thousands of hot dogs washed down by hundreds of gallons of soda and beer while watching thrilling sports and other events. Years before the professional National Basketball Association was formed, the venue hosted exciting college basketball double- and triple-headers. In fact, both the NCAA and NIT games were held at Madison Square Garden during the 1940s. Arthur took these rare game action shots featuring teams from all over the country.

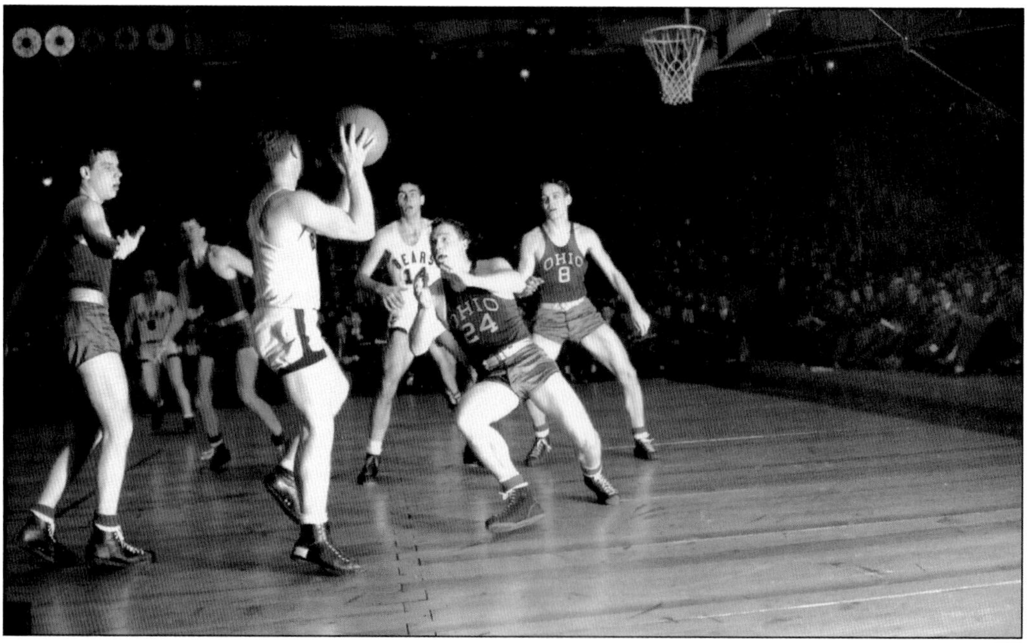

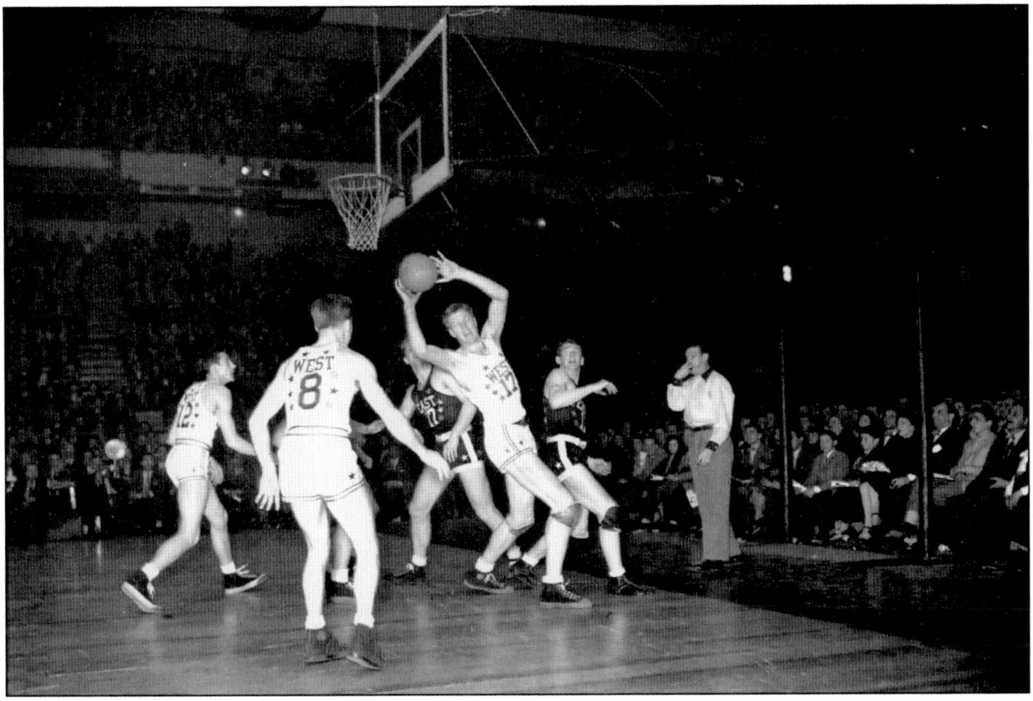


**College All-Stars at Madison Square Garden, 1940s.** From boxing, hockey, and basketball to political conventions, concerts, and the circus, Madison Square Garden has hosted thousands of exciting events. Each year, the 20,000-seat arena features numerous college basketball games, including these showing the East-West College All-Stars in the late 1940s.

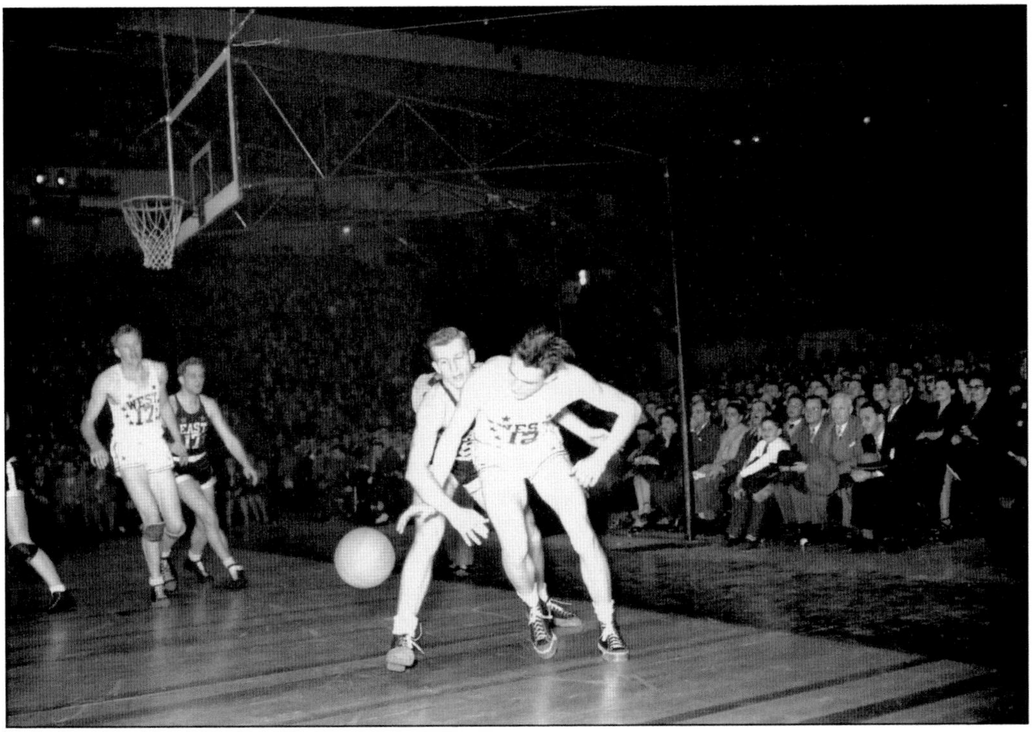

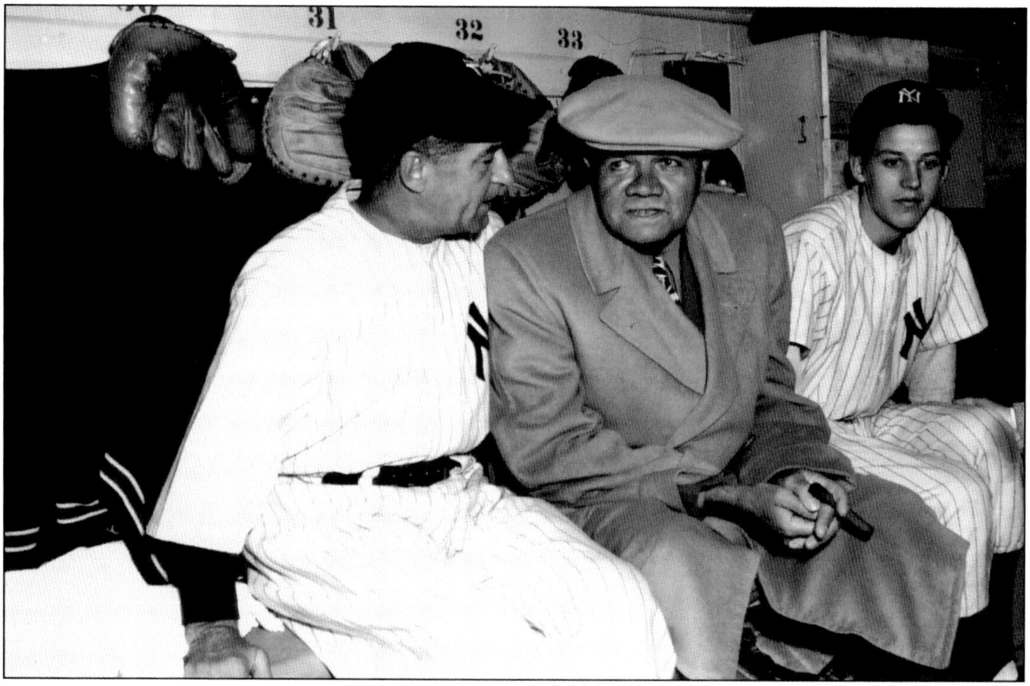

**BABE RUTH DAY, 1947.** On April 27, 1947, baseball legend Babe Ruth, diagnosed with a terminal case of throat cancer, attended Babe Ruth Day at Yankee Stadium. These photographs feature the Bambino in the New York dugout with manager Stanley Harris (above) and his good friend Emory Perry (below) during one of the last times he was feted by the Yankee faithful. On August 6, 1948, the Babe passed away. To this day, the former New York Yankee is still considered the greatest baseball player of all time.

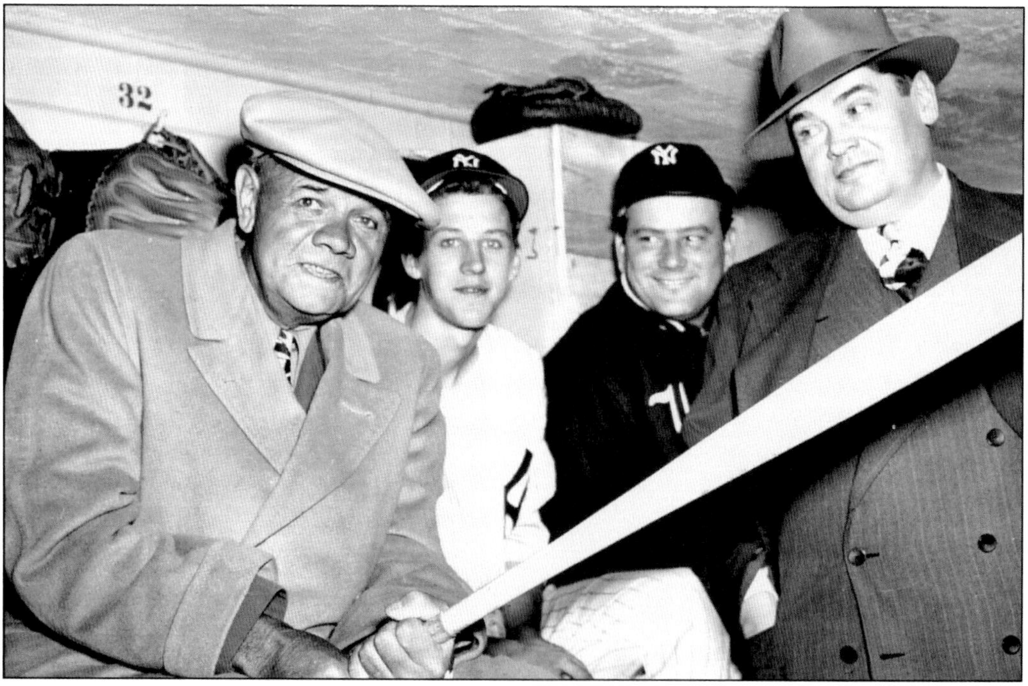

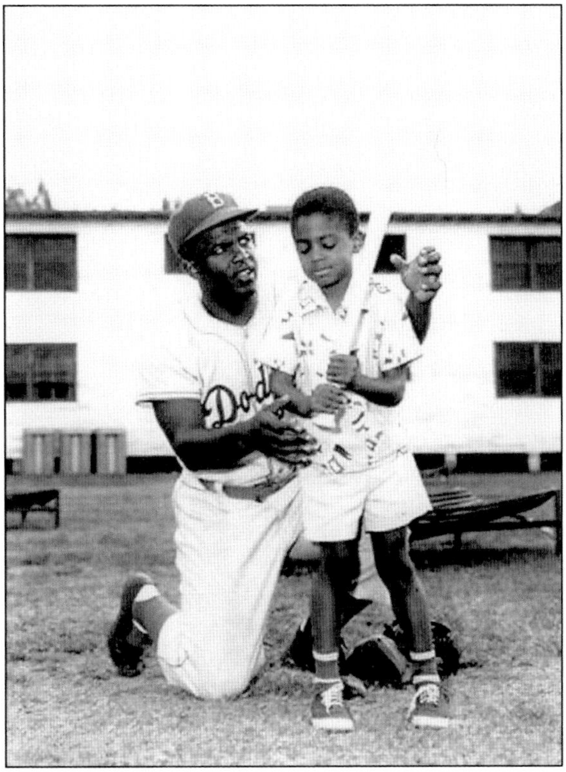

**BROOKLYN'S OWN JACKIE ROBINSON, C. 1955.** When Brooklyn Dodgers' owner Branch Rickey signed Jackie Robinson to play major-league baseball in 1947, thereby breaking the color barrier that existed for decades, it was not only a historic civil rights event of extraordinary magnitude, but Dodger fans were treated to one of the greatest ballplayers ever. The photograph to the right shows Robinson teaching a young player the ropes, and the image below captures him making a spectacular catch at second base.

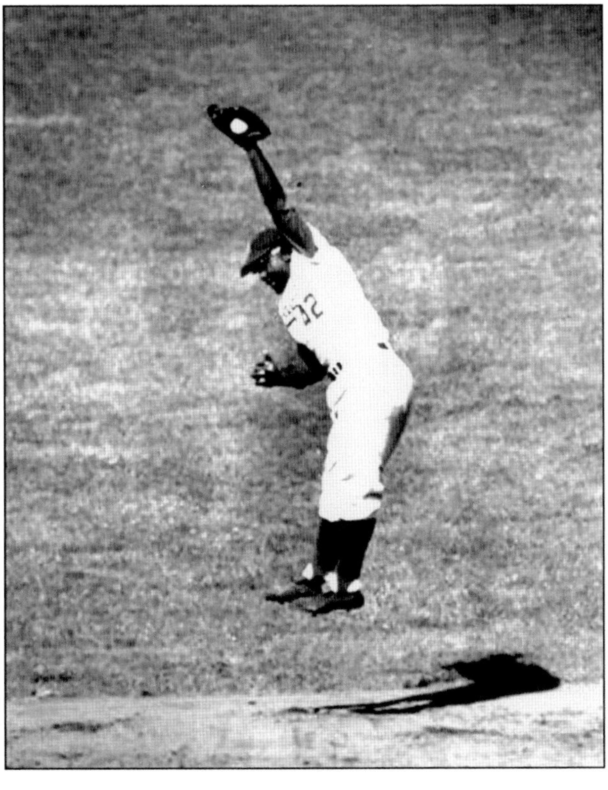

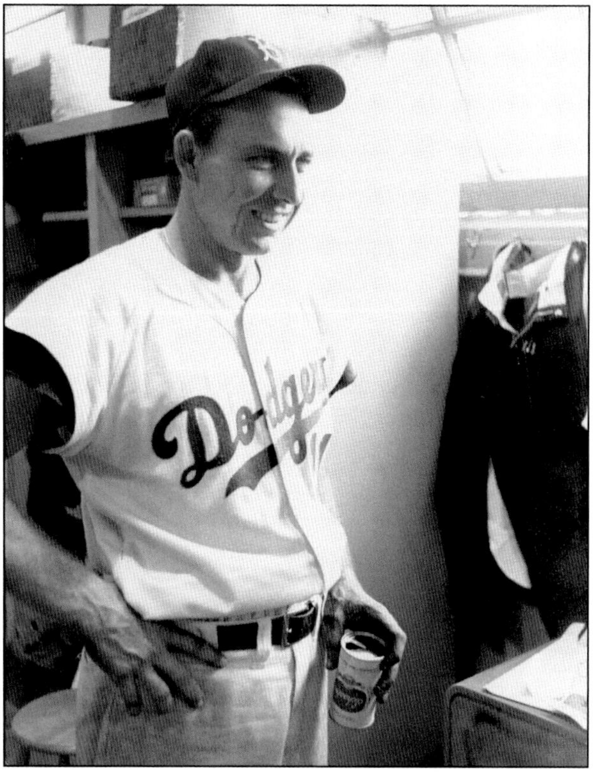


**BROOKLYN DODGERS, EARLY 1950S.** Although the New York Yankees dominated major-league baseball for decades, the Brooklyn "Trolley Dodgers" played in New York City for over 50 years, garnering widespread and loyal fan support. Here Arthur photographed two of the Dodgers stars who defined the team, first baseman Gil Hodges (left), relaxing in the locker room with an ice-cold beer, and outfielder Duke Snider (below), shortly before a game against the city's third team, the New York Giants. Giants star Willie Mays (No. 24) is on hand to watch batting practice.

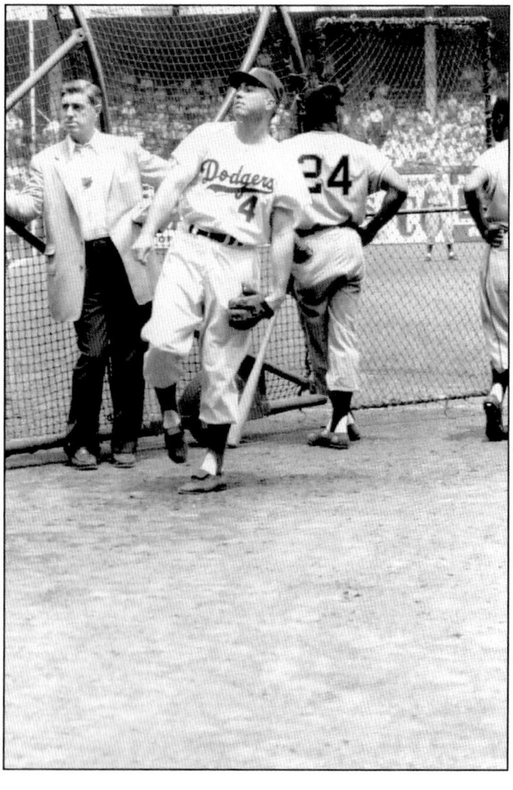

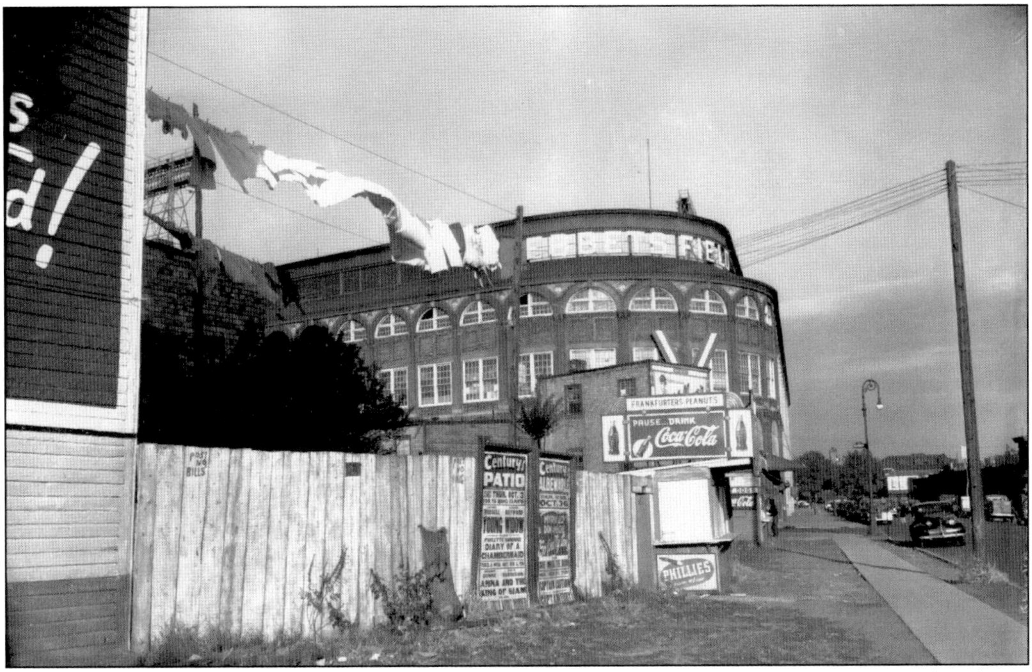


**EBBETS FIELD GOES DOWN, 1960.** Of all the ballparks that no longer exist, none has been romanticized more than Ebbets Field, home of the beloved Dodgers, which was located in the Flatbush section of Brooklyn. Brooklyn's favorite major-league franchise played at Ebbets Field from 1913 through 1957. Ebbets was the home field for the Dodgers' Jackie Robinson when he broke the color barrier in 1947 and for an adored team that won nine National League pennants and the World Series championship in 1955. The Dodgers played their last game at Ebbets Field on September 24, 1957, before departing for Los Angeles. They beat the Pittsburgh Pirates in front of only 6,702 fans.

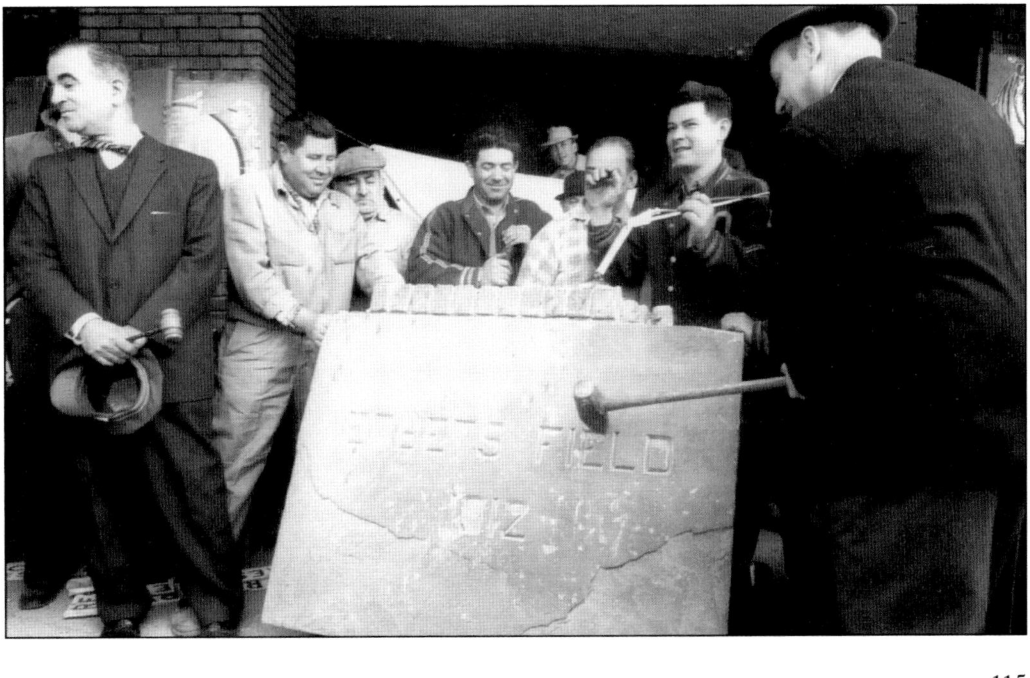

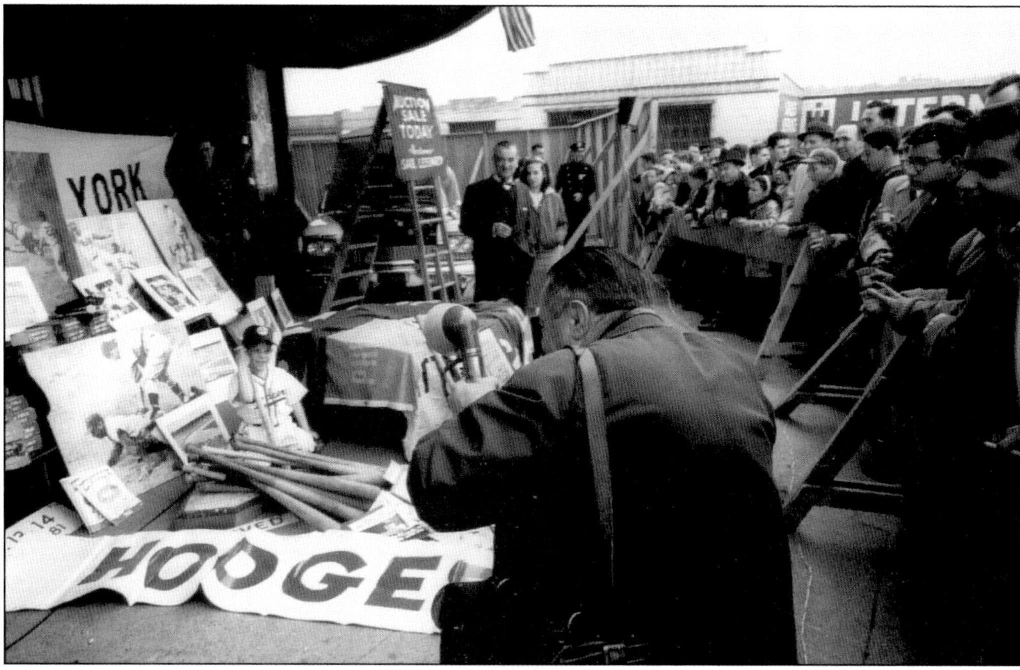


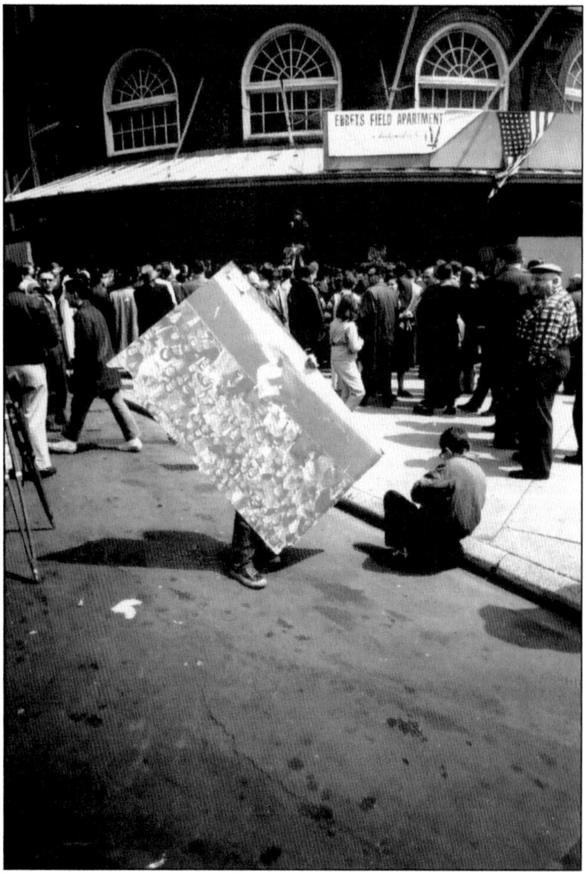


**A SAD FAREWELL, 1960.** When Ebbets Field was razed in 1960, Arthur was there to record an auction of stadium artifacts and memorabilia as well as the ballpark's demolition. The beloved park became the site of the Ebbets Field Apartments, which were renamed the Jackie Robinson Apartments in 1972, the year of Robinson's death.

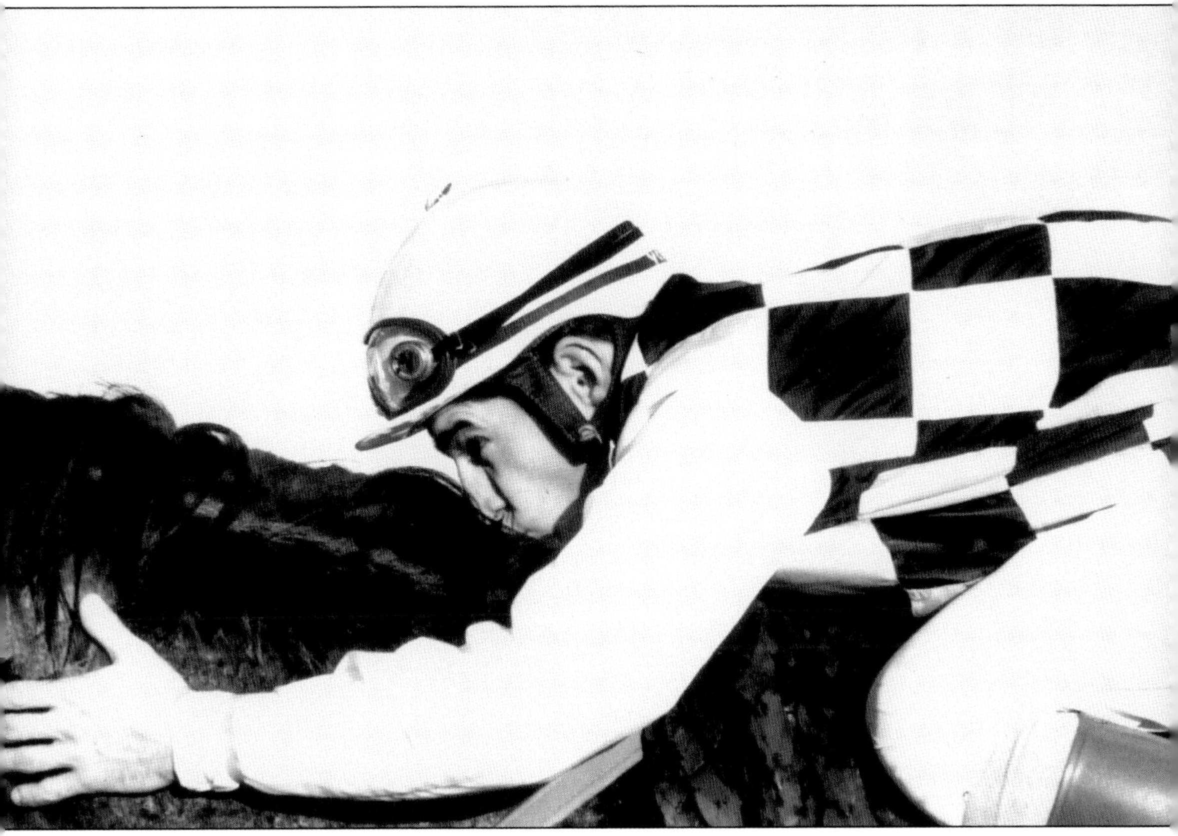

**THE EAGLE FLEW AWAY, 1960.** From his early days covering equestrian competitions at Duke, Arthur was at home photographing horses and their riders. This classic shot features the great jockey Manuel Ycaza kissing champion Thoroughbred Bald Eagle on his way to victory.

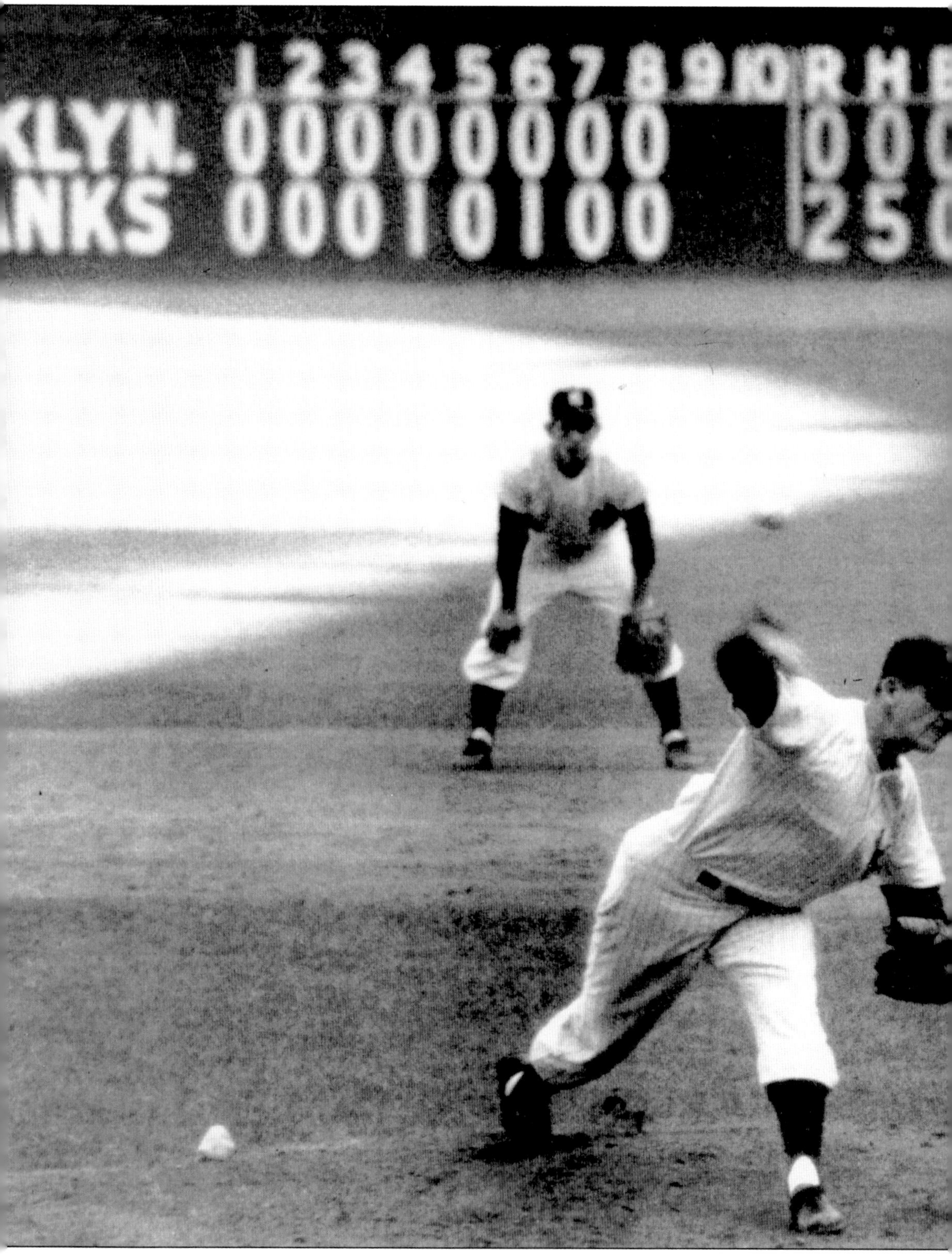
1 2 3 4 5 6 7 8 9 10 R H E
KLYN. 0 0 0 0 0 0 0 0 0 0
NKS 0 0 0 1 0 1 0 0 2 5

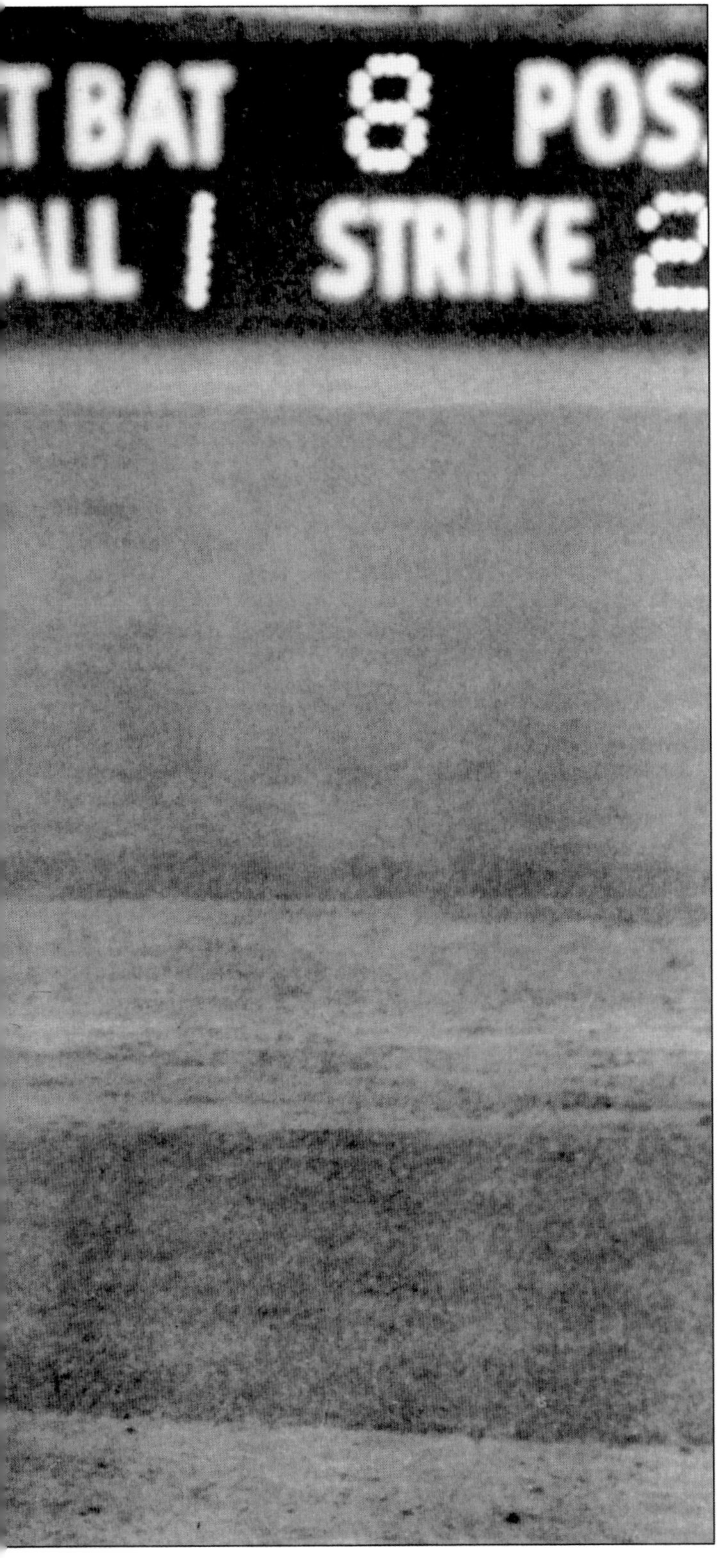


**THE PERFECT GAME, 1956.** As a young photographer, Arthur Rickerby had pioneered a switch from the bulky speed graphic to a 35 millimeter camera for sports and other news coverage. He used his 35 millimeter to snap the final pitch of Don Larsen's perfect game in Game Five of the 1956 World Series. It is among the most famous baseball photographs ever taken. This photograph of Larsen, Billy Martin at second base, and the New York Yankee Stadium scoreboard full of zeros behind them ran on the front page of most newspapers in America the next day.

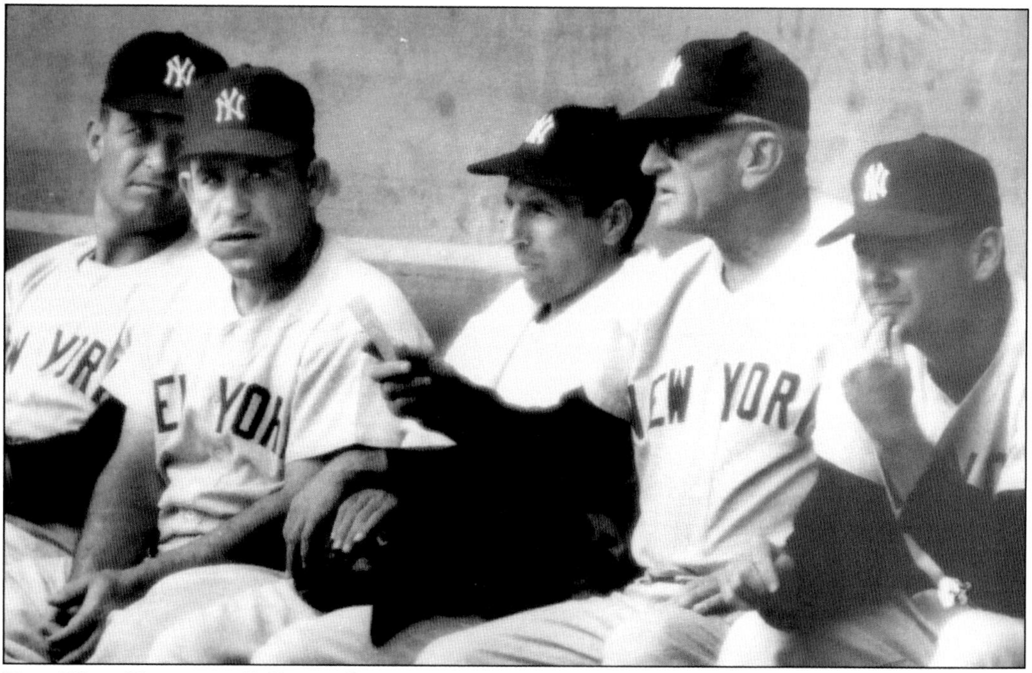

**THE "OLD PERFESSER" CASEY STENGEL, 1950S.** Known for his unique misuse of the English language, Casey Stengel was as smart a field general as baseball has ever produced. From 1949 through 1960, he managed the New York Yankees and led the team to 10 pennant championships and seven World Series. Here the "Old Perfesser" spouts his particular brand of "Stengelese" in the Yankee dugout.

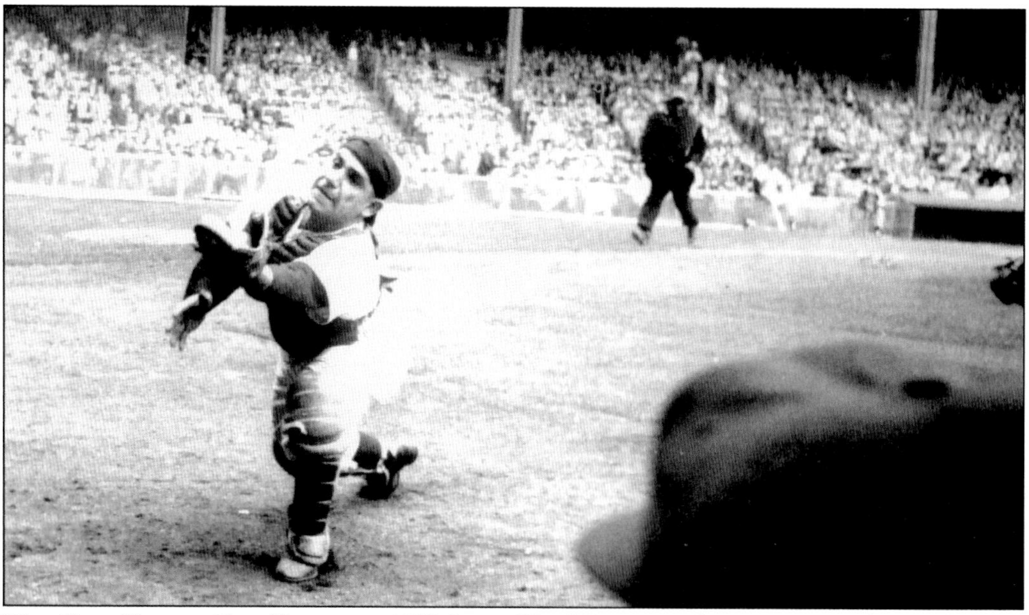

**NEW YORK YANKEE YOGI BERRA, C. 1958.** Larry "Yogi" Berra was the mainstay catcher of the most dominating baseball team of the 1950s, the New York Yankees. Taking a cue from Casey Stengel, Berra captured the imagination of baseball fans from the around the world with his malapropisms such as "It ain't over 'til it's over." This photograph catches Berra working his magic on the field.

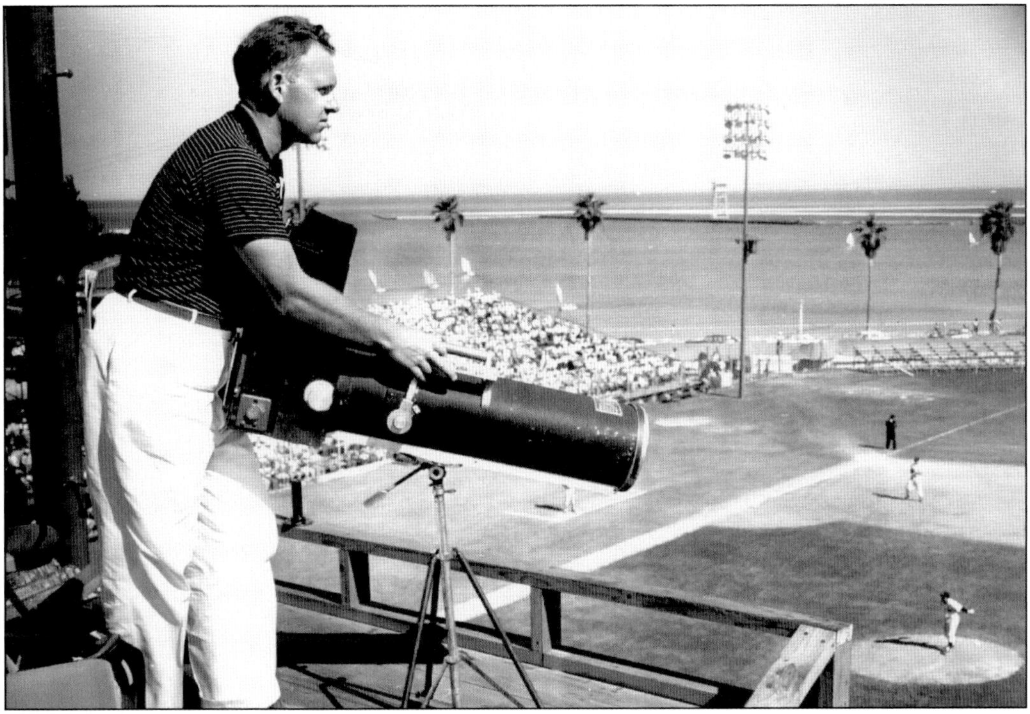

**THROUGH THE LENS OF ARTHUR RICKERBY, C. 1960.** Although Arthur Rickerby enjoyed covering his hometown favorite team, the New York Yankees, at spring training in St. Petersburg, Florida, he photographed many other major-league teams as well. These photographs show Arthur lining up his camera to capture the precise shot desired (above) and orchestrating another creative image featuring three players as his subjects (below).

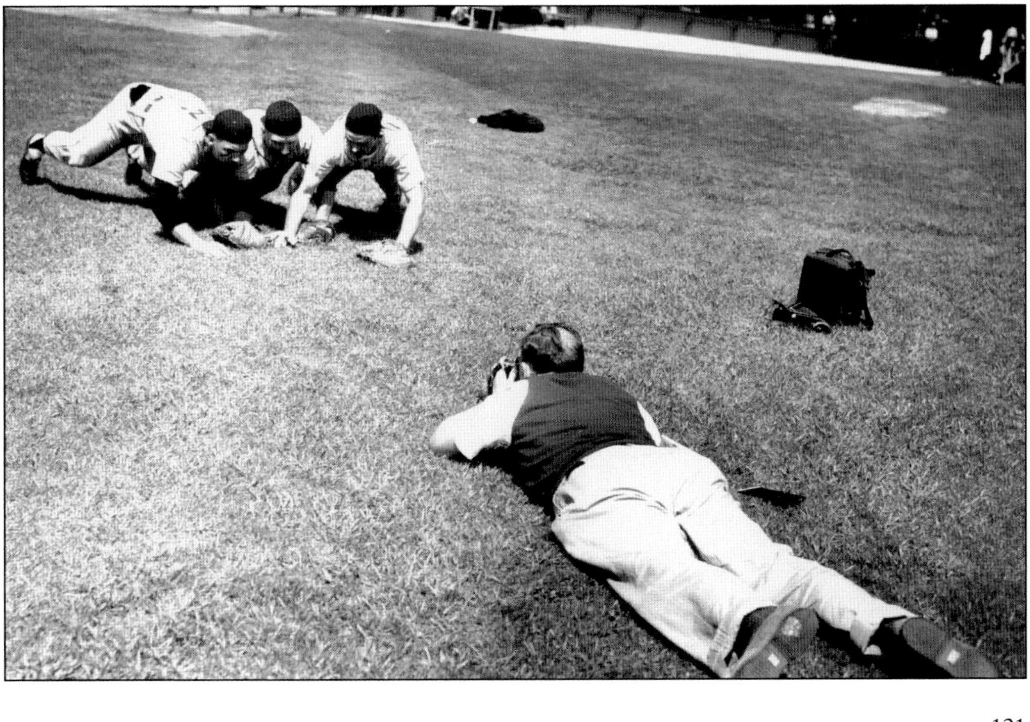

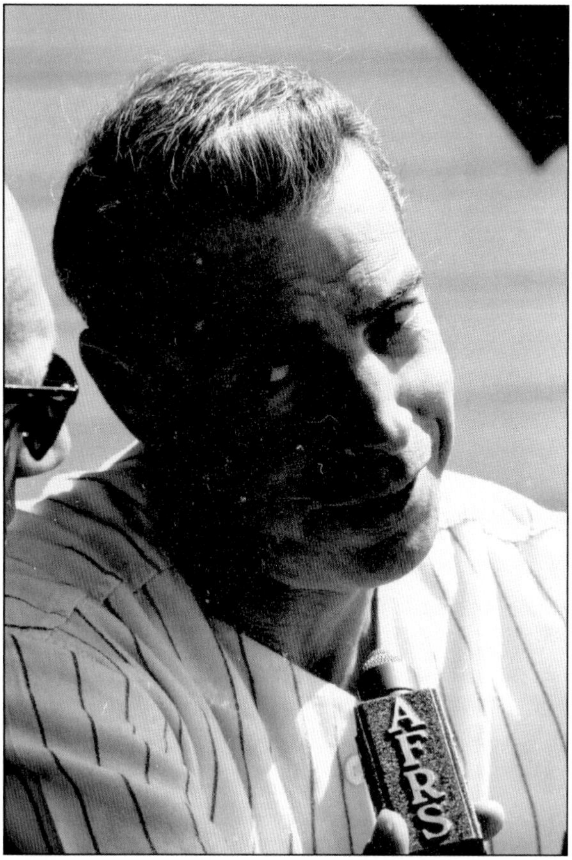


**THE YANKEE CLIPPER JOE DIMAGGIO, 1961.** During spring training for the 1961 major-league baseball season, the ever-popular Yankee Clipper, Joe DiMaggio, visited the team and created quite a stir. The photograph to the left shows Joltin' Joe, who had retired a decade earlier, addressing the media. Below, he sits in the St. Petersburg dugout alongside of Yankee greats Roger Maris, Elston Howard, and others.

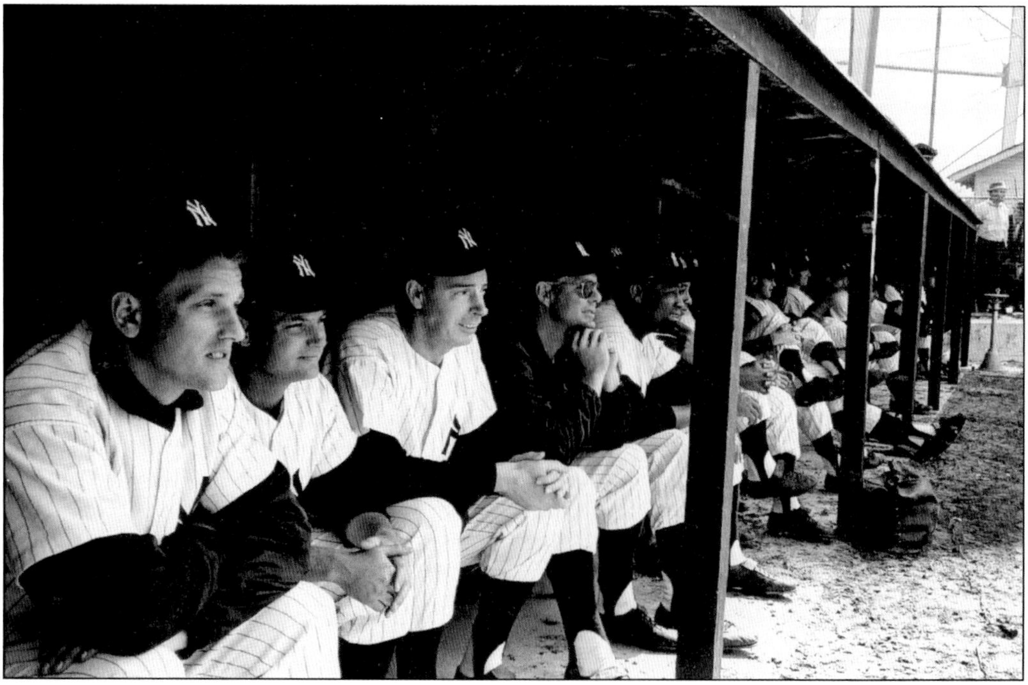

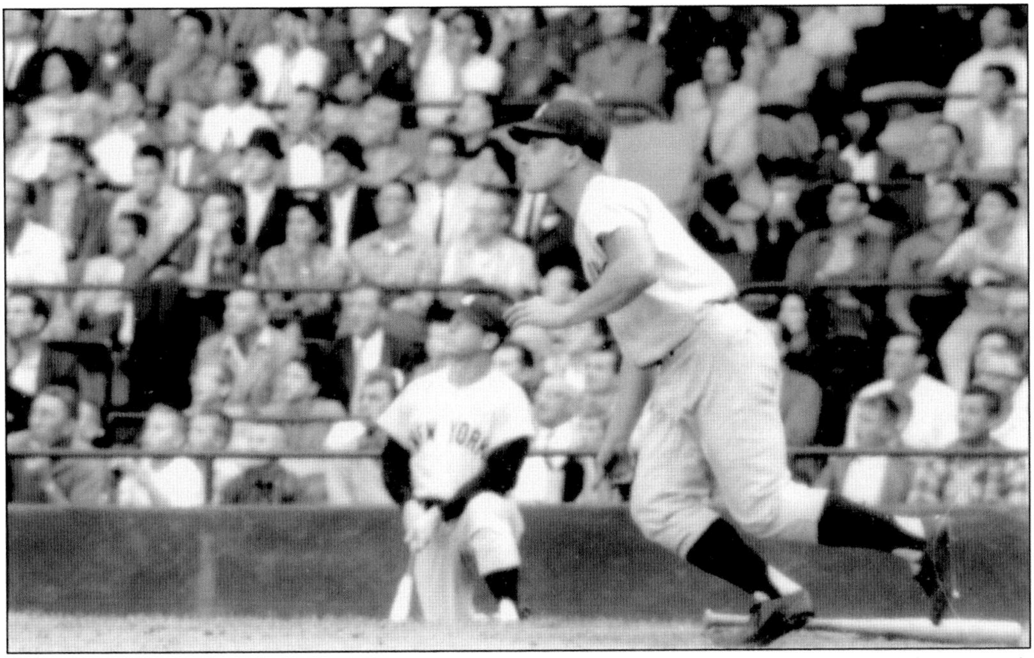

**THE M AND M BOYS, 1961.** The 1961 major-league baseball season was defined by the New York Yankees' Roger Maris and Mickey Mantle chasing the great Babe Ruth's single-season home run record of 60. Arthur was present at Yankee Stadium and recorded one of Roger Maris's 61 blasts with teammate Mickey Mantle on deck. After the home run, Mantle congratulates his friend Maris as he prepares to do more damage at the plate.

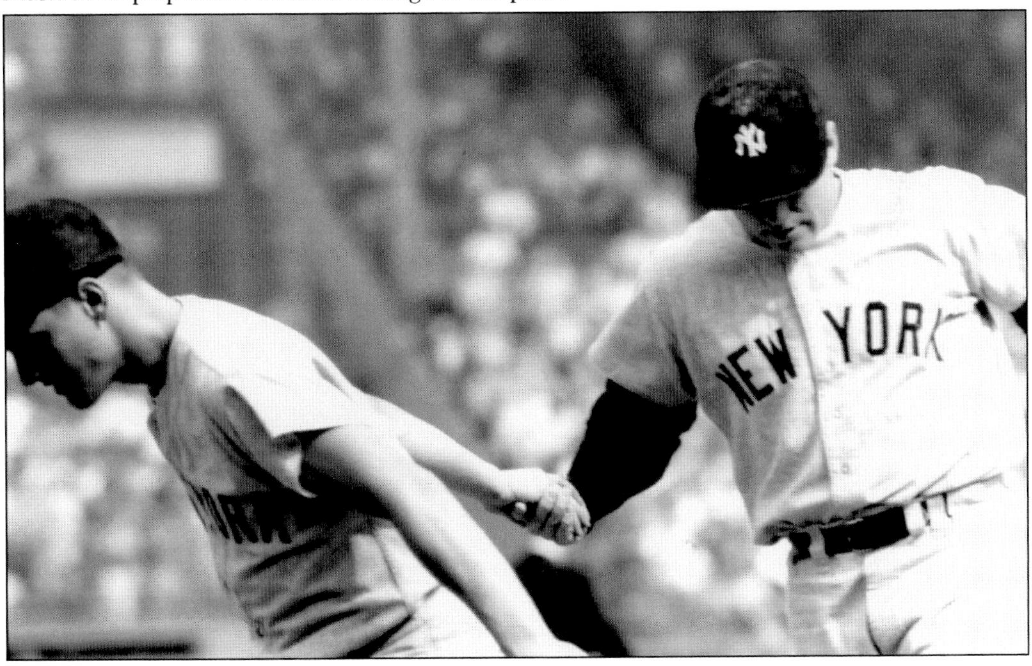

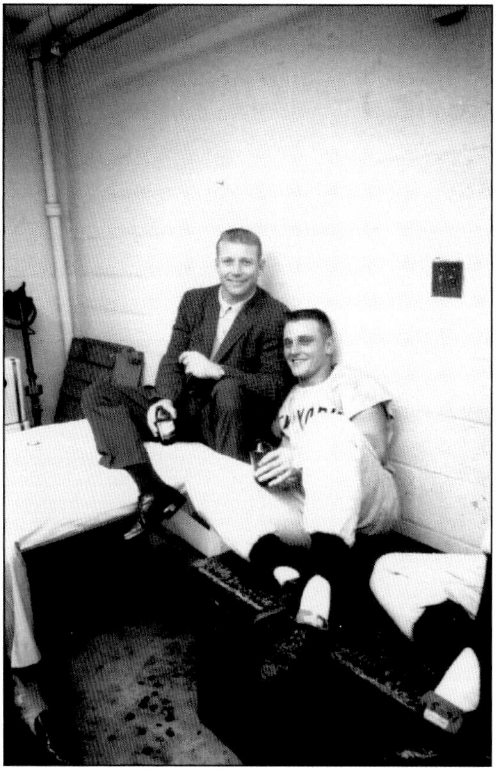

**Friends on and off the Field, 1961.** During the great home run chase of 1961, New York Yankee Roger Maris (right), who broke Babe Ruth's record by hitting 61 homers, became good friends with Mickey Mantle, who hit 54 home runs the same season. Here the boys are relaxing and smiling for their pal Arthur Rickerby.

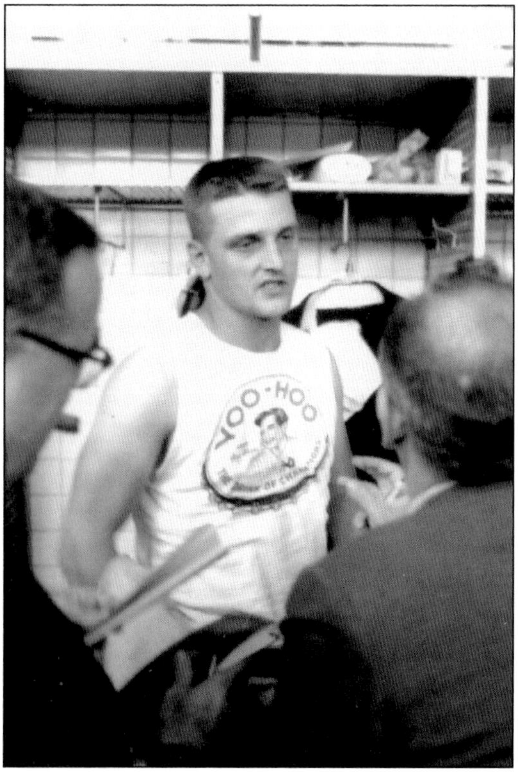


**The Stress of the Press, 1961.** Today baseball fans recall that it was not all fun and games for Roger Maris, a naturally reserved person, when he dealt with the New York press. After all, Maris was chasing the "unbreakable" home run record of 60 held by *the* New York sports icon, Babe Ruth, while also going head to head with longtime Yankee hero Mickey Mantle. In fact, it was such a stressful period for Maris that he began to prematurely lose his hair. Arthur, who had full access to the locker room after games, snapped this candid shot of Maris painstakingly answering reporters' questions. Note Maris's "Yoo Hoo" T-shirt featuring Yankee teammate Yogi Berra.

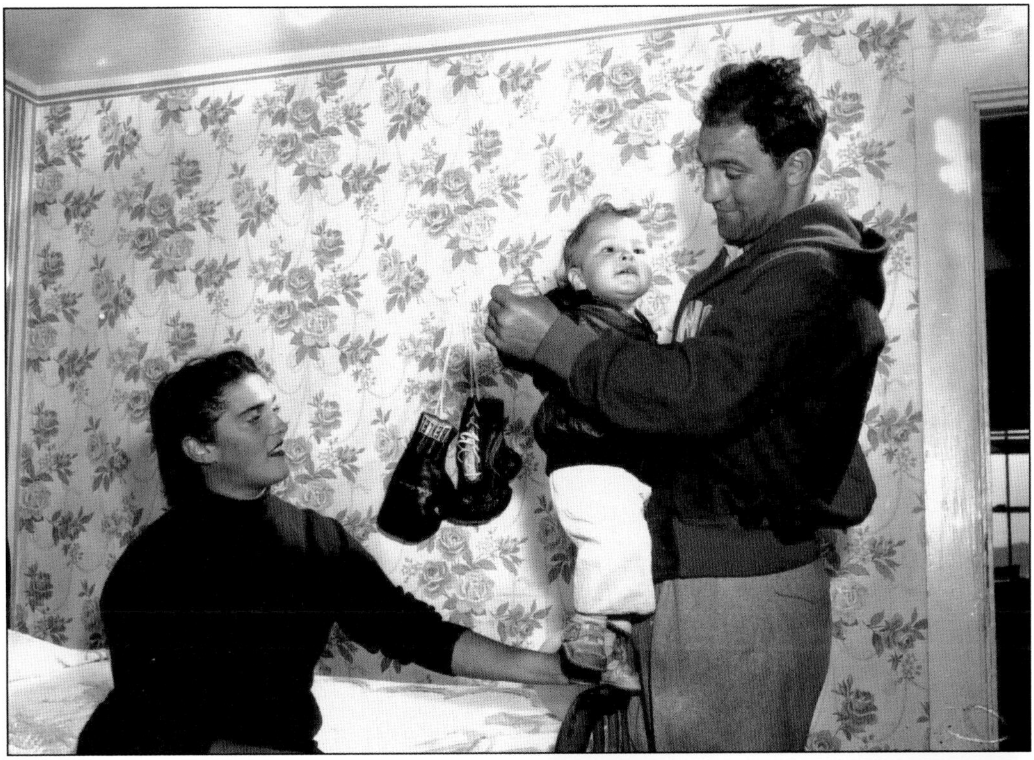

**THE ROCK, EARLY 1950S.** Born Rocco Francis Marchegiano in 1923, Rocky Marciano had overwhelming power and won all 49 fights in his professional boxing career. Arthur visited with Marciano and his family hours before one of the champ's heavyweight matches at Madison Square Garden (above). While ringside, Arthur recorded Marciano's intense face peering through the legs of his opponent (right).

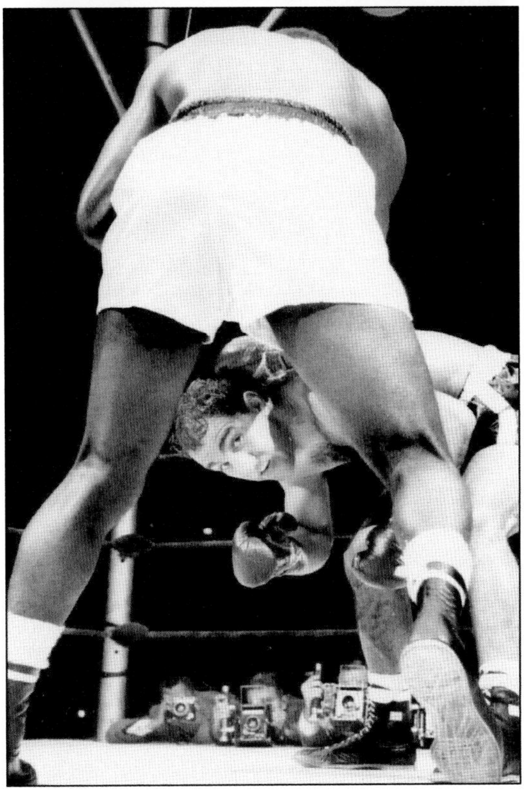

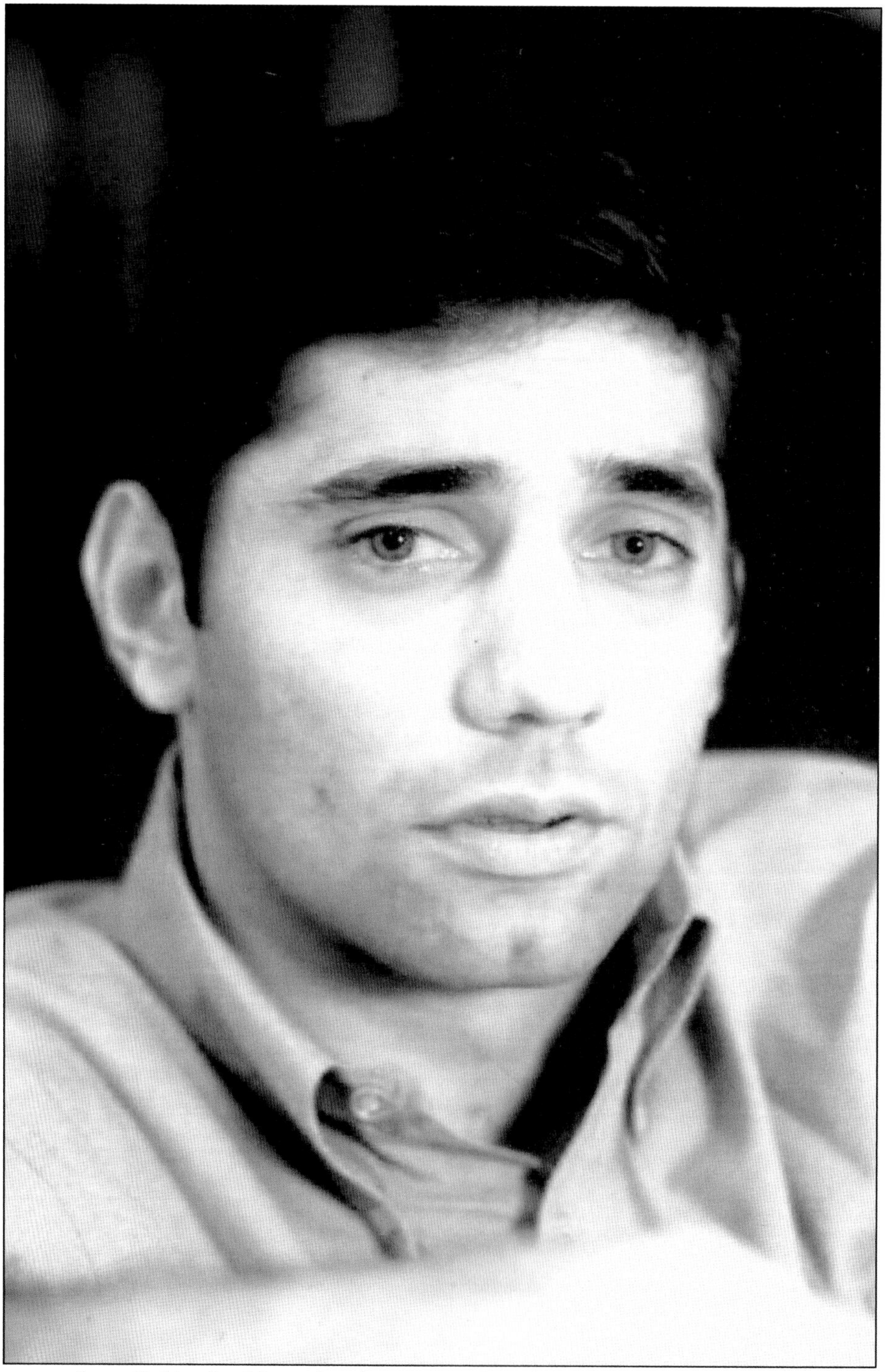

**BROADWAY JOE, 1960S.** Joe Namath is best remembered for when he led the New York Jets in 1969 to a stunning 16-7 upset of the heavily favored Baltimore Colts in Super Bowl III. Called "Broadway Joe" by the adoring New York press for his swinging bachelor lifestyle and movie star good looks, Arthur snapped this portrait when the quarterback was at the top of his game.

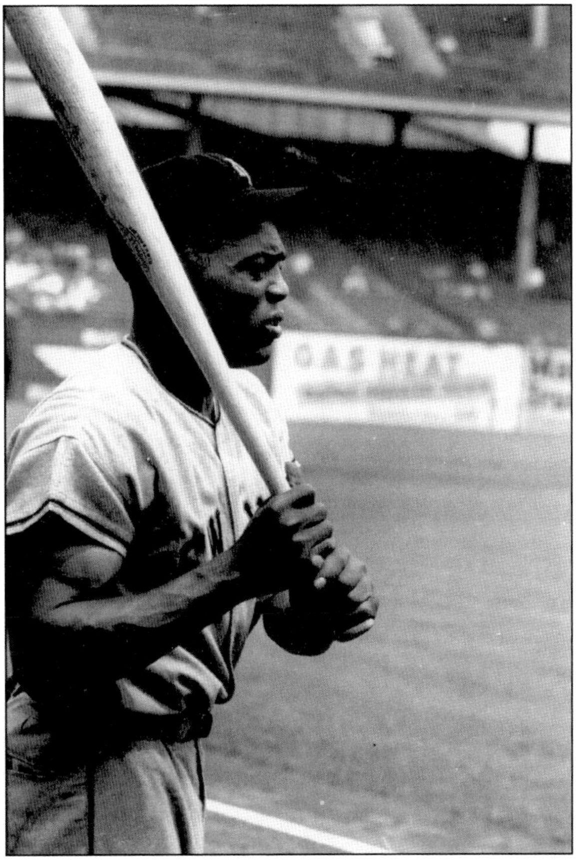


**THE "SAY HEY KID" WILLIE MAYS.** Many say that Willie Mays was the greatest all-around baseball player ever. Arthur took many photographs of the "Say Hey Kid," including young Mays, superstar of the New York Giants (right), as well as Mays during his first game as a member of the New York Mets (below). The image below was taken by Arthur during one of his very last assignments prior to his untimely death at the age of 51 in August 1972.

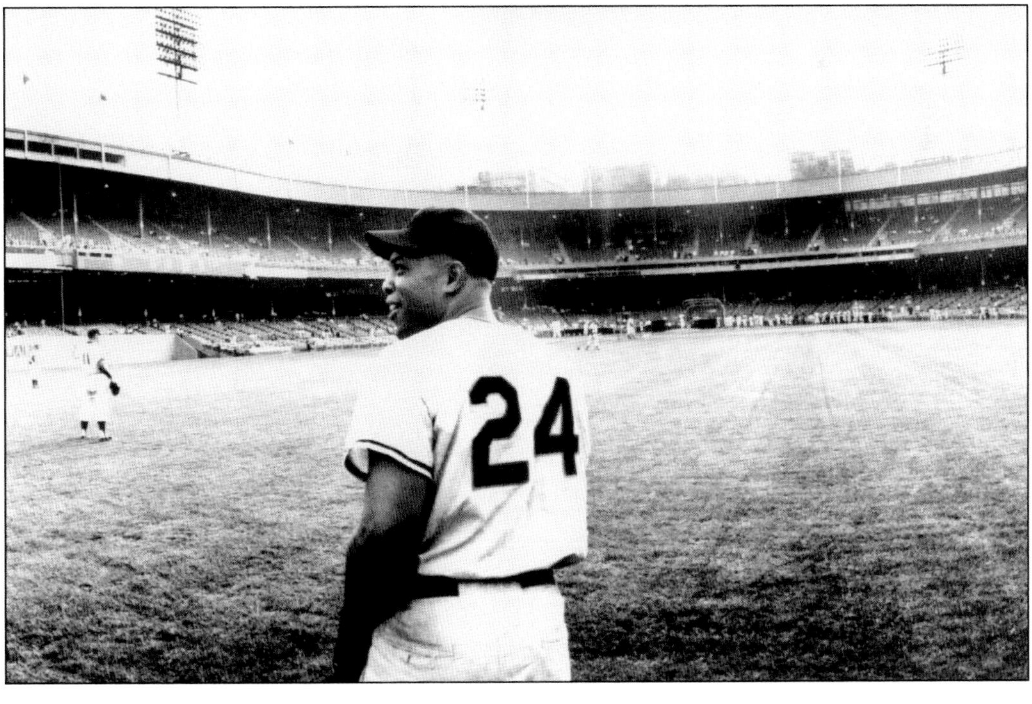